MW01352952

THE SOCIAL COSTS OF PORNOGRAPHY

THE SOCIAL COSTS OF PORNOGRAPHY

A COLLECTION OF PAPERS

Edited by

JAMES R. STONER, JR.

and

DONNA M. HUGHES

A project of the Witherspoon Institute in collaboration with the Social Trends Institute, Barcelona and New York, and the Institute for the Psychological Sciences, Arlington, Virginia

Published by the Witherspoon Institute
2010

Book and jacket design by Design4 Marketing Communications
Layout by Trejo Production
Printing by Thomson-Shore

Published in the United States by the Witherspoon Institute
16 Stockton Street, Princeton, New Jersey 08540

Library of Congress Control Number: 2010928708

ISBN: 9780981491134

Printed in the United States of America

TABLE OF CONTENTS

ACKNOWLEDGMENTS

Despite what jesters might say, studying pornography and its consequences is a troubling task, lightened in our case by the dedication of a group of true professionals. Luis Tellez of the Witherspoon Institute drew together a variety of scholars and supporters to initiate this project, and he oversaw its progress to completion, a task of several years. Roger Scruton and Gladys Sweeney of the Institute for the Psychological Sciences in Arlington, Virginia, were involved in the first conversations and helped bring many fine people to the initial consultation in Princeton in December 2008. Funding for that consultation, and for subsequent dissemination of its findings, was provided by the Social Trends Institute, the Caster Family Trust, and the Stuart Family Foundation. Planning of consultation details and gathering of papers afterwards fell to Patrick Hough, ever an attentive coordinator, and he was assisted by others on the Witherspoon staff, including Duncan Sahner and John Doherty. Mary Eberstadt's work on the companion *Statement of Findings and Recommendations* helped bring our own work into focus, and David Mills' superb line-editing improved many a draft. In the final production of the book, we were joined by a number of talented individuals: Bryan Ickes of Design4 Marketing Communications, who designed the book and its jacket; Margaret Trejo, who cheerfully and efficiently laid out the pages; and Megan Holobowicz and A. J. Marsh, who wrote and checked the index, respectively. Finally, more than anyone else, Alicia Brzycki's patience and persistence insured the completion of the book and its precision. She was effectively our managing editor or, as the quip went at Witherspoon, our "book quarterback," but in fact she kept the focus on the larger cause this volume is meant to serve.

Please note that this Collection of Papers *contains graphic language to convey the reality of contemporary pornography and its impact on men, women, and children.*

FOREWORD

Jean Bethke Elshtain

Pornography is as old as Western culture itself. Greek vases were often adorned with images that went beyond the erotic—at least to the ordinary eye—and embraced the pornographic. So long as human beings inhabit the earth, pornography will be present. But in what form? How pervasive is it? What harm might it do? Do we have solid evidence that attempts to curtail or curb pornography actually work?

I used to be much more of a "live and let live" person on this issue, years ago, in part because some of those who pushed for the censorship of pornography were so authoritarian. But the new technology has sent me in another direction. I just cannot, for example, fathom the ways in which child pornography is so pervasive and scoops up even babies into its disgusting maw. One doesn't even want to think about such matters, but think about them we must.

In a liberal society, such as our own, we are deeded a rather impoverished language with which to confront issues such as pornography: individualism, privacy, harm (or no-harm, as the case may be). To try to inject community, or the common good, or even shared public reason into the discussion is to court charges of censorship, moralistic prudery, and all the rest. The Supreme Court in the past has tried, and largely failed, to put the matter to rest. So where does this leave us? Are there no solid, flexible options at all?

Highly fraught matters

This volume explores the highly fraught matters that pornography presents. First, is there solid evidence that pornography harms people and that this harm extends beyond the individual user himself? Second, what moral perspectives can we bring to bear in order to raise public discourse about such matters? Third, can pornography be regulated and curbed constitutionally? Going beyond the hysteria that often (from all sides) accompanies these questions, the authors parse matters with solid evidence, wise analogies, acute clarification, and surprising even-handedness. I say "surprising" because *The Social Costs of Pornography: A Collection of Papers* is clearly on one side of the debate, and often one side or the other in such fraught matters gives no credit to, and allows no decent arguments from, its opponents. Not so here. Many of the arguments of opponents are rehearsed and responded to clearly and coherently.

Any serious confrontation with pornography must grapple with the "signs of the times." There is something new and clearly ominous about pornography today, namely, its ubiquity and ease of access, the ever more explicit and often violent forms that it takes, and its normalization.

No one is excluded from the new pornography's reach—neither the old nor the young, neither the able-bodied nor the disabled, no race, no sexual orientation—everything and everyone, it seems, is fair game. Astonishingly, many young people offer themselves up as pornographic subjects, filming and texting themselves in pornographic poses. Some would call them "erotic," I suppose. Minimally, one might say that self-pornography is peculiar because one violates one's own privacy.

Today also the sexual and the violent are so often fused into images of bodies, mostly females, destroyed, slaughtered in a variety of ingenious and cruel ways. Defenders of the use of such images even in mainstream television programs say they are, in fact, alerting people to cruelty against women and trying to fight it by displaying how terrible it really is. This is thin. Images may evoke pity and terror, yes, but they are as likely to incite and to excite, to cross yet another barrier. Those incited are keen for more ... and more ... and more yet again. On this score, we have solid, clear empirical evidence.

Even more troubling is the horror of child pornography. Almost beyond belief, babies as young as two months have been abused as pornographic subjects. Whether "real" or "virtual" (and herein lies another complexity), children, male and female, are ravished and demeaned in pornography geared to pedophiles, heterosexual and homosexual. Every taste and inclination is catered to; nothing is off-limits. You want gang-rape of a ten-year-old? That can be arranged. There are cases of a parent selling her child—yes, selling—to pornographers, usually to feed a drug habit. Those of us who observe these matters from a distance find it difficult to conjure how persons on the front lines of such activities and crimes manage to keep their humanity intact, to find a way to sleep at night with their moral sense securely in place. It cannot be easy.

Another "sign of the times" is the fact that pornography is now normalized. In the past it was largely isolated, confined to the "red light" districts in our cities. If you wanted to indulge in pornographic materials and shows, you trekked to that place and purchased its wares. These sites were sleazy and clearly marked as unsavory.

By insulating and isolating the red light districts, communities signaled that pornography was not something common and good, that they might not be able to stop it, but they can damn sure limit it and surround it with a sense of the marginal and the shameful.

We now live in a shameless age. Everything is revealed. There are no barriers of privacy any longer—that barrier was breached a long time ago. Ironic, is it not, that those violating the privacy that should protect the human body from public glare and misuse evoke "privacy" in order to degrade and to display that very body? But one of the many bizarre realities of our cultural moment.

I can recall the first time I saw a breast bared in the movies. I remember very little about the film—I don't think it was very good—but I can recall my reaction, a frisson that said to me a barrier had been breached and there was no way of repairing it. Of course, nudity in films can be done tastefully and delicately or crudely and pornographically. But to open up such images—no matter how well done—means, over time, their normalization. Then the temptation to go further and yet further and to shock rather than admire takes over.

What I am getting at in this list of "signs of the times" is that pornography cannot be treated as a highly abstract constitutional question. It penetrates lives and communities. It crosses boundaries of all kinds, geographic and moral. It affronts the dignity of the human person. Lives are frequently ruined in the process. I have known two marriages broken up by the addiction of one partner (the male in each case) to pornography. I do not refer to a few hours here or there, but to daily immersion in pornographic images for hours on end. The other spouse is neglected or transformed into another pornographic subject, or is enjoined to become such.

Modern technology being what it is and human nature being what it is, I assume that pornography will always be among us. I am no proponent of a utopia of punishment or sanctions. What we can do to try to stop it from spreading like an ugly fungus over all that it touches is to resist its allure ourselves, to criminalize—and then enforce the law—certain pornographic activities involving children, to enforce laws that now exist against cruelty and abuse of the sort that is often featured in modern pornography.

None of this is easy. A pornographer shut down one day will likely pop up the next somewhere else. It seems hopeless. But it is not. Any decent society will want ongoingly to signal that there are activities of which it disapproves, that it is by no means neutral about.

And it will do more. The most solid barrier against turning children into objects of pornographic abuse is a strong, intact family, a strong form of moral formation of the young so children come to respect and honor themselves and their own bodies, a wider social surround that creates barriers to sexual license and predation. The more transient, dislocated, drug-ridden, and broken-down a place is, the more likely it is that pornography will have a central role in that place. No place is immune, of course. But the evidence tells us that the gap between seeing and doing is eclipsed where social norms have collapsed and barriers to horrific behavior are loosened.

We should in doing all this be sensitive to the undeniable reality of the beauty of the human body as displayed in art, in sculpture, in literature. No one would call Michelangelo's magnificent "David" a pornographic statue. Some have, but the designation does not stick. The artist's appreciation of the human form is clear. His accomplishment is to represent that body in its beauty and dignity. What a contrast to the degradations of modern pornography in its slovenly or bestial forms.

Pornography's harm

It is very difficult to think about the ways anyone might be harmed by "David." It is very easy to contemplate the many ways we can all be harmed by contemporary pornography. This volume explores such questions wisely and well. But in order to deal with pornography wisely and well on the level of public conviction and public policy, we must first convince people that pornography is *not* an exclusively "private" matter, that its tentacles reach into the interstices of the human mind and into the heart and soul of human cultures and communities.

So: Welcome to this subject, yet again. It is likely not the first time the reader has confronted the question of pornography, and no doubt it will not be the last. I hope the analyses, the data, the arguments, and the images that flow forth from the pages of *The Social Costs of Pornography: A Collection of Papers* will assist the reader in the future to avoid the pitfalls of unrestrained libertarianism, on the one hand, and unrestrained top-down censoriousness, on the other. The "moral" need not be the cramped and cribbed "moralistic."

The point to be considered is: What sort of community is this? Is it reasonably decent and kind? Is it a fit place for human habitation, especially for the young? What happens to the most vulnerable among us? How do we ill-dignify the human body, and how do we forestall such affronts? These questions are not easy, but this learned volume helps push the debate forward in discerning ways.

THE SOCIAL COSTS OF PORNOGRAPHY

INTRODUCTION

James R. Stoner, Jr., and Donna M. Hughes

What are the costs and consequences of the widespread availability and use of pornography in society today? A generation or two ago, in the United States and throughout the Western world, it was decided that the social costs of pornography were not so high as to warrant the imposition on personal freedom that government suppression or regulation of pornography entailed.

In part because of changed attitudes, in part as a result of new constitutional doctrine that gave First Amendment protection to expression previously suppressed as obscene, America embarked on an experiment that effectively allowed the production and dissemination of pornography except when it involved children. Simultaneously, new technologies emerged that have broken down many of the physical barriers to pornography use. Now, instead of having to travel across town or to buy under the counter, consumers can access pornographic images and films from around the world in an instant on their home computers and on phones they carry in their pockets, much of it for free.

What are the results of this experiment and the new environment that accompanies it? The authors whose papers are collected in this volume have concluded that the evidence is unmistakable: The social costs of pornography today, insofar as they can be calculated, are high, and the risks of its continued easy availability may be greater still. As summarized in the companion document, *The Social Costs of Pornography: A Statement of Findings and Recommendations,* pornography has become increasingly available and increasingly "hard-core," and it harms not only innocent women and children but its users as well.

Some of the evidence of harm has been subjected to statistical analysis by social science methods; some of the evidence is clinical, which adds a personal immediacy. Moreover, philosophical analysis and reflection on the meaning of sexuality in human life has clarified the wrong to the person and the community that the use of pornography entails, while neuroscience is learning how to explain the addictive behavior now widely experienced by online pornography viewers and their need for ever more graphic or violent imagery. In short, pornography damages the moral ecology of contemporary society. It unravels lives, communities, and as Roger Scruton writes memorably below, love itself.

Most of the essays in this collection were originally delivered at a consultation called "The Social Costs of Pornography," held at Princeton University December 11–13, 2008, sponsored by the Witherspoon Institute of Princeton, New Jersey, in collaboration with the Social Trends Institute of Barcelona and New York, and the Institute for the Psychological Sciences of Arlington, Virginia. This was, to our knowledge, the first multidisciplinary scholarly exploration of the issue in the Internet Age, including among its presenters and participants sociologists, psychologists, psychiatrists, economists, political scientists, philosophers, lawyers, and journalists, as well as citizens who had been involved in the formulation of public policy on the issue over the years.

The group was not uniform in politics or in religion—there were members of both political parties, some noted as conservatives and others as feminists, some who were secular in orientation, others who were Christian (Catholic and Protestant), Jewish, and Muslim—and they did not aim to organize a specific proposal for public action. But over the three days they discovered a remarkable consensus among themselves that pornography was damaging society in new and troublesome ways, and that the late twentieth-century consensus that it is harmless entertainment that law and society could safely permit was thoroughly mistaken and must be challenged in the public square.

Our collection of the consultation papers—augmented with an additional paper and an appendix summarizing research findings on specific issues—is grouped under three headings. The first set of papers gathers and analyzes evidence of the harm done by contemporary pornography, viewed from a variety of perspectives. Over the past two decades, pornographers have used technology to make pornography more easily accessible, first with the VCR in the 1980s, then with the internet in the 1990s. As a consequence, the use of pornography has become privatized, moving from red light districts in seedy parts of town or adult bookstores along well-traveled highways to bedrooms, living rooms, and even offices.

During the technological migration, pornography moved into the cultural mainstream as well, becoming a central component of popular culture. Looking at the pervasive use of provocative imagery, Pamela Paul writes that the entire culture has become "pornified." The pornification of culture and the widespread use of pornography have negative consequences for individuals and couples. Contrary to the view that pornography will enhance sexual experiences, women and men are reporting that it has damaged their personal sexual satisfaction, their relationships, and their ability to be intimate with their spouses.

As Norman Doidge shows, men find that pornographic attitudes have invaded their minds and relationships as well as their computers. Previously, most research on the negative effects of pornography focused on how women were objectified and victimized. Today, the negative impact on men has been documented as well. As men's use of pornography increases, they become more desensitized and find it more difficult to achieve satisfaction and intimacy with their wives. Clinical findings reveal that pornography use can become addictive, and users find it very hard to stop even when facing the loss of their relationships, families, and jobs.

Violence is pervasive in pornography. As Mary Anne Layden documents, studies show that people who watch scenes of sexual violence are less likely to think violence is harmful. Sex offenders use pornography to groom victims. Anyone who looks at and becomes a user of pornography learns something from it. Users learn not only about specific sex acts, but about values, for pornography surreptitiously teaches behavior, beliefs, and attitudes. Teens are increasingly exposed to pornography, and some view it on a regular basis. No one knows what the impact of this early exposure will be on their ideas about sexuality or on their sexual behavior.

Today, women and teen girls are struggling to cope with a sexual cultural climate that has been molded by pornography, affecting their understanding of themselves and the character of their relationships with men, as Jill Manning and Ana Bridges each explain. Wives of pornography users are often devastated when they discover their husbands' secret habits. They feel betrayed and even more hurt and confused when their husbands can't or won't stop using it. A recent survey has found that 56% of divorce cases involved one partner compulsively using pornography.

The mainstreaming of pornography has led as well to more women consuming it. Women users exhibit the same problems as men users: They become desensitized to the content; they have difficulty forming long-term intimate relationships; and they are more likely to separate sexual gratification and emotional involvement.

Empirical evidence of this kind cannot be ignored, but it also cannot give a complete account of what is wrong about pornography. That demands ethical reflection: an understanding of the human person and the human good, and then a consideration of the use of pornography in light of that understanding. This is the subject of the second set of papers.

Scruton's essay offers what might be called a phenomenological account of human sexual desire, seeing the disorder of pornography in the search for sexual pleasure apart from desire for another person as a person, in other words, apart from love. Hadley Arkes takes a natural law approach to show that pornography is wrong in principle, not only for its harmful consequences, since it violates the natural exclusivity and intimacy of sexual relations, and he explains that what is wrong in principle cannot be ignored by law without teaching that wrong is right, or at least "all right." A Muslim reflection on sexual purity by Hamza Yusuf completes this part of the volume, drawing on Plato as well as the Koran.

There follow in the third set of papers several that address issues of law and policy in relation to the regulation of pornography. Actually, it is probably more precise to say that these essays lay out some of the challenges of bringing the power of law and public opinion to bear against the widespread availability and use of pornography, even in light of our new awareness of its social costs in the contemporary context, and they counsel caution and prudence in the design of remedies.

Historically, obscene materials were suppressed by the states and by the federal government, but around the middle of the twentieth century censorship began to relax, first in response to changes in public opinion, then as a result of the judiciary's extension of First Amendment protection to many materials that would have once been ruled obscene, finally as a consequence of a policy decision to stop prosecuting alleged obscenity when children were not involved.

While appreciating the wisdom in some of the earlier standards, as well as what was ill-advised in the old ways, both James Stoner and Gerard Bradley agree that the question is not one of nostalgia for a past era but of finding a way to address the serious harms of pornography in a context governed by constitutional doctrines and powerful interests that weigh against any effort at regulation. Although, as K. Doran shows, pornography is big business, and although, as Bradley reiterates, the value of public morality has been widely misunderstood, the situation is not hopeless in the face of mounting evidence of unmistakable wrong and measurable harm. In fact, even though contemporary constitutional law allows full regulation only of hard-core and child pornography, actual regulation in most jurisdictions and certainly on the internet does not at present approach what is constitutionally permitted. The question in the end is a matter of public opinion and political will.

While the companion *Statement of Findings and Recommendations* includes several proposals for reform in its conclusion, the present volume does not advocate a program for action. Rather, the aim of the authors has been to survey and try to understand a serious evil in society and to alert the public that pornography is an issue that deserves their attention. For many readers, perhaps especially those in the learned classes, hearing that alert will entail reconsidering opinions they formed long ago and now take for granted. We think, however, that the time has come for looking at the issue with fresh eyes: Pornography is different, the social context is different, and there is new evidence that pornography does immediate and sustained harm. What to make of the evidence and argument, and what to do in the face of it, we leave to every reader to discern.

PART ONE: EVIDENCE OF HARM

FROM PORNOGRAPHY TO PORNO TO PORN: HOW PORN BECAME THE NORM

Pamela Paul

"It's all mainstream now!"

That's what Seth Rogan's character Zack says to his best friend and intended love, Miri, in an effort to get her to make a pornographic film with him. The film is *Zack and Miri Make a Porno,* the latest gross-out comedy/romance from Kevin Smith, and one of many recent comedies (and romances, shockingly) to make light of pornography. Indeed, in Rogan's last romantic hit, *Knocked Up,* his character's "job" is creating a pornographic website. The women in the film? After a quick, symbolic "yuck!," they become willing participants.

It *is* all mainstream now. Over the past ten years, technological advances, cultural shifts, and social attitudes have transformed the pornography landscape. Today, men, women, and children are affected by the ubiquity and mainstreaming of pornography in unprecedented ways. The internet, in particular, has made pornography more anonymous, more accessible, and more affordable than ever before, bringing in new users, increasing use among existing fans, and catapulting many into sexual compulsiveness. Children are being exposed to pornography earlier than ever before, in ways that will profoundly affect their sexuality and their lives.

Not only is pornography itself more ubiquitous, the entire culture has become pornified. By that I mean that the aesthetics, values, and standards of pornography have seeped into mainstream popular culture. Young girls brazenly pose in pornographic ways on their MySpace pages, even creating porn-like videos of themselves gyrating and preening before untold numbers of strangers. Porn stars are regularly featured in the same tabloid magazines that profile actors, singers, and other celebrities, equating those who sell sex with those who create art on the basis of other talents (though, of course, one could argue the relative merits of that "art").

Pornography is everywhere

All of this would not be possible without the hyperspeed spread of pornography over the past two decades. Today, the number of people looking at pornography is staggering. Americans rent upwards of 800 million pornographic videos and DVDs (about one in five of all rented movies is porn), and the 11,000 porn films shot each year far outpaces Hollywood's yearly slate of 400. Four billion dollars a year is spent by consumers on video pornography in the United States, more than on football, baseball, and basketball. One in four internet users looks at a pornography website in any given month. Men look at pornography online more than they look at any other subject. And 66% of eighteen- to thirty-four-year-old men visit a pornographic site every month.

Pornography regularly makes headlines and sells products, even within the mainstream culture. In 2004, Janet Jackson notoriously bared her breast during the Super Bowl, in prime-time family television viewing hours. Shortly thereafter Paris Hilton's amateur sex video became an internet sensation. More media attention followed—Howard Stern fled to satellite radio and soon porn star Jenna Jameson and *Playboy* bunny Pamela Anderson were topping the best-seller lists with a memoir and a roman à clef, respectively. A glossy coffee table book of porn star portraits accompanied by essays from writers such as Salman Rushdie and Francine du Plessix Gray was published. Showtime ran a special in which porn stars, Jameson among them, bragged about the power women have in the pornography business. Today, celebrity couples boast about their trips to the hottest strip clubs. Characters on prime-time sitcoms extol the benefits of porn. Even mainstream women's magazines advise women to enliven their marital bedtime routine by turning on late-night Skinemax.

The message is that pornography is everywhere—and only ever-so-slightly scandalous. It is good for you, and especially good for relationships. Pornography is hip, sexy, and fun.

But particularly on the internet, where much of pornography today is consumed, the type of sexuality depicted often has more to do with violence, extreme fetishes, and mutual degradation than with fun, much less with sexual or emotional connection. For those who haven't double-clicked: These aren't airbrushed photos of the girl next door or images of coupling; they are vivid scenes of crying women enduring aggressive multiple penetration.

These are images created by pornographers for a single purpose: to help men masturbate and get them to pay for it. Sex, in pornography, is a commercialized product, devoid of emotion, stripped of humanity, an essentially empty experience. As one porn fan put it, after an evening of porn surfing, "You feel like, yeah, that was a release, but I don't know, maybe not the best thing. Like eating a bag of potato chips."

Bad for women and marriage

"You get into a slippery slope," cautions Massachusetts-based psychologist and sex therapist Aline Zoldbrod. "The majority of porn out there is degrading and has only gotten worse. The women are plasticized; there's no longer as much diversity or naturalism as there was two decades ago."

Zoldbrod believes many young men today are terrible lovers because they learn about sexuality from pornography. "In real life, sexually-speaking, women are slow cookers and men are microwaves. But in pornography, all a man does is touch a woman and she's howling in delight. Today, pornography is so widely used by young men, they learn these falsehoods. There's good evidence that the more porn men watch, the less satisfied they are with their partner's looks and sexual performance."

Advice columnists across North America receive letter after letter in which women complain about their partner's pornography. Men who watch a lot of porn seem to focus more intensely on the visual, even when in bed with a woman, asking her to emulate the look and moves of porn stars. Women have distorted body images and feel the need to remodel their appearances—no matter how they personally feel about pornography.

Though pressured to accept pornography as a sign of being sexy and hip, many women admit that in practice they are hurt by their boyfriend's use of porn. A twenty-four-year-old from Baltimore complained to me about how her boyfriend got lap dances at a strip club every month. "If he were to do that with a woman in front of me on the living room couch, that would be considered cheating. Why is it somehow okay just because he's at a strip club?" Another woman told me, "All of my girlfriends and I expect to find histories of pornographic websites on our computers after our boyfriends use it. They don't bother erasing the history if you don't give them a lot of hell." The implications troubled her. "I fear we are losing something very important—a healthy sexual worldview. I think, however, that we are using old ideas of pornography to understand its function in a much more complex modern world."

Women view men's relationship with pornography as a sign of betrayal, even cheating. A thirty-eight-year-old mother of two from Kentucky said finding her husband's secret stash of porn "pretty much wiped out the trust in our relationship." Once she knew about his years-long subterfuge, she recalled, "I would find myself worrying all the time. If I were going to take a trip for my job, I'd wonder about what he might look at while I was gone."

Pornography thus creates deception and distrust in relationships. Most women have no idea how often their boyfriends and husbands look at pornography because the men do not tell them. Usually the deception is deliberate, though many men deny to themselves how often they look at it, and most simply don't think about quantifying the amount they view. While men consider trust crucial for a healthy relationship, they seem willing to flout that trust when it comes to pornography—deceiving their significant others into thinking they're either not looking at it at all or are looking at it less frequently. Fitting pornography into one's life isn't always easy.

More women are installing programs such as Net Nanny® on their computers to limit their home computer internet access to PG websites. According to one filtering company, WiseChoice.net, more than half the company's 3,000 customers are adults who use the software not to block their kids' access but to keep themselves and other adults from looking at porn.[1] In a 2004 *Elle*/MSNBC.com poll, one in four women said she was concerned that her partner had an "out-of-control habit" with online pornography.

Matrimonial lawyers attest to a growing docket of cases in which pornography was a major source of tension, if not the cause of the divorce. "Pornography wrecks marriages," says Marcia Maddox, a Virginia-based attorney.

Bad for men

Yet lest pornography get written off as a "women's problem," consider the extensive negative effects of pornography on the primary users, men. According to a large-scale 1994 report summarizing eighty-one peer-reviewed research studies, most studies (70%) found that exposure to *nonaggressive* pornography has clear negative effects—and that is not the only kind of pornography most users view.[2]

Countless men have described to me how, while using pornography, they have lost the ability to relate to or be close to women. They have trouble being

---

1 Lynn Harris, "Stop Him Before He Clicks Again!" *Salon.com*, 15 April 2004, http://dir.salon.com/story/mwt/feature/2004/04/15/filters/index.html.

2 John S. Lyons, Rachel L. Anderson, and David B. Larsen, "A Systematic Review of the Effects of Aggressive and Nonaggressive Pornography," in *Media, Children, and the Family: Social Scientific, Psychodynamic, and Clinical Perspectives*, eds. Dolf Zillmann, Jennings Bryant, and Aletha Huston (Hillsdale, N.J.: Lawrence Erlbaum Associates, 1994), 305.

turned on by "real" women, and their sex lives with their girlfriends or wives collapse. These are men who seem like regular guys, but who spend hours each week with porn—usually online. And many of them admit they have trouble cutting down their use. They also find themselves seeking out harder and harder pornography.

In interviews for *Pornified*, a book I wrote about pornography's effects, men—even those who were avid porn fans—confessed that their pornography habits had damaged their sex lives. Men who use pornography say they are losing the ability to relate to, be close to, and achieve orgasm with real women.

A single twenty-something graphic designer told me he would find himself in bars, berating himself over the way he scanned potential dates. "I'd be saying, 'No, her breasts are too small, she's not worth it,' then wonder, 'Who have I become? Why am I judging women like this?'" After months of rampant use, he had to "restrict" himself in order to regain perspective.

A twenty-eight-year-old man explained, "I used to view porn online, but I began to find it more difficult to stay aroused when having sex with a real woman.... During a dry spell, I discovered iPorn, and the easiness of it made it easy to glut—to the point where now, even though the dry spell is over, real sex has lost some of its magic."

When they are having sex with real women, such men need to conjure images they've viewed in pornography in order to maintain their level of excitement. Other times, they want to focus on their partner, but find their minds filled with pornographic images instead—like getting a bad song trapped in their heads.

Men also told me that they found themselves wasting countless hours looking at pornography on their televisions and DVD players, and especially online. They looked at things they would have once considered appalling—bestiality, group sex, hard-core S&M, genital torture, child pornography.

They found the way they looked at women in real life warping to fit the pornography fantasies they consumed onscreen. Their daily interactions with women became pornified. Their relationships soured. They had trouble relating to women as individual human beings. They worried about the way they saw their daughters and girls their daughters' age. It wasn't only their sex lives that suffered—pornography's effects rippled out, touching all aspects of their existence. Their workdays became interrupted, their hobbies were tossed aside, their family lives were disrupted. Some men even lost their jobs, their wives, and their children. The sacrifice is enormous.

Nor is it only the most violent hard-core pornography that damages how the male users view women, including their wives and their girlfriends. Because pornography involves looking at women but not interacting with them, it elevates the physical while ignoring or trivializing all other aspects of the woman. A woman is literally reduced to her body parts and sexual behavior. Gary Brooks, a psychologist who studies pornography at Texas A&M University, explains that "soft-core pornography has a very negative effect on men as well. The problem with soft-core pornography is that it's voyeurism—it teaches men to view women as objects rather than to be in relationships with women as human beings."

But pornography doesn't just change how men view women—it changes their lives, including their relation to pornography. The first step is usually an increase in frequency and quantity of viewing: more times logging online or clicking the remote control, prolonged visits to certain websites, a tendency to fall into a routine. In a 2004 *Elle*/MSNBC.com poll, nearly 25% of men admitted that they were afraid they were "overstimulating" themselves with online sex.

In fact, routine is an essential ingredient in the financial success of high-tech porn. Wendy Seltzer, an advocate for online civil liberties, argues that pornographers should not even be concerned about piracy of their free material. "People always want this stuff. Seeing some of it just whets their appetite for more. Once they get through what's available for free, they'll move into the paid services."[3] And once they've indulged in more quantity, they want more quality—meaning more action, more intensity, more extreme situations. The user's impetus to find harder-core fare helps the entire industry.

Particularly on the internet, men find themselves veering off into forms of pornography they *never* thought they could find appealing. Those who start off with soft-core develop a taste for harder-core pornography.

Men who view a lot of pornography talk about their disgust the first time they chanced upon an unpleasant image or unsolicited child porn. But with experience, it doesn't bother the user as much—the shock wears thin quickly, especially given the frequent assault of such images he encounters on the internet. He learns to ignore or navigate around unwanted imagery, and the third time he sees an unpleasant image, it's merely an annoyance and a delay. At the same time that such upsetting imagery

---

3 John Schwartz, "The Pornography Industry vs. Digital Pirates," *New York Times*, 8 February 2004, final edition, sec. 3, p. 1.

becomes more tolerable, the imagery that had aroused him becomes less interesting, leading the user to ratchet up the extremity of the kind of pornography he seeks, looking for more shocking material than he started with.

The women's market

Having won over such a significant chunk of the male market, the pornography industry is eager to tap into the other potential 50% of the market: women. A number of companies are increasing production of pornography made by and for women, and the industry is keen to promote what it likes to view as women's burgeoning predilection for pornography. Playgirl TV announced its launch in 2004 with programming to include an "erotic soap opera" from a woman's point of view, a 1940s-style romantic comedy with "a sexual twist," and roundtable discussions of "newsworthy women's topics."

In recent years, women's magazines have regularly featured a discussion of pornography from a new perspective: how women can introduce it into their own lives. While many women continue to have mixed or negative feelings toward pornography, they are told to be realistic, to be "open-minded." Porn, they are told, is sexy, and if you want to be a sexually attractive and forward-thinking woman, you've got to catch on.

Today, the pornography industry and our pornified culture have convinced women that wearing a thong is a form of emancipation, learning to pole dance means embracing your sexuality, and taking your boyfriend for a lap dance is what every sexy and supportive girlfriend should do. In an *Elle* magazine poll, more than half of the respondents described themselves as "pro-stripping" (56%), and said that they weren't bothered if their partner went to strip clubs (52%).

Sociologist Michael Kimmel, who studies pornography and teaches sexuality classes at the State University of New York at Stony Brook, says, "Twenty years ago, my female students would say, 'Ugh, that's disgusting,' when I brought up pornography in class. The men would guiltily say, 'Yeah, I've used it.' Today, men are much more open about saying they use pornography all the time, and they don't feel any guilt. The women now resemble the old male attitude: They'll sheepishly admit to using it themselves." Women's attitudes have merged even more closely with men's.

The internet measurement firm comScore tracked close to thirty-two million women visiting at least one adult website in January 2004. Seven million of them were ages thirty-five to forty-four, while only 800,000 were over the age of sixty-five.[4] Nielsen NetRatings has found the figures to be somewhat lower, with ten million women visiting adult content websites in December 2003.[5] In a 2004 *Elle*/MSNBC.com poll, 41% of women said they have intentionally viewed or downloaded erotic films or photos, and 13% watched or sexually interacted with someone on a live webcam.

Yet as much as women are touted as the new pornography consumer, they still lag far behind men. The sensational headlines do little to reflect the reality of most women's experiences. Statistics belie the assertions of the pro-porn movement and the go-go girl mentality espoused by female pornography purveyors.

While some polls show that up to half of all women go online for sexual reasons, the percentage of women who say they do is likely exaggerated by the inclusion in the definition of "adult" internet content of erotica, dating, and informational sites, areas to which women are disproportionately drawn compared with men. Others feel that admitting they don't look at pornography at all is akin to affixing a "frigid" sticker to their chastity belts; better not to come off as uptight. Many women tracked through filtering programs visit pornographic sites by accident or out of curiosity, or are tracking down their male partner's usage.

Some attribute the rise in female consumption to an increased supply in pornography for women. That may be part of the reason, but there's more at play than a simple increase in supply—something has to explain the increased demand. Broader societal shifts in men's and women's roles in relationships and a corresponding swing in women's expectations and attitudes toward their sexuality are driving women to pornography, too.

Not a harmless "guy thing"

Many women try to treat porn as merely a harmless "guy thing," but they are profoundly disturbed when they are forced to come to terms with the way porn changes their lives—and the lives of their boyfriends or husbands. They find themselves constantly trying to measure up to the bodies and sexual performance of the women their men watch online and onscreen. They fear that they've lost the ability to turn their men on anymore—and quite often, they have.

---

4 *Countdown with Keith Olbermann*, MSNBC, 23 February 2004.

5 Mireya Navarro, "Women Tailor Sex Industry to Their Eyes," *New York Times*, 20 February 2004, final edition, sec. A, p. 1.

One twenty-four-year-old woman from Baltimore confided, "I find that porn's prevalence is a serious hindrance to my comfort level in relationships. Whether it's porn DVDs and magazines lying around the house, countless porn files downloaded on their computers, or even trips to strip clubs, almost every guy I have dated (as well as my male friends) is very open about his interest in porn. As a result, my body image suffers tremendously.... I wonder if I am insecure or if the images I see guys ogle every day has done this to me." She later confessed that she felt unable to air her concerns to anyone. "A guy doesn't think you're cool if you complain about it," she explained. "Ever since the internet made it so easy to access, there's no longer any stigma to porn."

A thirty-eight-year-old woman from a Chicago suburb described her husband's addiction to pornography: "He would come home from work, slide food around his plate during dinner, play for maybe half an hour with the kids, and then go into his home office, shut the door and surf internet porn for hours. I knew—and he knew that I knew. I put a filter on his browser that would email me every time a pornographic image was captured. . . . I continually confronted him on this. There were times I would be so angry I would cry and cry and tell him how much it hurt. . . . It got to the point where he stopped even making excuses. It was more or less: 'I know you know and I don't really care. What are you going to do about it?'"

For many wives and girlfriends, it becomes immediately clear that the kind of pornography their men are into is all about the men—about their needs, about what they want—not about their women or their relationships or their families. It's not surprising a woman ends up feeling second-rate. Not only does pornography dictate how women are supposed to look; it skews expectations of how they should act. Men absorb those ideals, but women internalize them as well. According to the nationally representative *Pornified*/Harris poll, commissioned for my 2004 book, most women (six out of ten) believe pornography affects how men expect them to look and behave. In fact, only about one out of seven women believes pornography *doesn't* raise men's expectations of women.

Men tell women their consumption of pornography is natural and normal, and if a woman doesn't like it, she is controlling, insecure, uptight, petty, or a combination thereof. The woman is demanding. She is unreasonable. He has to give up something he's cherished since boyhood. She's not supportive. She blows everything out of proportion. If it weren't for this attitude of hers, the relationship would be fine. For a woman to judge pornography as anything but positive is read as a condemnation of her man, or at the very least, of his sexual life. Discomfort with pornography also becomes a woman's discomfort with her own sexuality.

Still, the *Pornified*/Harris poll found that only one-fifth of Americans believe pornography improves the sex life of those who look at it. Indeed, two-thirds of respondents to this nationwide poll believe looking at pornography will *harm* a couple's relationship. And not surprisingly, half of Americans say pornography demeans women. Women are far more likely to believe this—58% compared with 37% of men. They are much less likely—20% compared with 34%—to believe that pornography *isn't* demeaning.

Of course, with increased viewing, the arousing effects of pornography become less obvious over time. While 60% of adults age fifty-nine and older believe pornography is demeaning toward women, only 35% of Gen Xers—the most tolerant and often heaviest users of pornography—agree.

Not a solo activity

In other words, despite appearances, pornography isn't precisely a solo activity. As interviews with men and women attest, it plays into how people approach and function in relationships. Whether a couple watches together, or one or both partners uses it alone, pornography plays a significant role not only in sex but in a couple's sense of trust, security, and fidelity. As Mark Schwartz, clinical director of the Masters and Johnson Clinic in St. Louis, Missouri, says, "Pornography is having a dramatic effect on relationships at many different levels and in many different ways—and nobody outside the sexual behavior field and the psychiatric community is talking about it."

Not knowing whom to turn to when their boyfriends turn away from them and toward pornography, many women write in to magazine advice columnists for help or ask for support in online forums. Female-oriented internet communities (chat rooms, bulletin boards, online forums, etc.) teem with discussions on the subject. Every week, advice columnists across the country address the issue; presumably many similar letters go unanswered in print.

Just one example: A woman writes to a local newspaper, "We've been together five years, lived together half that time. We have a loving, happy relationship. Recently, I discovered via the computer that he's fascinated by hard-core pornography, lots of it. When confronted, he said I have no right to be upset, though he's aware it offends me; he insisted I let it go. He's still spending hours looking at this and I'm disgusted. . . . I've tried to discuss how degrading and controlling this seems to me, but he's not willing to give it up. I know many people think it's harmless, but it's making me question whether I'm willing to continue a relationship with someone who can disregard my feelings so easily."[6]

The *Pornified*/Harris poll found that overall, 34% of women see men using pornography as cheating in absolutely all cases. Yet only 17% of men equated pornography with cheating. Indeed, most men who use pornography tend to see pornography as *not* cheating: A man has his needs, and he's fulfilling them in a way that prevents him from cheating on his wife with a real woman. According to the *Pornified*/Harris poll, 41% of men say pornography should never be considered cheating. Only 18% of women felt the same way.

Once she's discovered his pornography, what next? Psychotherapist Marlene Spielman says when a woman finds out about a partner's pornography habit, the result is usually a back and forth of very strong emotions. The woman typically feels hurt, angry, and betrayed. Confronted husbands often begin with denial before confessing the truth, followed by a big fight, blaming, and accusations. He may accuse her of driving him to it; she might point to his avoidance of problems in the relationship.

In the 2004 *Elle*/MSNBC.com poll, one in four divorced respondents said internet pornography and chat had contributed to their split. At the 2003 meeting of the American Academy of Matrimonial Lawyers, a gathering of the nation's divorce lawyers, attendees documented a startling trend. Nearly two-thirds of the attorneys present had witnessed a sudden rise in divorces related to the internet; 58% of those were the result of a spouse looking at excessive amounts of pornography online. According to the association's president, Richard Barry, "Eight years ago, pornography played almost no role in divorces in this country. Today, there are a significant number of cases where it plays a definite part in marriages breaking up."

The five lawyers from the office of matrimonial attorney Marcia Maddox are always working on at least one case involving pornography. In one, a wife found her husband's internet pornography while she and their daughter were working on a school project. Horrified, the woman hired a computer technician, who discovered a trove of hard-core pornography on the hard drive. The couple ended up getting a divorce; the mother was awarded sole custody.

---

6 "His Porn Habit Has Become a Hardcore Problem," *Toronto Star*, 4 July 2004, sec. B, p. 4.

The fact is, Maddox says, "Using pornography is like adultery. It's not *legally* adultery, which requires penetration. But there are many ways of cheating. It's often effectively desertion—men abandoning their family to spend time with porn." Often the judges find that even if children aren't directly exposed to a father's pornography, they are indirectly affected because their fathers ignore them in favor of porn. Visitation in such cases may be limited.

Mary Jo McCurley, an attorney who has practiced family law in Dallas since 1979, agrees. In the past five years, more and more cases are brought forth in which a husband's pornography habit is a factor. "We see cases in which the husband becomes so immersed in online porn it destroys the marriage," she explains. "Not only is it unsettling for the wife that he's using other women to get off, but it takes away from the time they could spend together as a couple."

In divorce cases these days, enormous amounts of time and money are spent recovering pornography from computers. "You can hire experts who specialize in digging through hard drives," McCurley says. "There are people who have made a profession out of it. It's become quite common in Texas divorce."

Bad for teenagers

The statistics are frightening, but even more appalling are the effects of pornography on the next generation. According to a 2001 study by the Kaiser Family Foundation, seven in ten fifteen-to-seventeen-year-olds admitted to "accidentally" stumbling across pornography online. Girls were more likely than boys to say they were "very upset" by the experience (35% versus 6%), although 41% of youth that age said that it wasn't a problem.

Statistics show nearly all—if not all—teenagers are exposed to pornography one way or another. A 2004 study by Columbia University found that 11.5 million teenagers (45%) have friends who regularly view internet pornography and download it.[7] (Incidentally, teenagers with a majority of friends who do so are three times more likely to smoke, drink, or use illegal drugs than are teens who have no such friends.)

The prevalence of teens with friends who view and download internet pornography increases with age, from nearly one-third of twelve-year-olds to nearly

7 Courtney C. Radsch, "Teenagers' Sexual Activity Is Tied to Drugs and Drink," *New York Times*, 30 August 2004, sec. A, p. 15.

two-thirds of seventeen-year-olds. Boys are significantly more likely than girls to have friends who view online pornography: 25% of twelve- and thirteen-year-old girls, and 46% of sixteen- and seventeen-year-old girls say they have friends who regularly view and download internet pornography, compared with 37% and 65% of boys in those age groups.[8]

Bear in mind that most of these statistics are already outdated.

Psychotherapists and family counselors across the country attest to the popularity of pornography among *pre*-adolescents. Even pre-adolescents are being treated for pornography addiction, says Judith Coché, a clinical psychologist who runs the Coché Center in Philadelphia and teaches psychiatry at the University of Pennsylvania. She describes one case in which the parents of an eleven-year-old girl found her creating her own pornographic website. When confronted, she said that pornography was considered "cool" among her friends. Perhaps it wasn't a very good idea, she admitted, but all of her friends were doing it. Her parents were horrified. Coché says, "Before the internet, I never encountered this."

"I've had my own therapy practice for over twenty-five years," she says. "I feel like I've seen everything." She pauses and says almost apologetically, "I've been walking around my practice saying, 'We have an epidemic on our hands.' The growth of pornography and its impact on young people is really, really dangerous. And the most dangerous part is that we don't even realize what's happening."

Pornography is wildly popular with teenage boys in a way that makes yesteryear's sneaked glimpses at *Penthouse* seem monastic. The prevalence of the internet among teenagers has made pornography just another online activity; there is little barrier to entry and almost no sense of taboo. Instead, pornography seems to be a natural right and an acceptable pastime. One teenage boy in Boston explained recently to the *New York Times*, "Who needs the hassle of dating when I've got online porn?"[9]

There is a reason for this. Like all good marketers, pornographers know it's important to reel consumers in while they're young. Pornography is integrated into

---

8 "National Survey of American Attitudes on Substance Abuse IX: Teen Dating Practices and Sexual Activity," The National Center on Addiction and Substance Abuse at Columbia University, August 2004: 23.

9 Benoit Denizet-Lewis, "Friends, Friends with Benefits and the Benefits of the Local Mall," *New York Times Magazine*, 30 May 2004.

the cable TV and videogame cultures, for example. MTV recently announced the launch of a Stan Lee/Hugh Hefner collaboration, *Hef's Superbunnies*, an "edgy, sexy animated series" from the creator of the *Spider-Man* comic book series featuring a buxom team of specially trained Playboy bunnies.[10]

Mainstream videogames regularly feature pornographic elements. One 2004 game, "The Guy Game," which features women exposing their breasts when they answer questions wrong in a trivia contest, didn't even get an "Adults-Only" rating. (The game manufacturer is being sued because one female included in the footage was only seventeen and didn't give her consent to be filmed.)[11] "BMX XXX" adds a pornographic sheen to bike stunts and racing. Another game, "Leisure Suit Larry: Magna Cum Laude," features full-on nudity as gamers live out the player lifestyle, trying to score hot babes. The manufacturers are fighting to obtain an "M" rating (the equivalent of a movie's "R") in order to ensure being carried at Walmarts across America.[12]

Marketers have extended the porn brand to everything from sporting equipment to clothing. Two snowboarding companies, Burton Snowboards and Sims, now offer boards—clearly marketed to teenagers, the backbone of the snowboarding market—emblazoned with images of *Playboy* bunnies and Vivid porn stars. Sims boasts that the boards with photographs of porn starts Jenna Jameson and Briana Banks are their best sellers.

Sexually cued to a computer

The effects of such ever-present pornography on kids who are still developing sexually has yet to be fully understood, Coché explains. She has talked to parents who have witnessed their sons playing computer games when pornographic pop-ups come onto the screen. "Pornography is so often tied into videogame culture and insinuates itself even into non-pornographic areas of the web. It's very hard for a twelve-year-old boy to avoid."

---

10 Cynthia Littleton, "Hugh Hefner, Stan Lee to Hop to 'Superbunnies,'" *Hollywood Reporter*, 7 September 2004.

11 Tor Thorsen, "Take-Two, Sony, and Microsoft Sued Over 'The Guy Game,'" *Gamespot.com*, 21 December 2004. Available at http://www.gamespot.com/news/6115478.html.

12 Chris Morris, "Video Games Get Raunchy," CNN *Money.com*, 13 May 2004, http://money.cnn.com/2004/05/11/technology/e3_nekkidgames/index.htm.

As a result, boys are learning to sexually cue to a computer, rather than to human beings. "This is where they're learning what turns them on. And what are they supposed to do about that? Whereas once boys would kiss a girl they had a crush on behind the school, we don't know how boys who become trained to cue sexually to computer-generated porn stars are going to behave, especially as they get older."

Kids also absorb pornography very differently from adults. Not only are they like sponges, they are also quite literal. Not only younger children, but even young teenagers are generally not sophisticated enough to differentiate between fantasy and reality. They learn direct lessons from pornography, with no filter, and with no concept of exaggeration, irony, or affect.

They learn what women supposedly look like, how they should act, and what they are supposed to do. They learn what women "want" and how men can give it to them. Watching pornography, boys and girls learn that women always want sex and that sex is divorced from relationships. They learn that men can have whomever they want and that women will respond the way men want them to. They learn that anal sex is the norm and instant female orgasm is to be expected. And they absorb these lessons avidly, emulating people they perceive to be role models.

"Kids today are going to run into pornography online, not erotica," explains Aline Zoldbrod. "They're getting a very bad model. Pornography doesn't show how a real couple negotiates conflict or creates intimacy." For girls especially, Zoldbrod believes, pornography is a "brutal way to be introduced to sexuality," since much of it is "rape-like" in its use of violence.

Still, many older kids at least partly recognize the negative side. When asked in the 2001 study by the Kaiser Family Foundation, 59% of fifteen- to twenty-four-year-olds said they thought seeing pornography online encouraged young people to have sex before they are ready, and half thought it would lead people to think unprotected sex is okay. Half thought internet pornography could lead to addiction and promote bad attitudes toward women. In a 2002 nationwide Gallup poll, 69% of teenage boys between the ages of thirteen and seventeen said that even if nobody ever knew about it, they would feel guilty about surfing pornography on the internet. Not surprising, an even greater number of girls—86%—felt the same way.

Interestingly, when asked about the effect of pornography for the *Pornified*/Harris poll, young people between the ages of eighteen and twenty-four were most likely of all generations to report negative consequences. Four in ten of them believe pornography harms relationships between men and women, compared with only three in ten twenty-five-to-forty-year-olds. The internet generation is also more likely to believe that pornography changes men's expectations of women's looks and behavior.

Adults also see the harm pornography does to young children and teenagers. When asked in the *Pornified*/Harris poll, "What is the greatest impact of pornography on children?" 30% of Americans said the fact that it distorts boys' expectations and understanding of women and sex, 25% said that it makes kids more likely to have sex earlier than they otherwise might have, 7% cited the way it distorts girls' body images and ideas about sex, and 6% said it makes kids more likely to look at pornography as adults (men were twice as likely as women to believe this).

Only 2% of Americans actually believe that pornography helps kids better understand sexuality. And only 9% think that it doesn't have any impact on children at all.

Pornography's effects

Pornography in all its permutations affects children's developing sexuality; the younger the age of exposure and the more hard-core the material, the more intense the effects. Boys who look at pornography excessively become men who connect arousal purely with the physical, losing the ability to become attracted by the particular features of a given partner. Instead, they recreate images from pornography in their brain while they're with a real person.

"It's sad that boys who are initiated to sex through these images become indoctrinated in a way that can potentially stay with them for the rest of their lives," Gary Brooks says. "Boys learn that you have sex in spite of your feelings, not because of your feelings. Meanwhile, girls are taught that you don't have intimacy without relationships."

No matter what kind of pornography teenagers look at, spending one's prepubescence and puberty using porn can have lifelong implications. Masters and Johnson's clinical director Mark Schwartz has seen fourteen- and fifteen-year-old boys who are addicted to pornography. "It's awful to see the effect it has on them," he says. "At such a young age, to have that kind of sexual problem."

Schwartz isn't surprised about the growing number of young addicts in the Internet Age. At that age, "your brain is much more susceptible," he explains. "Many of these boys are very smart and academically successful; a lot of computer geeks are the ones who get drawn in. It affects how they develop sexually. Think about a twelve-year-old boy looking at *Playboy* magazine. When you're talking about internet pornography, you can multiply that effect by the relative size of the internet itself."

Research trickling in has begun to document the effects of pornography on kids, a difficult area to study given obvious ethical challenges. Certainly, there aren't any parents who would consent to have their children view pornography in order to further research on the damage it causes.

Still, some evidence has been gathered. A recent study of 101 sexually abusive children in Australia documented increased aggressiveness in boys who use pornography. Almost all had internet access, and 90% admitted to seeing pornography online. One-fourth said an older sibling or a friend had shown them how to access pornography online, sometimes against their will; 25% said that using pornography was their primary reason for going online. When questioned separately, nearly all of their parents said they doubted their child would access any pornography via the internet.[13]

It wasn't like this

Touring around this country to promote my book *Pornified*, I heard again and again from concerned parents. "I know my fourteen-year-old son is looking at extremely hard-core pornography, but what can I do about it? He tells me he needs the computer for schoolwork." "I have a ten-year-old daughter. I don't want to even think about what boys her age are learning about the opposite sex online." "My daughter found pornography that my husband downloaded on the family computer." A pediatric nurse told me there was an incident in her practice in which *toddlers* acted out moves from a pornographic movie.

A day's worth of nationwide headlines inevitably brings up stories of children encountering pornography at the local library, child pornography arrests, and school incidents in which teachers are caught looking at pornography on school computers during school hours. It is terrible enough that adults are suffering the consequences of a pornified culture. But we must think about the kind of world we are introducing

---

13 Patrick Goodenough, "Online Porn Driving Sexually Aggressive Children," *CNSNews.com*, 25 November 2003.

to our children. Certainly everyone—liberals and conservatives alike—can agree with the statement, "It wasn't like this when we were kids." And I can't imagine anyone would have that thought without simultaneously experiencing a profound sense of fear and loss.

ACQUIRING TASTES AND LOVES: WHAT NEUROPLASTICITY TEACHES US ABOUT SEXUAL ATTRACTION AND LOVE

Norman Doidge

A. was a single, handsome young man who came to me because he was depressed. He had just gotten involved with a beautiful woman who had a boyfriend, and she had begun to encourage him to abuse her. She tried to draw A. into acting out sexual fantasies in which she dressed up as a prostitute, and he was to "take charge" of her and become violent in some way. When A. began to feel an alarming wish to oblige her, he got very upset, broke it off, and sought treatment. He had a history of involvement with women who were already attached to other men and emotionally out of control. His girlfriends had either been demanding and possessive or castratingly cruel. Yet these were the women who thrilled him. "Nice" girls, thoughtful, kind women, bored him, and he felt that any woman who fell in love with him in a tender, uncomplicated way was defective.

His own mother was a severe alcoholic, frequently needy, seductive, and given to emotional storms and violent rages throughout his childhood. A. recalled her banging his sister's head against the radiator and burning his stepbrother's fingers as a punishment for playing with matches. She was frequently depressed, often threatening suicide, and his role was to be on the alert, calm her, and prevent her. His relationship with her was also highly sexualized. She wore see-through nighties and talked to him as though he were a lover. He thought he recalled her inviting him into her bed when he was a child and had an image of himself sitting with his foot in her vagina while she masturbated. He had an exciting but furtive feeling about the scene. On the rare occasions when his father, who had retreated from his wife, was home, A. recalled himself as "perpetually short of breath," and trying to stop fights between his parents, who eventually divorced.

Taken from "Acquiring Tastes and Loves," from *The Brain That Changes Itself: Stories of Personal Triumph from the Frontiers of Brain Science*, by Norman Doidge, copyright © 2007 by Norman Doidge, used by permission of Viking Penguin, a division of Penguin Group (USA) Inc.

A. spent much of his childhood stifling his rage at both parents and often felt like a volcano about to burst. Intimate relationships seemed like forms of violence, in which others threatened to eat him alive, and yet by the time he had passed through childhood, it was for women who promised to do just that, and them alone, that he had acquired an erotic taste.

Human beings exhibit an extraordinary degree of sexual plasticity compared with other creatures. We vary in what we like to do with our partners in a sexual act. We vary where in our bodies we experience sexual excitement and satisfaction. But most of all we vary in whom or what we are attracted to. People often say they find a particular "type" attractive, or a "turn-on," and these types vary immensely from person to person.

For some, the types change as they go through different periods and have new experiences. One homosexual man had successive relations with men from one race or ethnic group, then with those from another, and in each period he could be attracted only to men in the group that was currently "hot." After one period was over, he could never be attracted to a man from the old group again. He acquired a taste for these "types" in quick succession and seemed more smitten by the person's category or type (i.e., "Asians" or "African-Americans") than by the individual. The plasticity of this man's sexual taste exaggerates a general truth: that the human libido is not a hardwired, invariable biological urge but can be curiously fickle, easily altered by our psychology and the history of our sexual encounters. And our libido can also be finicky. Much scientific writing implies otherwise and depicts the sexual instinct as a biological imperative, an ever-hungry brute, always demanding satisfaction—a glutton, not a gourmet. But human beings are more like gourmets and are drawn to types and have strong preferences; having a "type" causes us to defer satisfaction until we find what we are looking for, because attraction to a type is restrictive: the person who is "really turned on by blondes" may tacitly rule out brunettes and redheads.

Even sexual preference can occasionally change.[1] Though some scientists increasingly emphasize the inborn basis of our sexual preferences, it is also true that

1 The tendency of some heterosexuals to develop a homosexual attraction when members of the opposite sex are not available is well known (e.g., in prison or in the military), and these attractions tend to be "add-ons." According to Richard C. Friedman, researcher on male homosexuality, when male homosexuals develop a heterosexual attraction, it is almost always an "add-on" attraction, not a replacement (personal communication).

some people have heterosexual attractions for part of their lives—with no history of bisexuality—and then "add on" a homosexual attraction and vice versa.

Sexual plasticity may seem to have reached its height in those who have had many different partners, learning to adapt to each new lover; but think of the plasticity required of the aging married couple with a good sex life. They looked very different in their twenties, when they met, than they do in their sixties, yet their libidos adjust, so they remain attracted.

But sexual plasticity goes further still. Fetishists desire inanimate objects. The male fetishist can be more excited by a high-heeled shoe with a fur trim, or by a woman's lingerie, than by a real woman. Since ancient times some human beings in rural areas have had intercourse with animals. Some people seem to be attracted not so much to people as to complex sexual scripts, where partners play roles, involving various perversions, combining sadism, masochism, voyeurism, and exhibitionism. When they place an ad in the personals, the description of what they are looking for in a lover often sounds more like a job description than like that of a person they would like to know.

Given that sexuality is an instinct, and instinct is traditionally defined as a hereditary behavior unique to a species, varying little from one member to the next, the variety of our sexual tastes is curious. Instincts generally resist change and are thought to have a clear, nonnegotiable, hardwired purpose, such as survival. Yet the human sexual "instinct" seems to have broken free of its core purpose, reproduction, and varies[2] to a bewildering extent, as it does not in other animals, in which the sexual instinct seems to behave itself and act like an instinct.

No other instinct can so satisfy without accomplishing its biological purpose, and no other instinct is so disconnected from its purpose. Anthropologists have shown that for a long time humanity did not know that sexual intercourse was required for reproduction. This "fact of life" had to be learned by our ancestors, just as children must learn it today. This detachment from its primary purpose is perhaps the ultimate sign of sexual plasticity.

Love too is remarkably flexible, and its expression has changed through history. Though we speak of romantic love as the most *natural* of sentiments, in fact the con-

---

2 This plasticity is one reason why Freud called sex a "drive" as opposed to an instinct. A drive is a powerful urge that has instinctual roots but is more plastic than most instincts and is more influenced by the mind.

centration of our adult hopes for intimacy, tenderness, and lust in one person until death do us part is not common to all societies and has only recently become widespread in our own. For millennia most marriages were arranged by parents for practical reasons. Certainly, there are unforgettable stories of romantic love linked to marriage in the Bible, as in the Song of Songs, and linked to disaster in medieval troubadour poetry and, later, in Shakespeare. But romantic love began to gain social approval in the aristocracies and courts of Europe only in the twelfth century—originally between an unmarried man and a married woman, either adulterous or unconsummated, usually ending badly. Only with the spread of democratic ideals of individualism did the idea that lovers ought to be able to choose spouses for themselves take firmer hold and gradually begin to seem completely natural and inalienable.

It is reasonable to ask whether our sexual plasticity is related to neuroplasticity. Research has shown that neuroplasticity is neither ghettoized within certain departments in the brain nor confined to the sensory, motor, and cognitive processing areas we have already explored. The brain structure that regulates instinctive behaviors, including sex, called the hypothalamus, is plastic, as is the amygdala, the structure that processes emotion and anxiety.[3] While some parts of the brain, such as the cortex, may have more plastic potential because there are more neurons and connections to be altered, even noncortical areas display plasticity. It is a property of all brain tissue. Plasticity exists in the hippocampus[4] (the area that turns our memories from short-term to long-term ones) as well as in areas that control our breathing,[5] process primitive sensation,[6] and process pain.[7] It exists

---

3 The hypothalamus also regulates eating, sleeping, and important hormones. G. I. Hatton. 1997. Function-related plasticity in hypothalamus. *Annual Review of Neuroscience*, 20:375–97; J. LeDoux. 2002. *Synaptic self: How our brains become who we are*. New York: Viking; S. Maren. 2001. Neurobiology of Pavlovian fear conditioning. *Annual Review of Neuroscience*, 24:897–931, especially 914.

4 B. S. McEwen. 1999. Stress and hippocampal plasticity. *Annual Review of Neuroscience*, 22: 105–22.

5 J. L. Feldman, G. S. Mitchell, and E. E. Nattie. 2003. Breathing: Rhythmicity, plasticity, chemosensitivity. *Annual Review of Neuroscience*, 26:239–66.

6 E. G. Jones. 2000. Cortical and subcortical contributions to activity-dependent plasticity in primate somatosensory cortex. *Annual Review of Neuroscience*, 23:1–37.

7 G. Baranauskas. 2001. Pain-induced plasticity in the spinal cord. In C. A. Shaw and J. C. McEachern, eds., *Toward a theory of neuroplasticity*. Philadelphia: Psychology Press, 373–86.

in the spinal cord[8]—as scientists have shown; actor Christopher Reeve, who suffered a severe spinal injury, demonstrated such plasticity, when he was able, through relentless exercise, to recover some feeling and mobility seven years after his accident.

Merzenich puts it this way: "You cannot have plasticity in isolation . . . it's an absolute impossibility." His experiments have shown that if one brain system changes, those systems connected to it change as well.[9] The same "plastic rules"—use it or lose it, or neurons that fire together wire together—apply throughout. Different areas of the brain wouldn't be able to function together if that weren't the case.

Do the same plastic rules that apply to brain maps in the sensory, motor, and language cortices apply to more complex maps, such as those that represent our relationships, sexual or otherwise? Merzenich has also shown that complex brain maps are governed by the same plastic principles as simpler maps. Animals exposed to a simple tone will develop a single brain map region to process it. Animals exposed to a complex pattern, such as a melody of six tones, will not simply link together six different map regions but will develop a region that encodes the *entire* melody. These more complex melody maps obey the same plastic principles[10] as maps for single tones.

"The sexual instincts," wrote Freud, "are noticeable to us for their plasticity,[11] their capacity for altering their aims." Freud was not the first to argue that sexuality was plastic—Plato, in his dialogue on love, argued that human Eros took many

---

8 J. W. McDonald, D. Becker, C. L. Sadowsky, J. A. Jane, T. E. Conturo, and L. M. Schultz. 2002. Late recovery following spinal cord injury: Case report and review of the literature. *Journal of Neurosurgery (Spine 2)* 97:252–65; J. R. Wolpaw and A. M. Tennissen. 2001. Activity-dependent spinal cord plasticity in health and disease. *Annual Review of Neuroscience*, 24:807–43.

9 Merzenich has done experiments that show that when change occurs in a sensory processing area—the auditory cortex—it causes change in the frontal lobe, an area involved in planning, to which the auditory cortex is connected. "You can't change the primary auditory cortex," says Merzenich, "without changing what is happening in the frontal cortex. It's an absolute impossibility."

10 M. M. Merzenich, personal communication; H. Nakahara, L. I. Zhang, and M. Merzenich. 2004. Specialization of primary auditory cortex processing by sound exposure in the "critical period." *Proceedings of the National Academy of Sciences, USA*, 101(18): 7170–74.

11 S. Freud. 1932/1933/1964. *New introductory lectures on psycho-analysis*. Translated by J. Stratchey. In *Standard* edition of the complete psychological works of Sigmund Freud, vol. 22. London: Hogarth Press, 97.

forms[12]—but Freud laid the foundations for a neuroscientific understanding of sexual and romantic plasticity.

One of his most important contributions was his discovery of critical periods for sexual plasticity. Freud argued that an adult's ability to love intimately and sexually unfolds in stages, beginning in the infant's first passionate attachments to its parents. He learned from his patients, and from observing children, that early childhood, not puberty, was the first critical period for sexuality and intimacy, and that children are capable of passionate, protosexual feelings—crushes, loving feelings, and in some cases even sexual excitement, as A. was. Freud discovered that the sexual abuse of children is harmful because it influences the critical period of sexuality in childhood, shaping our later attractions and thoughts about sex. Children are needy and typically develop passionate attachments to their parents. If the parent is warm, gentle, and reliable, the child will frequently develop a taste for that kind of relationship later on; if the parent is disengaged, cool, distant, self-involved, angry, ambivalent, or erratic, the child may seek out an adult mate who has similar tendencies. There are exceptions, but a significant body of research now confirms Freud's basic insight that early patterns of relating and attaching to others, if problematic, can get "wired" into our brains[13] in childhood and repeated in adulthood. Many aspects of the sexual script that A. played out when he first came to see me were repetitions of his traumatic childhood situation, thinly disguised—such as his being attracted to an unstable woman who crossed normal sexual boundaries in furtive relationships, where hostility and sexual excitement were merged, while the woman's official partner was cuckolded and threatening to reenter the scene.

---

12 Plato's Eros is not identical with Freud's libido (or later Eros), but there is some overlap. Platonic Eros is the longing we feel in response to our awareness of our incompleteness as human beings. It is a longing to complete ourselves. One way we try to overcome our incompleteness is by finding another person to love and have sex with. But the speakers in Plato's *Symposium* also emphasize that this same Eros can take many forms, some of which don't appear erotic at first glance, and that erotic longing can have many different kinds of objects.

13 A. N. Schore. 1994. *Affect regulation and the origin of the self: The neurobiology of emotional development.* Hillsdale, N.J.: Lawrence Erlbaum Associates; A. N. Schore. 2003. *Affect dysregulation and disorders of the self.* New York: W. W. Norton & Co.; A. N. Schore. 2003. *Affect regulation and the repair of the self.* New York: W. W. Norton & Co.

The idea of the critical period was formulated around the time Freud started writing about sex and love, by embryologists[14] who observed that in the embryo the nervous system develops in stages, and that if these stages are disturbed, the animal or person will be harmed, often catastrophically, for life. Though Freud didn't use the term, what he said about the early stages of sexual development conforms to what we know about critical periods. They are brief windows of time when new brain systems and maps develop[15] with the help of stimulation from the people in one's environment.

Traces of childhood sentiments in adult love and sexuality are detectable in everyday behaviors. When adults in our culture have tender foreplay, or express their most intimate adoration, they often call each other "baby" or "babe." They use terms of endearment that their mothers used with them as children, such as "honey" and "sweetie pie," terms that evoke the earliest months of life when the mother expressed her love by feeding, caressing, and talking sweetly to her baby—what Freud called the oral phase, the first critical period of sexuality, the essence of which is summed up in the words "nurturance" and "nourish"—tenderly caring for, loving, *and* feeding. The baby feels merged with the mother, and its trust of others develops as the baby is held and nurtured with a sugary food, milk. Being loved, cared for, and fed are mentally associated in the mind and wired together in the brain in our first formative experience after birth.

When adults talk baby talk, using words such as "sweetie pie" and "baby" to address each other, and give their conversation an oral flavor, they are, according to Freud, "regressing," moving from mature mental states of relating to earlier phases of life. In terms of plasticity, such regression, I believe, involves unmasking old neuronal pathways that then trigger all the associations of that earlier phase. Regression can

---

14 M. C. Dareste. 1891. *Recherches sur la production artificielle des monstruosités.* [Studies of the artificial production of monsters.] Paris: C. Reinwald; C. R. Stockard. 1921. Developmental rate and structural expression: An experimental study of twins, "double monsters," and single deformities and their interaction among embryonic organs during their origin and development. *American Journal of Anatomy*, 28(2): 115–277.

15 In the first year of life, the average brain goes from weighing 400 grams at birth to 1000 grams at twelve months. We are so dependent on early love and the caregiving of others in part because large areas of our brain don't begin to develop until after we are born. The neurons in the prefrontal cortex, which helps us regulate our emotions, make connections in the first two years of life, but only with the help of people, which in most cases means the mother, who literally molds her baby's brain.

be pleasant and harmless, as in adult foreplay, or it can be problematic,[16] as when infantile aggressive pathways are unmasked and an adult has a temper tantrum.

Even "talking dirty" shows traces of infantile sexual stages. After all, why should sex be thought "dirty" at all? This attitude reflects a child's view of sex from a stage when it is conscious of toilet training, urination, and defecation and is surprised to learn that the genitals, which are involved in urination, and so close to the anus, are also involved in sex, and that Mommy permits Daddy to insert his "dirty" organ in a hole that is very close to her bottom. Adults are not generally bothered by this, because in adolescence they have gone through another critical period of sexual plasticity in which their brains reorganized again, so that the pleasure of sex becomes intense enough to override any disgust.

Freud showed that many sexual mysteries can be understood as critical-period fixations. After Freud, we are no longer surprised that the girl whose father left her as a child pursues unavailable men old enough to be her father, or that people raised by ice-queen mothers often seek such people out as partners, sometimes becoming "icy" themselves, because, never having experienced empathy in the critical period, a whole part of their brains failed to develop. And many perversions can be explained in terms of plasticity and the persistence of childhood conflicts. But the main point is that in our critical periods we can acquire sexual and romantic tastes and inclinations that get wired into our brains and can have a powerful impact for the rest of our lives. And the fact that we can acquire different sexual tastes contributes to the tremendous sexual variation between us.

The idea that a critical period helps shape sexual desire in adults contradicts the currently popular argument that what attracts us is less the product of our personal history than of our common biology. Certain people—models and movie stars, for instance—are widely regarded as beautiful or sexy. A certain strand of biology teaches us that these people are attractive because they exhibit biological signs of robustness, which promise fertility and strength: a clear complexion and symmetrical features mean a potential mate is free from disease; an hourglass figure is a sign a woman is fertile; a man's muscles predict he will be able to protect a woman and her offspring.

---

16 Sometimes regression is quite unanticipated, and otherwise mature adults become shocked at how "infantile" their behavior can become.

But this simplifies what biology really teaches. Not everyone falls in love with the body, as when a woman says, "I knew, when I first heard *that* voice, that he was for me," the music of the voice being perhaps a better indication of a man's soul than his body's surface. And sexual taste has changed over the centuries. Rubens's beauties were large by current standards, and over the decades the vital statistics of *Playboy* centerfolds and fashion models have varied from voluptuous to androgynous. Sexual taste is obviously influenced by culture and experience and is often acquired and then wired into the brain.

"Acquired tastes" are by definition learned, unlike "tastes," which are inborn. A baby needn't acquire a taste for milk, water, or sweets; these are immediately perceived as pleasant. Acquired tastes are initially experienced with indifference or dislike but later become pleasant—the odors of cheeses, Italian bitters, dry wines, coffees, patés, the hint of urine in a fried kidney. Many delicacies that people pay dearly for, that they must "develop a taste for," are the very foods that disgusted them as children.

In Elizabethan times lovers were so enamored of each other's body odors that it was common for a woman to keep a peeled apple in her armpit until it had absorbed her sweat and smell. She would give this "love apple" to her lover to sniff at in her absence. We, on the other hand, use synthetic aromas of fruits and flowers to mask our body odor from our lovers. Which of these two approaches is acquired and which is natural is not so easy to determine. A substance as "naturally" repugnant to us as the urine of cows is used by the Masai tribe in East Africa as a lotion for their hair—a direct consequence of the cow's importance in their culture. Many tastes we think "natural" are acquired through learning and become "second nature" to us. We are unable to distinguish our "second nature" from our "original nature" because our neuroplastic brains, once rewired, develop a new nature, every bit as biological as our original.

The current porn epidemic gives a graphic demonstration that sexual tastes can be acquired. Pornography, delivered by high-speed Internet connections, satisfies every one of the prerequisites for neuroplastic change.[17]

Pornography seems, at first glance, to be a purely instinctual matter: Sexually explicit pictures trigger instinctual responses, which are the product of millions of

---

17 In chapter 8, "Imagination," I give the scientific evidence that proves that we can change our brain maps simply by imagining things.

years of evolution. But if that were true, pornography would be unchanging. The same triggers, bodily parts and their proportions, that appealed to our ancestors would excite us. This is what pornographers would have us believe, for they claim they are battling sexual repression, taboo, and fear and that their goal is to liberate the natural, pent-up sexual instincts.

But in fact the content of pornography is a *dynamic* phenomenon that perfectly illustrates the progress of an acquired taste. Thirty years ago "hardcore" pornography usually meant the *explicit* depiction of sexual intercourse between two aroused partners, displaying their genitals. "Softcore" meant pictures of women, mostly, on a bed, at their toilette, or in some semiromantic setting, in various states of undress, breasts revealed.

Now hardcore has evolved and is increasingly dominated by the sadomasochistic themes of forced sex, ejaculations on women's faces, and angry anal sex, all involving scripts fusing sex with hatred and humiliation. Hardcore pornography now explores the world of perversion, while softcore is now what hardcore was a few decades ago, explicit sexual intercourse between adults, now available on cable TV. The comparatively tame softcore pictures of yesteryear—women in various states of undress—now show up on mainstream media all day long, in the pornification of everything, including television, rock videos, soap operas, advertisements, and so on.

Pornography's growth has been extraordinary; it accounts for 25 percent of video rentals and is the fourth most common reason people give for going online. An MSNBC.com survey of viewers in 2001 found that 80 percent felt they were spending so much time on pornographic sites that they were putting their relationships or jobs at risk. Softcore pornography's influence is now most profound because, now that it is no longer hidden, it influences young people with little sexual experience and especially plastic minds, in the process of forming their sexual tastes and desires. Yet the plastic influence of pornography on adults can also be profound, and those who use it have no sense of the extent to which their brains are reshaped by it.

During the mid- to late 1990s, when the Internet was growing rapidly and pornography was exploding on it, I treated or assessed a number of men who all had essentially the same story. Each had acquired a taste for a kind of pornography that, to a greater or lesser degree, troubled or even disgusted him, had a disturbing effect on the pattern of his sexual excitement, and ultimately affected his relationships and sexual potency.

None of these men were fundamentally immature, socially awkward, or withdrawn from the world into a massive pornography collection that was a substitute for relationships with real women. These were pleasant, generally thoughtful men, in reasonably successful relationships or marriages.

Typically, while I was treating one of these men for some other problem, he would report, almost as an aside and with telling discomfort, that he found himself spending more and more time on the Internet, looking at pornography and masturbating. He might try to ease his discomfort by asserting that everybody did it. In some cases he would begin by looking at a *Playboy*-type site or at a nude picture or video clip that someone had sent him as a lark. In other cases he would visit a harmless site, with a suggestive ad that redirected him to risqué sites, and soon he would be hooked.

A number of these men also reported something else, often in passing, that caught my attention. They reported increasing difficulty in being turned on by their actual sexual partners, spouses or girlfriends, though they still considered them objectively attractive. When I asked if this phenomenon had any relationship to viewing pornography, they answered that it initially helped them get more excited during sex but over time had the opposite effect. Now, instead of using their senses to enjoy being in bed, in the present, with their partners, lovemaking increasingly required them to fantasize that they were part of a porn script. Some gently tried to persuade their lovers to act like porn stars, and they were increasingly interested in "fucking" as opposed to "making love." Their sexual fantasy lives were increasingly dominated by the scenarios that they had, so to speak, downloaded into their brains, and these new scripts were often more primitive and more violent than their previous sexual fantasies. I got the impression that any sexual creativity these men had was dying and that they were becoming addicted to Internet porn.

The changes I observed are not confined to a few people in therapy. A social shift is occurring. While it is usually difficult to get information about private sexual mores, this is not the case with pornography today, because its use is increasingly public. This shift coincides with the change from calling it "pornography" to the more casual term "porn." For his book on American campus life, *I Am Charlotte Simmons,* Tom Wolfe spent a number of years observing students on university campuses. In the book one boy, Ivy Peters, comes into the male residence and says, "Anybody got porn?"[18]

Wolfe goes on, "This was not an unusual request. Many boys spoke openly about how they masturbated at least once every day, as if this were some sort of prudent maintenance of the psychosexual system." One of the boys tells Ivy Peters, "Try the third floor. They got some one-hand magazines up there." But Peters responds, "I've built up a tolerance to magazines . . . I need videos." Another boy says, "Oh, f'r Chrissake, I.P., it's ten o'clock at night. In another hour the cum dumpsters will start coming over here to spend the night . . . And you're looking for porn videos and a knuckle fuck." Then Ivy "shrugged and turned his palms up as if to say, 'I want porn. What's the big deal?'"

The big deal is his tolerance. He recognizes that he is like a drug addict who can no longer get high on the images that once turned him on. And the danger is that this tolerance will carry over into relationships, as it did in patients whom I was seeing, leading to potency problems and new, at times unwelcome, tastes. When pornographers boast that they are pushing the envelope by introducing new, harder themes, what they don't say is that they must, because their customers are building up a tolerance to the content. The back pages of men's risqué magazines and Internet porn sites are filled with ads for Viagra-type drugs—medicine developed for older men with erectile problems related to aging and blocked blood vessels in the penis. Today young men who surf porn are tremendously fearful of impotence, or "erectile dysfunction" as it is euphemistically called. The misleading term implies that these men have a problem in their penises, but the problem is in their heads, in their sexual brain maps. The penis works fine when they use pornography. It rarely occurs to them that there may be a relationship between the pornography they are consuming and their impotence. (A few men, however, tellingly described their hours at computer porn sites as time spent "masturbating my brains out.")

One of the boys in Wolfe's scene describes the girls who are coming over to have sex with their boyfriends as "cum dumpsters." He too is influenced by porn images, for "cum dumpsters," like many women in porn films, are always eager, available receptacles and therefore devalued.

The addictiveness of Internet pornography is not a metaphor. Not all addictions are to drugs or alcohol. People can be seriously addicted to gambling,

---

18 T. Wolfe. 2004. *I Am Charlotte Simmons*. New York: HarperCollins, 92–93.

even to running. All addicts show a loss of control of the activity, compulsively seek it out despite negative consequences, develop tolerance so that they need higher and higher levels of stimulation for satisfaction, and experience withdrawal if they can't consummate the addictive act.

All addiction involves long-term, sometimes lifelong, neuroplastic change in the brain. For addicts, moderation is impossible, and they must avoid the substance or activity completely if they are to avoid addictive behaviors. Alcoholics Anonymous insists that there are no "former alcoholics" and makes people who haven't had a drink for decades introduce themselves at a meeting by saying, "My name is John, and I am an alcoholic." In terms of plasticity, they are often correct.

In order to determine how addictive a street drug is, researchers at the National Institutes of Health (NIH) in Maryland train a rat to press a bar until it gets a shot of the drug. The harder the animal is willing to work to press the bar, the more addictive the drug. Cocaine, almost all other illegal drugs, and even nondrug addictions such as running make the pleasure-giving neurotransmitter dopamine more active[19] in the brain. Dopamine is called the reward transmitter, because when we accomplish something—run a race and win—our brain triggers its release. Though exhausted, we get a surge of energy, exciting pleasure, and confidence and even raise our hands and run a victory lap. The losers, on the other hand, who get no such dopamine surge, immediately run out of energy, collapse at the finish line, and feel awful about themselves. By hijacking our dopamine system, addictive substances give us pleasure without our having to work for it.

Dopamine, as we saw in Merzenich's work, is also involved in plastic change. The same surge of dopamine that thrills us also consolidates the neuronal connections responsible for the behaviors that led us to accomplish our goal. When Merzenich used an electrode to stimulate an animal's dopamine reward system while playing a sound, dopamine release stimulated plastic change,[20] enlarging the representation for the sound in the animal's auditory map. An important link with porn is that dopamine is also released in sexual excitement,[21] increasing the sex drive in

---

19 E. Nestler. 2001. Molecular basis of long-term plasticity underlying addiction. *Nature Reviews Neuroscience*, 2(2): 119–28.

20 S. Bao, V. T. Chan, L. I. Zhang, and M. M. Merzenich. 2003. Suppression of cortical representation through backward conditioning. *Proceedings of the National Academy of Sciences, USA*, 100(3): 1405–8.

21 T. L. Crenshaw. 1996. *The alchemy of love and lust*. New York: G. P. Putnam's Sons, 135.

both sexes, facilitating orgasm, and activating the brain's pleasure centers. Hence the addictive power of pornography.

Eric Nestler, at the University of Texas, has shown how addictions cause permanent changes in the brains of animals. A single dose of many addictive drugs will produce a protein, called iFosB (pronounced "delta Fos B"), that accumulates in the neurons. Each time the drug is used, more iFosB accumulates, until it throws a genetic switch, affecting which genes are turned on or off. Flipping this switch causes changes that persist long after the drug is stopped, leading to irreversible damage to the brain's dopamine system and rendering the animal far more prone to addiction. Nondrug addictions, such as running and sucrose drinking, also lead to the accumulation of iFosB and the same permanent changes in the dopamine system.[22]

Pornographers promise healthy pleasure and relief from sexual tension, but what they often deliver is an addiction, tolerance, and an eventual decrease in pleasure. Paradoxically, the male patients I worked with often craved pornography but didn't like it.

The usual view is that an addict goes back for more of his fix because he likes the pleasure it gives and doesn't like the pain of withdrawal. But addicts take drugs when there is *no* prospect of pleasure, when they know they have an insufficient dose to make them high, and will crave more even before they begin to withdraw. Wanting and liking are two different things.

An addict experiences cravings because his plastic brain has become sensitized[23] to the drug or the experience. Sensitization is different from tolerance. As tolerance develops, the addict needs more and more of a substance or porn to get a pleasant effect; as sensitization develops, he needs less and less of the substance to crave it intensely. So sensitization leads to increased wanting, though not necessarily liking.[24] It is the accumulation of iFosB, caused by exposure to an addictive substance or activity, that leads to sensitization.

---

22 E. Nestler. 2003. *Brain plasticity and drug addiction.* Presentation at "Reprogramming the Human Brain" Conference, Center for Brain Health, University of Texas at Dallas, April 11.

23 K. C. Berridge and T. E. Robinson. 2002. The mind of an addicted brain: Neural sensitization of wanting versus liking. In J. T. Cacioppo, G. G. Bernston, R. Adolphs, et al., eds., *Foundations in social neuroscience.* Cambridge, Mass.: MIT Press, 565–72.

24 It is possible to judge whether an animal or a person likes the taste of a food by its facial expressions. Berridge and Robinson have shown, by manipulating dopamine levels while animals eat, that it is possible to make them want more food, even though they don't like it.

Pornography is more exciting than satisfying because we have two separate pleasure systems in our brains,[25] one that has to do with exciting pleasure and one with satisfying pleasure. The exciting system relates to the "appetitive" pleasure that we get imagining something we desire, such as sex or a good meal. Its neurochemistry is largely dopamine-related, and it raises our tension level.

The second pleasure system has to do with the satisfaction, or consummatory pleasure,[26] that attends actually having sex or having that meal, a calming, fulfilling pleasure. Its neurochemistry is based on the release of endorphins, which are related to opiates and give a peaceful, euphoric bliss.

Pornography, by offering an endless harem of sexual objects, hyperactivates the appetitive system. Porn viewers develop new maps in their brains, based on the photos and videos they see. Because it is a use-it-or-lose-it brain, when we develop a map area, we long to keep it activated. Just as our muscles become impatient for exercise if we've been sitting all day, so too do our senses hunger to be stimulated.

The men at their computers looking at porn were uncannily like the rats in the cages of the NIH, pressing the bar to get a shot of dopamine or its equivalent. Though they didn't know it, they had been seduced into pornographic training sessions that met all the conditions required for plastic change of brain maps. Since neurons that fire together wire together, these men got massive amounts of practice wiring these images into the pleasure centers of the brain, with the rapt attention necessary for plastic change. They imagined these images when away from their computers, or while having sex with their girlfriends, reinforcing them. Each time they felt sexual excitement and had an orgasm when they masturbated, a "spritz of dopamine," the reward neurotransmitter, consolidated the connections made in the brain during the sessions. Not only did the reward facilitate the behavior; it provoked none of the

---

25 N. Doidge. 1990. Appetitive pleasure states: A biopsychoanalytic model of the pleasure threshold, mental representation, and defense. In R. A. Glick and S. Bone, eds., *Pleasure beyond the pleasure principle*. New Haven: Yale University Press, 138–73.

26 Certain depressed people have trouble experiencing any pleasure at all, and their appetitive and consummatory systems do not function. They can't anticipate having a good time, and should they be dragged out to a meal or some other pleasant activity, they can't enjoy it. But some people who are depressed, while unable to anticipate having fun, will, if dragged out to a meal or social event, find their spirits lifting because, even though the appetitive system is not working properly, the consummatory system is.

embarrassment they felt purchasing *Playboy* at a store. Here was a behavior with no "punishment," only reward.

The content of what they found exciting changed as the Web sites introduced themes and scripts that altered their brains without their awareness. Because plasticity is competitive, the brain maps for new, exciting images increased at the expense of what had previously attracted them—the reason, I believe, they began to find their girlfriends less of a turn-on.

The story of Sean Thomas,[27] first published in England's *Spectator*, is a remarkable account of a man descending into a porn addiction, and it sheds light on how porn changes brain maps and alters sexual taste, as well as the role of critical-period plasticity in the process. Thomas wrote, "I never used to like pornography, not really. Yes, in my teens in the Seventies I used to have the odd copy of *Playboy* under my pillow. But on the whole I didn't really go for skin mags or blue movies. I found them tedious, repetitive, absurd, and very embarrassing to buy." He was repelled by the bleakness of the porn scene and the garishness of the mustachioed studs who inhabited it. But in 2001, shortly after he first went online, he got curious about the porn everyone said was taking over the Internet. Many of the sites were free—teasers, or "gateway sites," to get people into the harder stuff. There were galleries of naked girls, of common types of sexual fantasies and attractions, designed to press a button in the brain of the surfer, even one he didn't know he had. There were pictures of lesbians in a Jacuzzi, cartoon porn, women on the toilet smoking, coeds, group sex, and men ejaculating over submissive Asian women. Most of the pictures told a story.

Thomas found a few images and scripts that appealed to him, and they "dragged me back for more the next day. And the next. And the next." Soon he found that whenever he had a spare minute, he would "start hungrily checking out Net Porn."

Then one day he came across a site that featured spanking images. To his surprise, he got intensely excited. Thomas soon found all sorts of related sites, such as "Bernie's Spanking Pages" and the "Spanking College."

---

27 S. Thomas. 2003. How Internet porn landed me in hospital. *National Post*, June 30, A14. These quotes are from the *National Post* version of an article originally published in the *Spectator*, June 28, 2003, called "Self abuse."

"This was the moment," he writes, "that the real addiction set in. My interest in spanking got me speculating: What other kinks was I harboring? What other secret and rewarding corners lurked in my sexuality that I would now be able to investigate in the privacy of my home? Plenty, as it turned out. I discovered a serious penchant for, inter alia, lesbian gynecology, interracial hardcore, and images of Japanese girls taking off their hotpants. I was also into netball players with no knickers, drunk Russian girls exposing themselves, and convoluted scenarios where submissive Danish actresses were intimately shaved by their dominant female partners in the shower. The Net had, in other words, revealed to me that I had an unquantifiable variety of sexual fantasies and quirks and that the process of satisfying these desires online only led to more interest."

Until he happened upon the spanking pictures, which presumably tapped into some childhood experience or fantasy about being punished, the images he saw interested him but didn't compel him. Other people's sexual fantasies bore us. Thomas's experience was similar to that of my patients: Without being fully aware of what they were looking for, they scanned hundreds of images and scenarios until they hit upon an image or sexual script that touched some buried theme that really excited them.

Once Thomas found that image, he changed. That spanking image had his *focused attention*, the condition for plastic change. And unlike a real woman, these porn images were available all day, every day on the computer.

Now Thomas was hooked. He tried to control himself but was spending at least five hours a day on his laptop. He surfed secretly, sleeping only three hours a night. His girlfriend, aware of his exhaustion, wondered if he was seeing someone else. He became so sleep deprived that his health suffered, and he got a series of infections that landed him in a hospital emergency room and finally caused him to take stock. He began inquiring among his male friends and found that many of them were also hooked.

Clearly there was something about Thomas's sexuality, outside his awareness, that had suddenly surfaced. Does the net simply reveal quirks and kinks, or does it also help create them? I think it creates new fantasies out of aspects of sexuality that have been outside the surfer's conscious awareness, bringing these elements together to form new networks. It is not likely that thousands of men have witnessed, or even imagined, submissive Danish actresses intimately shaved by their dominant female partners in the shower. Freud discovered that such fantasies take hold of the mind because of the *individual* components in them. For instance, some heterosexual men are interested in porn scenarios where older, dominant women initiate younger women into lesbian sex. This may be because boys in early childhood often feel dominated by their mothers, who are the "boss," and dress, undress, and wash them. In early childhood some boys may pass through a period when they strongly identify with their mothers and feel "like a girl," and their later interest in lesbian sex can express their residual unconscious female identification.[28] Hardcore porn unmasks some of the early neural networks that formed in the critical periods of sexual development and brings all these early, forgotten, or repressed elements together to form a new network, in which all the features are wired together. Porn sites generate catalogs of common kinks and mix them together in images. Sooner or later the surfer finds a killer combination that presses a number of his sexual buttons at once. Then he reinforces the network by viewing the images repeatedly, masturbating, releasing dopamine and strengthening these networks. He has created a kind of "neosexuality," a rebuilt libido that has strong roots in his buried sexual tendencies. Because he often develops tolerance, the pleasure of sexual discharge must be supplemented with the pleasure of an aggressive release, and sexual and aggressive images are increasingly mingled—hence the increase in sadomasochistic themes in hardcore porn.

Critical periods lay the groundwork for our types, but falling in love in adolescence or later provides an opportunity for a second round of massive plastic change. Stendhal, the nineteenth-century novelist and essayist, understood that love could lead to radical changes in attraction. Romantic love triggers such powerful emotion that we can reconfigure what we find attractive, even overcoming "objective" beauty. In *On Love* Stendhal describes a young man, Alberic, who meets a woman more beautiful than his mistress. Yet Alberic is far more drawn to his mistress than to this woman because his mistress promises him so much more happiness. Stendhal calls this "Beauty Dethroned by Love." Love has such power to change attraction that Alberic is turned on by a minor defect on his mistress's face, her pockmark. It excites him because "he has experienced so many emotions in the presence of that pockmark, emotions for the most part exquisite and of the most absorbing interest,

---

28 E. Person. 1986. The omni-available woman and lesbian sex: Two fantasy themes and their relationship to the male developmental experience. In G. I. Fogel, F. M. Lane, and R. S. Liebert, eds., *The psychology of men*. New York: Basic Books, 71–94, especially 90.

that whatever his emotions may have been, they are renewed with incredible vividness at the sight of this sign, even observed on the face of another woman . . . in this case ugliness becomes beauty."[29]

This transformation of taste can happen because we do not fall in love with looks alone. Under normal circumstances finding another person attractive can prompt a readiness to fall in love, but that person's character and a host of other attributes, including his ability to make us feel good about ourselves, crystallize the process of falling in love. Then being in love triggers an emotional state so pleasurable that it can make even pockmarks attractive, plastically rewiring our aesthetic sense. Here is how I believe it works.

In 1950 "pleasure centers" were discovered[30] in the limbic system, a part of the brain heavily involved in processing emotion. In Dr. Robert Heath's experiments on humans—an electrode was implanted into the septal region of the limbic system and turned on—these patients experienced a euphoria so powerful that when the researchers tried to end the experiment, one patient pleaded with them not to. The septal region also fired when pleasant subjects were discussed with the patients and during orgasm. These pleasure centers were found to be part of the brain's reward system, the mesolimbic dopamine system. In 1954 James Olds and Peter Milner showed that when they inserted electrodes into an animal's pleasure center while teaching it a task, it learned more easily because learning felt so pleasurable and was rewarded.

When the pleasure centers are turned on, everything we experience gives us pleasure. A drug like cocaine acts on us by lowering the threshold at which our pleasure centers will fire, making it easier for them to turn on. It is not simply the cocaine that gives us pleasure. It is the fact that our pleasure centers now fire so easily that makes whatever we experience feel great.[31] It is not just cocaine that can lower the threshold at which our pleasure centers fire. When people with bipolar disorder (formerly called manic depression) begin to move toward their manic highs, their

---

29 Stendhal also described how young girls at the theater fell in love with famously "ugly" actors, such as Le Kain, who in their performances evoked powerful, pleasurable emotions. By the end of the performance, the girls exclaimed, "Isn't he beautiful!" See Stendhal. 1947. *On love*. Translated by H.B.V. under the direction of C. K. Scott-Moncrieff. New York: Grosset & Dunlap, 44, 46–47.

30 R. G. Heath. 1972. Pleasure and pain activity in man. *Journal of Nervous and Mental Disease*, 154(1): 13–18.

31 N. Doidge, 1990.

pleasure centers begin firing more easily. And falling in love also lowers the threshold at which the pleasure centers will fire.[32]

When a person gets high on cocaine, becomes manic, or falls in love, he enters an enthusiastic state and is optimistic about everything, because all three conditions lower the firing threshold for the *appetitive* pleasure system, the dopamine-based system associated with the pleasure of anticipating something we desire. The addict, the manic, and the lover are increasingly filled with hopeful anticipation and are sensitive to anything that might give pleasure—flowers and fresh air inspire them, and a slight but thoughtful gesture makes them delight in all mankind. I call this process "globalization."[33]

Globalization is intense when falling in love and is, I believe, one of the main reasons that romantic love is such a powerful catalyst for plastic change. Because the pleasure centers are firing so freely, the enamored person falls in love not only with the beloved but with the world and romanticizes his view of it. Because our brains are experiencing a surge of dopamine, which consolidates plastic change, any pleasurable experiences and associations we have in the initial state of love are thus wired into our brains.

Globalization not only allows us to take more pleasure in the world, it also makes it harder for us to experience pain and displeasure or aversion. Heath showed that when our pleasure centers fire,[34] it is more difficult for the nearby pain and aversion centers to fire too. Things that normally bother us don't. We love being in love not only because it makes it easy for us to be happy but also because it makes it harder for us to be unhappy.

Globalization also creates an opportunity for us to develop new tastes in what we find attractive, like the pockmark that gave Alberic such pleasure. Neurons that fire together wire together, and feeling pleasure in the presence of this normally unappealing pockmark causes it to get wired into the brain as a source of delight. A similar mechanism occurs when a "reformed" cocaine addict passes the seedy alleyway where he first took the drug and is overwhelmed with cravings so powerful

---

32 Ibid.

33 Ibid.

34 Unfortunately, the tendency of our pleasure and pain centers to inhibit each other also means that a person who is depressed, and who has aversive centers firing, finds it more difficult to enjoy things he normally would.

that he goes back to it. The pleasure he felt during the high was so intense that it caused him to experience the ugly alleyway as enticing, by association.

There is thus a literal chemistry of love, and the stages of romance reflect the changes in our brain during not only the ecstasies but also love's throes. Freud, one of the first people to describe the psychic effects of cocaine and, as a young man, the first to discover its medical uses, got a glimpse of this chemistry. Writing to his fiancée, Martha, on February 2, 1886, he described taking cocaine while composing the letter. Because cocaine acts on the system so quickly, the letter, as it unfolds, gives us a marvelous window into its effects. He first describes how it makes him talkative and confessional. His initial self-deprecatory remarks vanish as the letter goes on, and soon he feels fearless, identifiying with his brave ancestors defending the Temple in Jerusalem. He likens cocaine's ability to cure his fatigue to the magical cure he gets from being with Martha romantically. In another letter he writes that cocaine reduces his shyness and depression, makes him euphoric, enhances his energy, self-esteem, and enthusiasm, and has an aphrodisiac effect. He is describing a state akin to "romantic intoxication,"[35] when people feel the initial high, talk all night, and have increased energy, libido, self-esteem, and enthusiasm, but because they think everything is good, they may also have impaired judgment—all of which occurs with a dopamine-promoting drug like cocaine. Recent fMRI (functional magnetic resonance imaging) scans of lovers[36] looking at photos of their sweethearts show that a part of the brain with great concentrations of dopamine is activated; their brains looked like those of people on cocaine.

But the pains of love also have a chemistry. When separated for too long, lovers crash and experience withdrawal, crave their beloved, get anxious, doubt themselves, lose their energy, and feel run-down if not depressed. Like a little fix, a letter, an e-mail, or a telephone message from the beloved provides an instant shot of energy. Should they break up, they get depressed—the opposite of the manic high. These "addictive symptoms"—the highs, crashes, cravings, withdrawal, and fixes—are subjective signs of plastic changes occurring in the structure of our brains, as they adapt to the presence or absence of the beloved.

---

35 M. Liebowitz. 1983. *The chemistry of love.* Boston: Little, Brown & Co.

36 A. Bartels and S. Zeki. 2000. The neural basis for romantic love. *NeuroReport,* 11(17): 3829–34; see also H. Fisher. 2004. *Why we love: The nature and chemistry of romantic love.* New York: Henry Holt and Co.

A tolerance, akin to tolerance for a drug, can develop in happy lovers as they get used to each other. Dopamine likes novelty. When monogamous mates develop a tolerance for each other[37] and lose the romantic high they once had, the change may be a sign, not that either of them is inadequate or boring, but that their plastic brains have so well adapted to each other that it's harder for them to get the same buzz they once got from each other.

Fortunately, lovers can stimulate their dopamine, keeping the high alive, by injecting novelty into their relationship. When a couple go on a romantic vacation or try new activities together, or wear new kinds of clothing, or surprise each other, they are using novelty to turn on the pleasure centers, so that everything they experience, *including each other*, excites and pleases them. Once the pleasure centers are turned on and globalization begins, the new image of the beloved again becomes associated with unexpected pleasures and is plastically wired into the brain, which has evolved to respond to novelty. We must be learning if we are to feel fully alive, and when life, or love, becomes too predictable and it seems like there is little left to learn, we become restless—a protest, perhaps, of the plastic brain when it can no longer perform its essential task.

Love creates a generous state of mind. Because love allows us to experience as pleasurable situations or physical features that we otherwise might not, it also allows us to unlearn negative associations, another plastic phenomenon.

The science of unlearning is a very new one. Because plasticity is competitive, when a person develops a neural network, it becomes efficient and self-sustaining and, like a habit, hard to unlearn. Recall that Merzenich was looking for "an eraser" to help him speed up change and unlearn bad habits.

Different chemistries are involved in learning than in unlearning. When we learn something new, neurons fire together and wire together, and a chemical process occurs at the neuronal level called "long-term potentiation," or LTP, which strengthens the connections between the neurons. When the brain unlearns associations and disconnects neurons, another chemical process occurs, called "long-term depression," or LTD (which has nothing to do with a depressed mood state). Unlearning and weakening connections between neurons is just as plastic a process, and just

---

37 Tolerance occurs when the brain is inundated with a substance—in this case dopamine—and in response the receptors on the neurons for that substance "down regulate," or decrease in number, so more of the substance is required to get the same effect.

as important, as learning and strengthening them. If we only strengthened connections, our neuronal networks would get saturated. Evidence suggests that unlearning existing memories is necessary to make room for new memories in our networks.[38]

Unlearning is essential when we are moving from one developmental stage to the next. When at the end of adolescence a girl leaves home to go to college in another state, for example, both she and her parents undergo grief and massive plastic change, as they alter old emotional habits, routines, and self-images.

Falling in love for the first time also means entering a new developmental stage and demands a massive amount of unlearning. When people commit to each other, they must radically alter their existing and often selfish intentions and modify all other attachments, in order to integrate the new person in their lives. Life now involves ongoing cooperation that requires a plastic reorganization of the brain centers that deal with emotions, sexuality, and the self. Millions of neural networks have to be obliterated and replaced with new ones—one reason that falling in love feels, for so many people, like a loss of identity. Falling in love may also mean falling out of love with a past love; this too requires unlearning at a neural level.

A man's heart is broken by his first love when his engagement breaks off. He looks at many women, but each pales in comparison to the fiancée he came to believe was his one true love and whose image haunts him. He cannot unlearn the pattern of attraction to his first love. Or a woman married for twenty years becomes a young widow and refuses to date. She cannot imagine she will ever fall in love again, and the idea of "replacing" her husband offends her. Years pass, and her friends tell her it is time to move on, to no avail.

Often such people cannot move on because they cannot yet grieve; the thought of living without the one they love is too painful to bear. In neuroplastic terms, if the romantic or the widow is to begin a new relationship without baggage, each must first rewire billions of connections in their brains. The work of mourning is piecemeal,[39] Freud noted; though reality tells us our loved one is gone, "its orders cannot be obeyed

---

38 E. S. Rosenzweig, C. A. Barnes, and B. L. McNaughton. 2002. Making room for new memories. *Nature Neuroscience*, 5(1): 6–8.

39 S. Freud. 1917/1957. *Mourning and melancholia.* Translated by J. Stratchey. In *Standard* edition of the complete psychological works of Sigmund Freud, vol. 14. London: Hogarth Press, 237–58, especially 245.

at once." We grieve by calling up one memory at a time, reliving it, and then letting it go. At a brain level we are turning on each of the neural networks that were wired together to form our perception of the person, experiencing the memory with exceptional vividness, then saying good-bye one network at a time. In grief, we *learn* to live without the one we love, but the reason this lesson is so hard is that we first must *unlearn* the idea that the person exists and can still be relied on.

Walter J. Freeman, a professor of neuroscience at Berkeley, was the first to make the connection between love and massive unlearning. He has assembled a number of compelling biological facts that point toward the conclusion that massive neuronal reorganization occurs at two life stages: when we fall in love and when we begin parenting. Freeman argues that massive plastic brain reorganization—far more massive than in normal learning or unlearning—becomes possible because of a brain neuromodulator.

Neuromodulators are different from neurotransmitters. While neurotransmitters are released in the synapses to excite or inhibit neurons, neuromodulators enhance or diminish the overall effectiveness of the synaptic connections and bring about enduring change. Freeman believes that when we commit in love, the brain neuromodulator oxytocin is released, allowing existing neuronal connections to melt away so that changes on a large scale can follow.

Oxytocin is sometimes called the commitment neuromodulator because it reinforces bonding in mammals. It is released when lovers connect and make love—in humans oxytocin is released in both sexes during orgasm[40]—and when couples parent and nurture their children. In women oxytocin is released during labor and breast-feeding. An fMRI study shows that when mothers look at photos of their children, brain regions[41] rich in oxytocin are activated. In male mammals a closely related neuromodulator called vasopressin is released when they become fathers. Many young people who doubt they will be able to handle the responsibilities of parenting are not aware of the extent to which oxytocin may change their brains, allowing them to rise to the occasion.

---

40 W. J. Freeman. 1999. *How brains make up their minds.* London: Weidenfeld & Nicolson, 160; J. Panksepp. 1998. *Affective neuroscience: The foundations of human and animal emotions.* New York: Oxford University Press, 231; L. J. Young and Z. Wang. 2004. The neurobiology of pair bonding. *Nature Neuroscience,* 7(10): 1048–54.

41 A. Bartels and S. Zeki. 2004. The neural correlates of maternal and romantic love. *NeuroImage,* 21:1155–66.

Studies of a monogamous animal called the prairie vole have shown that oxytocin, which is normally released in their brains during mating, makes them pair off for life. If a female vole has oxytocin injected into her brain, she will pair-bond for life with a nearby male. If a male vole is injected with vasopressin, it will cuddle with a nearby female. Oxytocin appears also to attach children to parents, and the neurons that control its secretion may have a critical period of their own. Children reared in orphanages without close loving contact often have bonding problems when older. Their oxytocin levels remain low for several years after they have been adopted by loving families.[42]

Whereas dopamine induces excitement, puts us into high gear, and triggers sexual arousal, oxytocin induces a calm, warm mood that increases tender feelings and attachment and may lead us to lower our guard. A recent study shows that oxytocin also triggers trust. When people sniff oxytocin and then participate in a financial game, they are more prone to trust[43] others with their money. Though there is still more work to be done on oxytocin in humans, evidence suggests that its effect is similar to that in prairie voles: It makes us commit to our partners and devotes us to our children.[44]

But oxytocin, Freeman argues, works in a unique way, related to unlearning. In sheep, oxytocin is released in the olfactory bulb, a part of the brain involved in odor perception, with each new litter. Sheep and many other animals bond with, or "imprint" on, their offspring by scent. They mother their own lambs and reject the unfamiliar. But if oxytocin is injected into a mother ewe when exposed to an unfamiliar lamb, she will mother the strange lamb[45] too.

Oxytocin is not, however, released with the first litter—only with those litters that follow—suggesting to Freeman that the oxytocin plays the role of *wiping out* the neural circuits that bonded the mother with her first litter, so she can bond with

---

42 A. B. Wismer Fries, T. E. Ziegler, J. R. Kurian, S. Jacoris, and S. D. Pollak. 2005. Early experience in humans is associated with changes in neuropeptides critical for regulating social behavior. *Proceedings of the National Academy of Sciences, USA,* 102(47): 17237–40.

43 M. Kosfeld, M. Heinrichs, P. J. Zak, U. Fischbacher, and E. Fehr. 2005. Oxytocin increases trust in humans. *Nature,* 435(7042): 673–76.

44 The ancient Greeks, with simple elegance, described our tendency to develop powerful, not always rational, loving attachments to family and friends, as "love of one's own," and oxytocin seems to be one of several neurochemicals that promote it.

45 C. S. Carter. 2002. Neuroendocrine perspectives on social attachment and love. In J. T. Cacioppo, G. G. Bernston, R. Adolphs, et al., eds., 853–90, especially 864.

her second. (Freeman suspects that the mother bonds with her first litter using other neurochemicals.[46]) Oxytocin's ability to wipe out learned behavior has led some scientists to call it an amnestic hormone.[47] Freeman proposes that oxytocin melts down existing neuronal connections[48] that underlie existing attachments, so new attachments can be formed. Oxytocin, in this theory, does not teach parents to parent. Nor does it make lovers cooperative and kind; rather, it makes it possible for them to learn new patterns.

There is some dispute over the idea that oxytocin is solely responsible for this new burst of learning, for change in our existing attachments, or how it might facilitate these changes. Neuroscientist Jaak Pankseep argues that oxytocin, in combination with other brain chemicals, is so overwhelmingly good at reducing our feeling of separation-distress that the pain of losing previous attachments makes less of an impression than it would otherwise. This relative lack of distress may also free us to learn new things and form new bonds, while partially reconfiguring our existing relationships.

Freeman's theory helps to explain how love and plasticity affect each other. Plasticity allows us to develop brains so unique—in response to our individual life experiences—that it is often hard to see the world as others do, to want what they want, or to cooperate. But the successful reproduction of our species requires cooperation. What nature provides, in a neuromodulator like oxytocin, is the ability for two brains in love to go through a period of heightened plasticity, allowing them to mold to each other and shape each other's intentions and perceptions. The brain

---

46 Personal communication.

47 T. R. Insel. 1992. Oxytocin—a neuropeptide for affiliation: Evidence from behavioral, receptor, autoradiographic, and comparative studies. *Psychoneuroendocrinology*, 17(1): 3–35, especially 12; Z. Sarnyai and G. L. Kovács. 1994. Role of oxytocin in the neuroadaptation to drugs of abuse. *Psychoneuroendocrinology*, 19(1): 85–117, especially 86.

48 W. J. Freeman. 1995. *Societies of brains: A study in the neuroscience of love and hate.* Hillsdale, N.J.: Lawrence Erlbaum Associates, 122–23;W. J. Freeman, 1999, 160–61. Freeman points out that hormones that influence behavior, such as estrogen or thyroid, generally need to be released steadily in the body to have their effects. But oxytocin is released only briefly, which strongly suggests that its role is *setting the stage for a new phase,* in which new behaviors replace existing behaviors. Unlearning may be especially important in mammals because the cycle of reproduction and rearing the young takes so long and requires such a deep bond. For a mother to switch from being totally preoccupied with one litter to caring for the next requires a massive alteration in her goals, intentions, and the neuronal circuits involved.

for Freeman is fundamentally an organ of socialization, and so there must be a mechanism that, from time to time, undoes our tendency to become overly individualized, overly self-involved, and too self-centered.

As Freeman says, "The deepest meaning of sexual experience lies not in pleasure, or even in reproduction, but in the opportunity it affords to surmount the solipsistic gulf, opening the door, so to speak, whether or not one undertakes the work to go through. It is the afterplay, not the foreplay, that counts in building trust."[49]

Freeman's concept reminds us of many variations on love: the insecure man who leaves a woman quickly after making love during the night, because he fears being overly influenced by her should he stay through the morning; the woman who tends to fall in love with whomever she has sex with. Or the sudden transformation of the man who barely noticed children into a devoted father; we say "he's matured" and "the kids come first," but he may have had some help from oxytocin, which allowed him to go beyond his deep-seated patterns of selfish concern. Contrast him with the inveterate bachelor[50] who never falls in love and becomes more eccentric and rigid with each passing year, plastically reinforcing his routines through repetition.

Unlearning in love allows us to change our image of ourselves—for the better, if we have an adoring partner. But it also helps account for our vulnerability when we fall in love and explains why so many self-possessed young men and women, who fall in love with a manipulative, undermining, or devaluing person, often lose all sense of self and become plagued with self-doubt, from which it may take years to recover.

Understanding unlearning, and some of the fine points of brain plasticity, turned out to be crucial in the treatment of my patient A. By the time A. went to college, he found himself replaying his critical-period experience and being attracted to emotionally disturbed, already attached women very much like his mother, feeling it was his job to love and rescue them.

---

49 W. J. Freeman, 1995, 122–23.

50 One typical explanation for the rigidity of aging bachelors or bachelorettes, who want to marry but have become too fussy, is that they fail to fall in love because they have become increasingly rigid through living alone. But perhaps they also become increasingly rigid because they fail to fall in love and never get the surge of oxytocin that may facilitate plastic change. In a similar vein, one can ask how much of people's ability to parent well is enhanced by the prior experience of having fallen in love—in a mature way—allowing them to unlearn selfishness and open themselves up to another. If each mature love experience has the potential to help us unlearn earlier, more selfish intentions and become less self-centered, a mature adult love would be one of the best predictors of the ability to parent well.

A. was caught in two plastic traps.

The first was that a relationship with a thoughtful, stable woman who might have helped him unlearn his love for problem women, and teach him a new way to love, simply didn't turn him on, though he wished it would. So he was stuck with a destructive attraction, formed in his critical period.

His second, related trap can also be understood plastically. One of his most tormenting symptoms was the almost perfect fusion in his mind of sex with aggression. He felt that to love someone was to consume her, to eat her alive, and that to be loved was to be eaten alive. And his feeling that sexual intercourse was a violent act upset him greatly, yet excited him. Thoughts of sexual intercourse immediately led to thoughts of violence, and thoughts of violence, to sex. When he was effective sexually, he *felt* he was dangerous. It was as though he lacked separate brain maps for sexual and violent feelings.

Merzenich has described a number of "brain traps"[51] that occur when two brain maps, meant to be separate, merge. As we have seen, he found that if a monkey's fingers were sewn together and so forced to move at the same time, the maps for them would fuse, because their neurons fired together and hence wired together. But he also discovered that maps fuse in everyday life. When a musician uses two fingers together frequently enough while playing an instrument, the maps for the two fingers sometimes fuse, and when the musician tries to move only one finger, the other moves too. The maps for the two different fingers are now "dedifferentiated." The more intensely the musician tries to produce a single movement, the more he will move both fingers, strengthening the merged map. The harder the person tries to get out of the brain trap, the deeper he gets into it, developing a condition called "focal dystonia." A similar brain trap occurs in Japanese people who, when speaking English, can't hear the difference between *r* and *l* because the two sounds are not differentiated in their brain maps. Each time they try to say the sounds properly, they say them incorrectly, reinforcing the problem.

---

51 M. M. Merzenich, F. Spengler, N. Byl, X. Wang, and W. Jenkins. 1996. Representational plasticity underlying learning: Contributions to the origins and expressions of neurobehavioral disabilities. In T. Ono, B. L. McNaughton, S. Molochnikoff, E. T. Rolls, and H. Nishijo, eds., *Perception, memory and emotion: Frontiers in neuroscience*. Oxford: Elsevier Science, 45–61, especially 50.

This is what I believe A. experienced. Each time he thought of sex, he thought of violence. Each time he thought of violence, he thought of sex, reinforcing the connection in the merged map.

Merzenich's colleague Nancy Byl, who works in physical medicine, teaches people who can't control their fingers to redifferentiate their finger maps.[52] The trick is not to try to move the fingers separately, but to relearn how to use their hands the way they did as babies. When treating guitarists with focal dystonias who have lost control of their fingers, for example, she first instructs them to stop playing guitar for a while, to weaken the merged map. Then they just hold an unstrung guitar for a few days. Then a single string with a different feel from a normal guitar string is put on the guitar, and they feel it carefully, but with only one finger. Finally they use a second finger, on a separate string. Eventually the fused brain maps for their fingers separate into two distinct maps, and they can play again.

A. came into psychoanalysis. Early on we sorted out why love and aggression had fused, tracing the roots of his brain trap to his experience with his drunken mother who often gave free rein to sexual and violent feelings simultaneously. But when he still couldn't change what attracted him, I did something similar to what Merzenich and Byl do to redifferentiate maps. For a long period in the therapy, whenever A. expressed any kind of physical tenderness outside the sexual arena untainted by aggression, I pointed it out and asked him to observe it closely, reminding him that he was capable of a positive feeling and capable of intimacy.

When violent thoughts came up, I got him to search his experience to find even a single instance in which aggression or violence was untainted with sex or was even praiseworthy, as in justified self-defense. Whenever these areas came up—a pure

---

52 N. N. Byl, S. Nagarajan, and A. L. McKenzie. 2003. Effect of sensory discrimination training on structure and function inpatients with focal hand dystonia: A case series. *Archives of Physical Medicine and Rehabilitation,* 84(10): 1505–14. Merzenich has helped Japanese people trying to speak English without an accent get out of their brain traps (see page 122). Knowing that the basis for this problem lies in the absence of a differentiated auditory cortex for certain sounds, Merzenich and his collaborators set out to differentiate them. Using the same kind of approach as *Fast For-Word,* he radically modified the *r* and *l* sounds, so that the difference was *grossly* exaggerated and the Japanese listeners could pick it up. Then the team gradually normalized the sounds, while the subjects were listening. It was essential for the speakers to always pay very close attention throughout the exercises, something they didn't do in normal speech. It took about ten to twenty hours of training to learn to make the distinction. "You can teach anybody to speak an accentless second language as an adult," Merzenich says, "but it requires very intense training."

physical tenderness, or aggression that wasn't destructive—I drew his attention to them. As time passed, he was able to form two different brain maps, one for physical tenderness, which had nothing to do with the seductiveness he experienced with his mother, and another for aggression—including healthy assertiveness—which was quite different from the senseless violence he'd experienced when his mother was drunk.

Separating sex and violence in his brain maps allowed him to feel better about relationships and sex, and improvement followed in stages. While he wasn't immediately able to fall in love with or become excited by a healthy woman, he did fall in love with a woman who was a bit healthier than his previous girlfriend, and he benefited from the learning and unlearning that that love provided. This experience allowed him to enter progressively healthier relationships, unlearning more each time. By the end of therapy he was in a healthy, satisfying, happy marriage; his character, and his sexual type, had been radically transformed.

The rewiring of our pleasure systems, and the extent to which our sexual tastes can be acquired, is seen most dramatically in such perversions as sexual masochism, which turns physical pain into sexual pleasure. To do this the brain must make pleasant that which is inherently unpleasant, and the impulses that normally trigger our pain system are plastically rewired into our pleasure system.

People with perversions[53] often organize their lives around activities that mix aggression and sexuality, and they often celebrate and idealize humiliation, hostility, defiance, the forbidden, the furtive, the lusciously sinful, and the breaking of taboos; they feel special for not being merely "normal." These "transgressive" or defiant attitudes are essential to the enjoyment of perversion. The idealization of the perverse, and the devaluation of "normalcy," is brilliantly captured in Vladimir Nabokov's novel *Lolita*, in which a middle-aged man idolizes and has sex with a prepubescent, twelve-year-old girl, while showing contempt for all older females.

---

53 The notion of "perversion" implies that our sexual drive is like a river that most naturally flows in a certain channel, until something happens that puts it off course and diverts, or perverts, its direction. People who call themselves "kinky" concede the point, a kink being something with a twist in it.

Sexual sadism[54] illustrates plasticity in that it fuses two familiar tendencies, the sexual and the aggressive, each of which can give pleasure separately, and brings them together so when they are discharged, the pleasure is doubled. But masochism goes much further because it takes something inherently unpleasant, pain, and turns it into a pleasure, altering the sexual drive more fundamentally and more vividly demonstrating the plasticity of our pleasure and pain systems.

For years the police, through raids on S&M establishments, knew more about serious perversions than most clinicians. While patients with milder perversions often come for treatment of such problems as anxiety or depression, those with serious perversions seldom seek therapy because, generally, they enjoy them.

Robert Stoller, M.D., a California psychoanalyst, did make important discoveries[55] through visits to S&M and B&D (bondage and discipline) establishments in Los Angeles. He interviewed people who practiced hardcore sadomasochism, which inflicts real pain on the flesh, and discovered that masochistic participants had all had serious physical illnesses as children and had undergone regular, terrifying, painful medical treatment. "As a result," writes Stoller, "they had to be confined severely and for long periods [in hospitals] without the chance to unload their frustration, despair and rage openly and appropriately. Hence the perversions."[56] As children, they consciously took their pain, their inexpressible rage, and reworked it in daydreams, in altered mental states, or in masturbation fantasies, so they could

---

54 True, some reject the idea that in perversion, aggression gets linked with sexuality. The literary critic Camille Paglia argues that sexuality is by nature aggressive. "My theory," she says, "is that whenever sexual freedom is sought or achieved, sadomasochism will not be far behind." She attacks feminists who believe that sex is all sugar and spice and who argue that it is patriarchal society that makes sex violent. Sex, for Paglia, is about power; society is not the source of sexual violence; sex, the irrepressible natural force, is. If anything, society is the force that inhibits the inherent violence of sex. Paglia is certainly more realistic than those who would deny that perversion is rife with aggression. But in assuming that sex is fundamentally aggressive, and sadomasochistic, she doesn't allow for the plasticity of human sexuality. Just because sex and aggression can unite in a plastic brain, and appear "natural," doesn't mean that that is their only possible expression. We have seen that certain brain chemicals released in sex, such as oxytocin, cause us to be tender to each other. It is no more accurate to say that fully realized sexuality is always violent than to say it is always gentle and sweet. C. Paglia. 1990. *Sexual personae*. New Haven: Yale University Press, 3.

55 R. J. Stoller. 1991. *Pain and passion: A psychoanalyst explores the world of S & M*. New York: Plenum Press.

56 Ibid., 25.

replay the story of the trauma with a happy ending and say to themselves, *This time, I win*. And the way they won was by eroticizing their agony.

The idea that an "inherently" painful feeling can become pleasurable may at first strike us as hard to believe, because we tend to assume that each of our sensations and emotions is inherently either pleasurable (joy, triumph, and sexual pleasure) or painful (sadness, fear, and grief). But in fact this assumption does not hold up. We can cry tears of happiness and have bittersweet triumphs; and in neuroses people may feel guilty about sexual pleasure, or no pleasure at all, where others would feel delight. An emotion that we think inherently unpleasurable, such as sadness, can, if beautifully and subtly articulated in music, literature, or art, feel not only poignant but sublime. Fear can be exciting in frightening movies or on roller coasters. The human brain seems able to attach many of our feelings and sensations either to the pleasure system or to the pain system, and each of these links or mental associations requires a novel plastic connection in the brain.

The hardcore masochists whom Stoller interviewed must have formed a pathway that linked the painful sensations they had endured to their sexual pleasure systems, resulting in a new composite experience, voluptuous pain. That they all suffered in early childhood strongly suggests that this rewiring occurred during the critical periods of sexual plasticity.

In 1997 a documentary appeared that sheds light on plasticity and masochism: *Sick: The Life and Death of Bob Flanagan, Supermasochist*. Bob Flanagan performed his masochistic acts in public as a performance artist and exhibitionist and was articulate, poetic, and at times very funny.

In Flanagan's opening scenes we see him naked, humiliated, pies being thrown in his face, fed with a funnel. But images flash of his being physically hurt and choked, hinting at far more disturbing forms of pain.

Bob was born in 1952 with cystic fibrosis, a genetic disorder of the lungs and pancreas in which the body produces an excessive amount of abnormally thick mucus that clogs the air passages, making it impossible to breathe normally, and leads to chronic digestive problems. He had to fight for every breath and often turned blue from lack of oxygen. Most patients born with this disease die as children or in their early twenties.

Bob's parents noticed he was in pain from the moment he came home from the hospital. When he was eighteen months old, doctors discovered pus between his lungs and began treating him by inserting needles deep into his chest. He began to dread these procedures and screamed desperately. Throughout childhood he was hospitalized regularly and confined nearly naked inside a bubblelike tent so doctors could monitor his sweat—one of the ways cystic fibrosis is diagnosed—while he felt mortified that his body was visible to strangers. To help him breathe and fight infections, doctors inserted all sorts of tubes into him. He was also aware of the severity of his problem: Two of his younger sisters had also had cystic fibrosis; one died at six months, the other at twenty-one years.

Despite the fact that he had become a poster boy for the Orange County Cystic Fibrosis Society, he began to live a secret life. As a young child, when his stomach hurt relentlessly, he would stimulate his penis to distract himself. By the time he was in high school, he would lie naked at night and secretly cover himself with thick glue, for he knew not what reason. He hung himself from a door with belts in painful positions. Then he began to insert needles into the belts to pierce his flesh.

When he was thirty-one, he fell in love with Sheree Rose, who came from a very troubled family. In the film we see Sheree's mother openly belittle her husband, Sheree's father, who, Sheree claims, was passive and never showed her affection. Sheree describes herself as being bossy since childhood. She is Bob's sadist.

In the film Sheree uses Bob, with his consent, as her slave. She humiliates him, cuts into the skin near his nipples with an X-Acto knife, puts clamps on his nipples, force-feeds him, chokes him with a cord till he turns blue, forces a large steel ball—as big as a billiard ball—into his anus, and puts needles in his erogenous zones. His mouth and lips are sutured shut with stitches. He writes of drinking Sheree's urine from a baby bottle. We see him with feces on his penis. His every orifice is invaded or defiled. These activities give Bob erections and lead to great orgasms in the sex that often follows.

Bob survives both his twenties and his thirties and in his early forties has become the oldest living survivor of cystic fibrosis. He takes his masochism on the road, to S&M clubs and art museums, where he enacts his masochistic rituals in public, always wearing his oxygen mask to breathe.

In one of the final scenes a naked Bob Flanagan takes a hammer and nails his penis, right through its center, to a board. He then matter-of-factly removes the nail so that blood spurts all over the camera lens, like a fountain, from the deep hole through his penis.

It is important to describe precisely what Flanagan's nervous system could endure, in order to understand the extent to which completely novel brain circuits can develop, linking the pain system to the pleasure system.

Flanagan's idea that his pain must be made pleasurable colored his fantasies from early childhood. His remarkable history confirms that his perversion developed out of his unique life experience and is linked to his traumatic memories. As an infant, he was tied into the crib in the hospital so he couldn't escape and hurt himself. By age seven his confinement had turned into a love of constriction. As an adult, he loved bondage and being handcuffed or tied up and hung for long periods in positions that torturers might use to break their victims. As a child, he was required to endure the powerful nurses and doctors who hurt him; as an adult, he voluntarily gave this power to Sheree, becoming her slave, whom she could abuse while practicing pseudomedical procedures on him. Even subtle aspects of his childhood relationship to his doctors were repeated in adulthood. The fact that Bob gave Sheree his consent repeated an aspect of the trauma because, after a certain age, when the doctors took blood, pierced his skin, and hurt him, he gave them permission, knowing his life depended on it.

This mirroring of childhood traumas through the repetition of such subtle details is typical of perversions. Fetishists—who are attracted to objects—have the same trait. A fetish, Robert Stoller said, is an object[57] that tells a story, that captures scenes from childhood trauma and eroticizes them. (One man who developed a fetish for rubber underwear and raincoats was a childhood bedwetter, forced to sleep on rubber sheets, which he found humiliating and uncomfortable. Flanagan had a number of fetishes, for medical paraphernalia and the blunt metals from hardware stores—screws, nails, clamps, and hammers—all of which he used, at various times, for erotic-masochistic stimulation, to penetrate, pinch, or pound his flesh.)

Flanagan's pleasure centers were no doubt rewired in two ways. First, emotions such as anxiety that are normally unpleasant became pleasant. He explains that he is constantly flirting with death because he was promised an early death and is trying to master his fear. In his 1985 poem, "Why," he makes clear that his super-masochism allows him to feel triumphant, courageous, and invulnerable after a life of vulnerability. But he goes beyond simply mastering fear. Humiliated by doctors who stripped him and put him in a plastic tent to measure his sweat, he now proudly

57 More precisely, Stoller wrote, "a fetish is a story masquerading as an object."

strips in museums. To master his feelings of being exposed and humiliated as a child, he becomes a triumphant exhibitionist. Shame is made into a pleasure, converted into shamelessness.

The second aspect of his rewiring is that physical pain becomes pleasure. Metal in flesh now feels good, gives him erections, and makes him have orgasms. Some people under great physical stress release endorphins, the opiumlike analgesics that our bodies make to dull our pain and that can make us euphoric. But Flanagan explains he is not dulled to pain—he is drawn to it. The more he hurts himself, the more sensitized to pain he becomes, and the more pain he feels. Because his pain and pleasure systems are connected, Flanagan feels real, intense pain, and it feels good.

Children are born helpless and will, in the critical period of sexual plasticity, do anything to avoid abandonment and to stay attached to adults, even if they must learn to love the pain and trauma that adults inflict. The adults in little Bob's world inflicted pain on him "for his own good." Now, by becoming a supermasochist, he ironically treats pain as though it is good for him. He is utterly aware that he is stuck in the past, reliving infancy, and says he hurts himself "because I am a big baby, and I want to stay that way." Perhaps the fantasy of *staying* the tortured baby is an imaginary way of keeping himself from the death that awaits him should he allow himself to grow up. If he can stay Peter Pan, endlessly "tormented" by Sheree, at least he will never grow up and die prematurely.

At the end of the film we see Flanagan dying. He stops making jokes and begins to look like a cornered animal, overwhelmed with fear. The viewer sees how terrified he must have been as a little boy, before he discovered the masochistic solution to tame his pain and terror. At this point, we learn from Bob that Sheree has been talking of splitting up—evoking every suffering child's worst fear, abandonment. Sheree says the problem is that Bob is no longer submitting to her. He looks utterly brokenhearted—and in the end, she stays, and nurses him tenderly.

In his final moments, almost in shock, he asks plaintively, "Am I dying? I don't understand it . . . What is going on? . . . I'd never believe this." So powerful were his masochistic fantasies, games, and rituals, in which he embraced painful death, that it seems he thought he had actually beaten it.

As for the patients who became involved in porn, most were able to go cold turkey once they understood the problem and how they were plastically reinforcing it. They found eventually that they were attracted once again to their mates. None of these men had addictive personalities or serious childhood traumas, and when they understood what was happening to them, they stopped using their computers for a period to weaken their problematic neuronal networks, and their appetite for porn withered away. Their treatment for sexual tastes acquired later in life was far simpler than that for patients who, in their critical periods, acquired a preference for problematic sexual types. Yet even some of these men were able, like A., to change their sexual type, because the same laws of neuroplasticity that allow us to acquire problematic tastes also allow us, in intensive treatment, to acquire newer, healthier ones and in some cases even to lose our older, troubling ones. It's a use-it-or-lose-it brain, even where sexual desire and love are concerned.

PORNOGRAPHY AND VIOLENCE: A NEW LOOK AT THE RESEARCH

Mary Anne Layden

Pornography is a potent teacher of both beliefs and behaviors, and in fact provides the ideal conditions for learning. It can teach not only specific sexual behaviors, but general attitudes toward women and children, what relationships are like, and the nature of sexuality. Certainly some important reactions are inborn and instinctual, but the great majority of our beliefs and behaviors have been learned. Once we learn them, we also learn if it is acceptable to engage in the behaviors and are sometimes stimulated to do just that. For many reasons, as we shall see, pornography is a very effective teacher of beliefs and behaviors, and one that also teaches its users that the behaviors are acceptable and stimulates them to do so. However, what it teaches and what it stimulates can be toxic.

Factors affecting learning

We learn better using images than words, because images carry more information in a more compact form. A split-second look at an image can convey more information than a split-second look at words. Words are often perceived as opinions, while images are often perceived as events or facts. We argue in our head against words or opinions, but much less often against events or facts, particularly images. The vast majority of pornography is visual.

We also learn better when aroused. If something activates our sympathetic nervous system, we are more prepared to remember the information received at that point. The arousal may come from excitement, fear, disgust, or sexual tension. Pornography can produce any of these emotions. We tend to remember any experience we have in those aroused states.

And learning is better if it is reinforced. Behavior that is rewarded is likely to be repeated while behavior that is punished is less likely to be repeated. Sexual arousal and orgasm are extremely rewarding experiences. We may be innately predisposed to enjoy the rewards of sexual arousal and orgasm, but we learn how and when and with whom we can experience those pleasures. If a novel sexual behavior produces an orgasm, we are more likely to repeat that behavior and add it to our sexual template and repertoire.

Learning is also better if we see others perform a behavior and observe what happens. Seeing others who are modeling behaviors rewarded or punished will have some of the same effects on us as if we were rewarded or punished ourselves. We don't have to directly experience those rewards and consequences. We learn to repeat or avoid those behaviors by seeing their effect on the models.

Imagery that contains role models who are demonstrating sexual behavior and being rewarded for it, that produces sexual arousal in the viewer and is followed by an orgasm, can be extremely effective in producing deeply learned beliefs and behaviors.

Pornography can offer all these elements—images, arousal, reinforcement, the example of others—so it is a potent teacher of both beliefs and behaviors. It provides the ideal conditions for learning.

One category of beliefs we learn is called "permission-giving beliefs."[1] These beliefs give us permission to engage in a behavior we would like to engage in or are already engaging in. They tell us there is no need to stop, change, or reduce the behavior—they tell us, for example, that what we are doing is normal, that it doesn't hurt anyone, and that everybody is doing it.

Marshall has stated that "this may be pornography's most insidious influence; namely, the acceptance of the attitudes (some obvious, some more subtle) expressed in pornography. Pornographic depictions of sexuality distort the truth about desires of women and children, and legitimize men's sense of entitlement, and use of force, violence, and degrading acts by the male actors."[2] In other words, pornography has the ability not only to teach social attitudes and behaviors, but also to give permission to engage in them. Permission-giving beliefs become releasers of behavior.

Pornography is an ideal teacher of these releaser beliefs. It can teach specific sexual behaviors and general attitudes toward women and children, teach what relationships are like, and teach the nature of sexuality, thus giving permission for a wide range of actions. For example, a male masturbating to the images of smiling children having sex with adults or of sexually aroused women being beaten, raped, or

---

1 Aaron T. Beck, *Prisoners of Hate: The Cognitive Basis of Anger, Hostility, and Violence* (New York: HarperCollins, 1999).

2 William L. Marshall, "Revisiting the Use of Pornography by Sexual Offenders: Implications for Theory and Practice," *Journal of Sexual Aggression* 6, nos. 1 and 2 (2000): 67.

degraded, is learning that the subjects enjoy and desire this treatment and is thereby being taught that he has permission to act this way himself.

So pornography can be a teacher, a releaser, and a trigger of behaviors. Pornography is not only potent but multifaceted in its effect. Pornography can teach what to do, with whom to do it, when and how often to do it, that it's okay to do it, and then stimulate the urge to do it now.

It is not surprising that many psychologists call internet pornography the new "crack cocaine" when you note the combination of the power of pornography with the ready, 24/7 availability of pornography on any computer, much of it free, accessible in the privacy and anonymity of the home.

Some of the messages of pornography teach beliefs and behaviors. Some of these behaviors are pathological, illegal, or both, and are toxic on many levels. The illegal behaviors are rape, child molestation, pedophilia, prostitution, domestic violence, sexual harassment, and some paraphilias (e.g., sexual deviances such as exhibitionism, voyeurism, and bestiality). Some of pornography's messages about relationships, sexuality, and women may be damaging and pathological, even if the behaviors are not illegal.

This learning produces effects in attitudes toward sexual violence, relationships, the attractiveness of a partner, and women's liberation; and in sexual violence behaviors, pedophilia, sexual harassment, prostitution, sexual deviance, and physically risky behavior.

Pornography and attitudes toward sexual violence

The rape myth is a set of beliefs that women are responsible for rape, like to be raped, want to be raped, and suffer few negative outcomes because of it. A number of studies have looked at the acceptance of the rape myth after exposing the subjects to sexual imagery, both violent and non-violent, and one study also asked subjects about their typical pornography use.

Males shown imagery of a woman aroused by sexual violence, and then shown pornography that involved rape, were more likely than those who hadn't to say that the rape victim suffered less, that she enjoyed it, and that women in general enjoy rape.[3] Japanese males exposed to a depiction of rape in which the woman enjoyed

---

3 James Check and Neil M. Malamuth, "An Empirical Assessment of Some Feminist Hypotheses About Rape," *International Journal of Women's Studies* 8, no. 4 (September–October 1985): 414–23.

the rape were more likely to believe that women in general enjoy rape and that they make false accusations of rape when compared with males exposed to a depiction in which the women showed pain.[4]

Males who viewed sexual violence obtained higher scores on scales measuring acceptance of both interpersonal violence and the rape myth when compared with males who viewed either a physically violent or a neutral film.[5] The increase in attitudes supporting sexual violence following exposure to pornography is greater if the pornography is violent than if it is non-violent.[6]

A similar effect is seen even when the pornography is not violent. Males who were shown non-violent scenes that sexually objectified and degraded women and were then exposed to material that depicted rape were more likely to indicate that the rape victim experienced pleasure and "got what she wanted."[7] Even *women* who were exposed to pornography as a child had a greater acceptance of the rape myth than those who were not exposed as children.[8] Both males and females who were exposed to pornography recommended a sentence for a rapist that was half that recommended by those who had been shown non-pornographic imagery. These subjects appear to have trivialized the crime of rape.[9]

One study not only exposed subjects to pornographic imagery but also asked them about their typical pornography use.[10] High pornography users were higher than low pornography users on scales measuring acceptance of the rape myth,

---

4 Ken-Ichi Ohbuchi et al., "Effects of Violent Pornography Upon Viewers' Rape Myth Beliefs: A Study of Japanese Males," *Psychology, Crime, and Law* 7, no. 1 (1994): 71–81.

5 Monica G. Weisz and Christopher Earls, "The Effects of Exposure to Filmed Sexual Violence on Attitudes Toward Rape," *Journal of Interpersonal Violence* 10, no. 1 (1995): 71–84.

6 Mike Allen et al., "Exposure to Pornography and Acceptance of the Rape Myth," *Journal of Communication* 45, no. 1 (1995): 5–26.

7 Michael Milburn, Roxanne Mather, and Sheree Conrad, "The Effects of Viewing R-Rated Movie Scenes that Objectify Women on Perceptions of Date Rape," *Sex Roles* 43, nos. 9 and 10 (2000): 645–64.

8 Shawn Corne et al., "Women's Attitudes and Fantasies About Rape as a Function of Early Exposure to Pornography," *Journal of Interpersonal Violence* 7, no. 4 (1992): 454–61.

9 Dolf Zillmann and Jennings Bryant, "Effects of Massive Exposure to Pornography," in *Pornography and Sexual Aggression*, eds. Neil M. Malamuth and Edward Donnerstein (New York: Academic Press, 1984).

10 James Check and Ted Guloien, "The Effects of Repeated Exposure to Sexually Violent Pornography, Nonviolent Dehumanizing Pornography, and Erotica," in *Pornography: Research Advances and Policy Considerations*, eds. Dolf Zillmann and Jennings Bryant (Hillsdale, N.J.: Lawrence Erlbaum Associates, 1989), 159–84.

acceptance of violence against women, adversarial sex beliefs, reported likelihood of committing rape and forced sex acts, and sexual callousness. High pornography users who were shown non-violent dehumanizing pornography show higher scores in reported likelihood of committing rape, sexual callousness, and sexually aggressive behaviors than high pornography users who weren't shown pornography.

These studies indicate that the use of pornography, even that which does not include sexual violence, changes beliefs about rape and sexual violence. If women like to be raped and deserve to be raped, there isn't any need for sexual restraint or frustration of sexual desire. Rape pornography teaches men that when a woman says no, the man does not need to stop. So a man may learn that there isn't any need to pay attention to a woman who is resisting, crying, screaming, struggling, or saying no, because ultimately she wants it and will enjoy it. He can conclude that her resistance is a sham and is part of a sex dance that leads to orgasm. He may assume that even her resistance is sexy and sexually arousing because it is part of the sexual template.

In other words, pornography makes violence sexy.[11]

Pornography and sexual violence behaviors

Attitudes supporting sexual violence lead to an increased likelihood of sexually violent behavior. Some studies have looked at likelihood of future behavior measures, while other studies have looked at actual (self-reported) past behaviors.

Pornography can start to cross the line between thought and behavior in the kinds of fantasies that can produce an erection. One study exposed males to an arousing rape or non-rape presentation. Afterwards, they asked the males to try to reach as high a level of sexual arousal as they could without any direct stimulation of the penis. In doing so, those who had been exposed to the rape presentation were more likely to create sexually violent fantasies in order to arouse themselves than those exposed to the non-rape presentation. So for some of these males, rape fantasies were now part of their sexual template and were arousing.[12]

---

11 Diana E. H. Russell, *Making Violence Sexy: Feminist Views on Pornography* (New York: Teachers College Press, 1993).

12 Neil M. Malamuth, "Rape Fantasies as a Function of Exposure to Violent Sexual Stimuli," *Archives of Sexual Behavior* 10, no. 1 (1981): 33–47.

Another study examined measures of the likelihood of future sexually violent behavior as well as past actual sexually violent behaviors. It found that all types of pornography (soft-core, hard-core, violent, and rape) are correlated with using verbal coercion, drugs, and alcohol to sexually coerce women. The future likelihood of raping a woman was correlated with the use of *all* types of pornography, including soft-core pornography. All types of pornography other than soft-core were correlated with actual rape. Those reporting higher past exposure to violent pornography were six times more likely to report having raped than those reporting low past exposure.[13]

Similarly, men who engaged in date rape reported that they "very frequently" read *Playboy, Penthouse, Chic, Club, Forum, Gallery, Genesis, Oui,* or *Hustler.*[14] The correlation between rape rates and circulation rates for eight pornographic magazines (the same magazines minus *Hustler*) indicated that states with higher circulation rates had higher rape rates.[15]

Adolescent boys who read pornographic material were more likely to be involved in active sexual violence.[16] Juvenile sex offenders (juvenile rapists and child molesters) were more likely to have been exposed to pornography (42% had been exposed) than juveniles who were not sex offenders (29%), and also to have been exposed at an early age (five to eight years old), while juvenile child molesters had been more frequently exposed to pornography than those who did not molest children.[17] Another study reported that twenty-nine of the thirty juvenile offenders studied had been exposed to X-rated magazines or videos, and the average age of

---

13 Scot B. Boeringer, "Pornography and Sexual Aggression: Associations of Violent and Nonviolent Depictions with Rape and Rape Proclivity," *Deviant Behavior* 15, no. 3 (1994): 289–304.

14 Robin Warshaw, *I Never Called It Rape* (New York: HarperCollins, 1988).

15 Larry Baron and Murray Straus, "Sexual Stratification, Pornography, and Rape in the United States," in *Pornography and Sexual Aggression*, eds. Neil M. Malamuth and Edward Donnerstein (New York: Academic Press, 1984).

16 Silvia Bonino et al., "Use of Pornography and Self-Reported Engagement in Sexual Violence Among Adolescents," *European Journal of Developmental Psychology* 3, no. 3 (2006): 265–88.

17 Michelle E. Ford and Jean Ann Linney, "Comparative Analysis of Juvenile Sexual Offenders, Violent Nonsexual Offenders and Status Offenders," *Journal of Interpersonal Violence* 10, no. 1 (1995): 56–70.

first exposure was about 7.5 years.[18] Only 11% of juvenile sex offenders said that they did not use sexually explicit material.[19] Ironically, given these figures, exposing adults to pornography decreases the number of adults who believe that pornography needs to be restricted from children.[20] Having been exposed to pornography, they normalize the use of pornography not only for adults but for children as well.

Similarly, adult sex offenders showed a high rate of using hard-core pornography: child molesters (67%), incest offenders (53%), and rapists (83%) were significantly higher in use than non-offenders (29%). Child molesters (37%) and rapists (35%) were more likely to use pornography as an instigator to offending than were incest offenders (13%).[21] It is an interesting finding that while these offenders used rape and child pornography to instigate their offenses, they did not exclusively do so; they often used adult and consensual pornography. Even adult consensual pornography can be used to instigate these offenses.

Pornography's effect depends upon not just what you are exposed to, but also how often. The more frequently men used pornography and the more violent the pornography they used, the more likely they were to coerce others into sex, including to use physical coercion (i.e., rape).[22]

Pornography's effect also depends upon individuals' characteristics as well as how often they use pornography. Males who were high in hostile masculinity and sexual promiscuity and who used pornography frequently were significantly more likely to be physically and sexually aggressive than males who were low in these three factors.[23] However, this study was unable to determine if those individual charac-

---

18 Edward Wieckowski et al., "Deviant Sexual Behavior in Children and Young Adolescents: Frequency and Patterns," *Sexual Abuse: A Journal of Research and Treatment* 10, no. 4 (1998): 293–304.

19 Judith Becker and Robert Stein, "Is Sexual Erotica Associated with Sexual Deviance in Adolescent Males?," *International Journal of Law and Psychiatry* 14, nos. 1 and 2 (1991): 85–95.

20 Zillmann and Bryant, "Effects of Massive Exposure to Pornography."

21 William L. Marshall, "The Use of Sexually Explicit Stimuli by Rapists, Child Molesters, and Non-Offenders," *Journal of Sex Research* 25, no. 2 (1988): 267–88.

22 Mary Koss and Cheryl Oros, "Sexual Experiences Survey: A Research Instrument Investigating Sexual Aggression and Victimization," *Journal of Consulting and Clinical Psychology* 50, no. 3 (June 1982): 455–57.

23 Neil M. Malamuth, Tamara Addison, and Mary Koss, "Pornography and Sexual Aggression: Are There Reliable Effects and Can We Understand Them?," *Annual Review of Sex Research* 11 (2000): 26–68.

teristics of hostile masculinity and promiscuity might have been produced by pornography use at an earlier point in life.

Much of the research has focused on the males who perpetrate the behaviors. However, there are studies that have focused on the female victims. One study questioned 100 women who presented to a rape crisis center. Twenty-eight percent said that their abuser used pornography. Of those whose abuser used pornography, 40% said the pornography was part of the abuse, being used either during the abuse or just prior to it, and 43% said that it affected the nature of the abuse. None of them thought it decreased the frequency of the abuse, but 21% thought it increased the frequency and 14% believed it increased the level of violence. In fact, 18% thought their abuser became more sadistic with the use of pornography. Of the total, 12% said the abuser imitated the pornography, and 14% said someone had tried to force them to do something he had seen in pornography.[24]

Another study found that 24% of women surveyed indicated that they had been upset by someone trying to get them to do something they had seen in pornography. Those who said this were more likely to have been victims of threatened or actual sexual assault.[25]

A meta-analysis of thirty-three studies (meta-analyses examine findings across a large number of studies) revealed that exposure to either violent or non-violent pornography increases behavioral aggression.[26] These studies taken as a whole indicate that many types of pornography and frequent use of pornography are connected to negative behaviors—both violent fantasies or actual violent assaults—with violent pornography having the strongest negative effect. These patterns are seen in adults and in minors, and are found in studies focused on perpetrators and victims.

Pedophilia, sexual harassment, and domestic violence

Being charged with a child pornography offense is a good predictor of who might get the diagnosis of pedophilia. It appears to be a better predictor of pedophilia than actually having raped a child. Individuals who have been charged with a child

---

24 Raquel Bergen and Kathleen Bogle, "Exploring the Connection Between Pornography and Sexual Violence," *Violence and Victims* 15, no. 3 (2000): 227–34.

25 Charlene Senn, "The Research on Women and Pornography: The Many Faces of Harm," in *Making Violence Sexy*, ed. Diana E. H. Russell (New York: Teachers College Press, 1993).

26 Allen et al., "Exposure to Pornography."

pornography offense, whether or not they have committed a sexual offense against children, are more likely to be pedophiles than are individuals who have offended against children but do not use child pornography. Fantasy may be a more accurate predictor than behavior because individuals have more options and more control of their options in fantasies than in behaviors that depend upon the availability of others.[27]

Forms of sexual violence perpetrated against women other than rape are affected by the use of pornography. Many women will be sexually harassed on their jobs and elsewhere. The likelihood of sexually harassing another is significantly correlated with the volume of past exposure to sexually explicit materials.[28]

Domestic violence is another form of violence against women. The violence may typically be physical and emotional, but these are often combined with sexual violence. Battered women experienced significantly more sexual violence than women who were not battered.[29] For example, 39% of the battered women said that their partners had tried to get them to act out pornographic scenes they had been shown, compared with 3% of other women.[30]

The batterer's use of pornography and alcohol significantly increases a battered woman's odds of being sexually abused. Pornography alone increases the odds of sexual violence by a factor of almost two, and the combination of pornography and alcohol increases the odds of sexual violence by a factor of three.[31]

Forty percent of abused women indicated that their partner used violent pornography. Of those whose partners used pornography, 53% said that they had been asked or forced to enact scenes they had been shown, and 26% had been reminded of pornography by an abuser during the abuse. Of the 40% who had been raped, 73% stated that their partners had used pornography.

---

27 Michael C. Seto, James Cantor, and Ray Blanchard, "Child Pornography Offenses Are a Valid Diagnostic Indicator of Pedophilia," *Journal of Abnormal Psychology* 115, no. 3 (2006): 610–15.

28 Azy Barak et al., "Sex, Guys, and Cyberspace: Effects of Internet Pornography and Individual Differences on Men's Attitudes Toward Women," *Journal of Psychology and Human Sexuality* 11, no. 1 (1999): 63–91.

29 Evelyn Sommers and James V. P. Check, "An Empirical Investigation of the Role of Pornography in the Verbal and Physical Abuse of Women," *Violence and Victims* 2, no. 1 (1987): 189–209.

30 Ibid.

31 Janet H. Shope, "When Words Are Not Enough: The Search for the Effect of Pornography on Abused Women," *Violence Against Women* 10, no. 1 (2004): 56–72.

These studies may not indicate that pornography causes battering, but they do suggest that battering may be expanded to include sexual violence when pornography is involved.

Prostitution, partners, and deviance

Men who go to prostitutes are twice as likely to have watched a pornographic movie over the last year (66%) than a national sample (33%). Men who go to prostitutes frequently are more likely to have seen a pornographic movie (74%) than those who have gone to a prostitute only once (53%). The same pattern is seen with the use of pornographic magazines; men who go to prostitutes frequently are more likely to have seen a pornographic magazine in the last year (75%) than men who have gone to a prostitute only once (56%).[32]

Exposure to pornography leads men to rate their female partners as less attractive than they would have had they not been exposed.[33] They are less satisfied with their partners' attractiveness, sexual performance, and level of affection. They expressed a greater desire for sex without emotional involvement.[34] Undergraduate men who regularly viewed pornography spontaneously generated more sexual terms to describe the construct "women" than did those who viewed pornography less regularly.[35]

Paraphilias are psychiatric disorders of sexuality as defined by the *Diagnostic and Statistical Manual* of the American Psychiatric Association. Paraphilia used to be called sexual perversion or sexual deviance. These are behaviors in which the object of the sexual desire is abnormal (e.g., an animal), or the behavior itself is sexually abnormal (e.g., sadomasochism). Some paraphilias can be engaged in alone (e.g., fetishism), and some involve people who do not consent (e.g., exhibitionism).

---

32 Martin A. Monto, "Focusing on the Clients of Street Prostitutes: A Creative Approach to Reducing Violence Against Women" (paper submitted to the US Department of Justice, 1999, available at http://www.ncjrs.gov/pdffiles1/nij/grants/182859.pdf).

33 James B. Weaver, Jonathan L. Masland, and Dolf Zillmann, "Effect of Erotica on Young Men's Aesthetic Perception of Their Female Sexual Partners," *Perceptual and Motor Skills* 58 (1984): 929–30.

34 Dolf Zillmann and Jennings Bryant, "Pornography's Impact on Sexual Satisfaction," *Journal of Applied Social Psychology* 18, no. 5 (1988): 438–53.

35 Deborrah E. S. Frable, Anne E. Johnson, Hildy Kellman, "Seeing Masculine Men, Sexy Women, and Gender Differences: Exposure to Pornography and Cognitive Constructs of Gender," *Journal of Personality* 65, no. 2 (1997): 311–55.

Sexual deviance can be learned. Some men may initially look at deviant pornography out of curiosity. Some may move up to harder kinds because softer material no longer arouses them. Either way they may learn deviant beliefs and behavior from it. Things that used to lead to disgust now seem less unusual and more common and even normal, and over time, come to seem sexy. Through pornography males who never would have considered sex that involves feces (coprophilia), urine (urophilia), and animals (bestiality) may now learn about, get aroused by, and engage in these very things.

Individuals who already suffer from these deviances significantly prefer pornography that portrays their own deviance, but they also like other deviant pornography, especially sadomasochistic pornography, though to a lesser extent.[36] Those who were exposed to pornography were more likely to believe that unusual and pathological sexual behaviors were more common and more normal. Their belief in how often others engaged in sex with animals, sex in groups, and sex with violence was double in those exposed to pornography when compared with those who were not.[37] These beliefs are permission-giving beliefs and become releasers of behavior.

Relationships, women's liberation, and risky behavior

The use of pornography has several other negative effects. One is a changed understanding of relationships. For males, more pornography use was associated with greater acceptance of sex outside of marriage for married individuals, greater acceptance of sex before marriage, and less child-centeredness during marriage.[38] The reduced desire for children is especially pronounced in a reduced desire for female children.[39]

---

36 Niklas Långström and Michael C. Seto, "Exhibitionistic and Voyeuristic Behavior in a Swedish National Population Survey," *Archives of Sexual Behavior* 35, no. 4 (2006): 427–35; Niklas Långström and Kenneth J. Zucker, "Transvestic Fetishism in the General Population: Prevalence and Correlates," *Journal of Sex and Marital Therapy* 31, no. 2 (2005): 87–95.

37 Zillmann and Bryant, "Effects of Massive Exposure to Pornography."

38 Jason S. Carroll et al., "Generation XXX: Pornography Acceptance and Use Among Emerging Adults," *Journal of Adolescent Research* 23, no. 1 (2008): 6–30.

39 Dolf Zillmann, "The Effects of Prolonged Consumption of Pornography," in *Pornography: Research Advances and Policy Considerations*, eds. Dolf Zillmann and Jennings Bryant (Hillsdale, N.J.: Lawrence Erlbaum Associates, 1989), 127–58.

Those who were shown pornography reduced their support for the women's liberation movement. This is true for both men and women.[40]

For males, more pornography use is correlated with more alcohol use and more binge-drinking.[41]

Pornography also encourages physically risky behavior. In pornography no one is shown contracting and dying from AIDS, and there aren't any negative consequences ever shown for having deviant kinds of sex.

Yet deviant kinds of sexual behavior carry a number of physical risks. The most obvious one is acquiring sexually transmitted diseases, including HIV. These can lead to other diseases and disorders (e.g., cervical cancer and infertility). Sexual behavior involving feces and urine can lead to influenza, pneumonia, hepatitis A, hepatitis C, and intestinal parasites. Anal sex can cause ripping of the anal tissue, anal fissures, and puncturing of internal organs. The tearing of anal tissue makes it easier for the HIV virus to enter the body.

Pornography portrays sex with as many strangers as possible as normal, desirable, and without consequences, and those who use pornography do have more sex partners than do other people.[42] The factor most associated with HIV transmission is increased number of partners.

Summary

The large body of research on pornography reveals that it functions as a teacher of, a permission-giver for, and a trigger of many negative behaviors and attitudes that can severely damage not only the users but many others, including strangers. The damage is seen in men, women, and children, and in both married and single adults. It involves pathological behaviors, illegal behaviors, and some behaviors that are both illegal and pathological. Pornography is a widely influential and very toxic teacher.

---

40 Zillmann and Bryant, "Effects of Massive Exposure to Pornography."

41 Carroll et al., "Generation XXX."

42 Ibid.

THE IMPACT OF PORNOGRAPHY ON WOMEN: SOCIAL SCIENCE FINDINGS AND CLINICAL OBSERVATIONS

Jill C. Manning

On a recent business trip, I encountered a teenage young woman wearing a pink tank top that read "*Future Porn Star*" across the chest. This three-word aspiration naturally caught my attention due to my clinical work with individuals, couples, and families who are grappling with the impact of pornography and sexually compulsive behavior. Various questions crossed my mind: What motivates a young woman to advertise such a statement? What does it mean? Who is she hoping it will offend, attract, or . . . arouse? Who is profiting from this kind of merchandise? If it is a joke, how and when did working in the sex industry become funny, as opposed to desperate or oppressive? And of course, What's *next?*

Pornography has long since left the seedy back alley of the pre–Hugh Hefner era to take a socially and economically legitimized place in mainstream popular culture and the global economy.[1] The pink tank top symbolically underscored that the impact of pornography in today's social milieu, and on women in particular, is complex, multifaceted, and unprecedented. Women no longer can be categorically described as the objectified, the victimized, or the consumed, as today they are also the objectifiers, the producers, and the consumers. Pornography, it could be argued, is altering the cultural Zeitgeist and the lived reality of women in ways we may not come to identify or fully appreciate until society has paid significant social costs.

This paper will attempt to summarize pornography's impact upon women through social science findings, cultural trends, and clinical observations.

A sexualized social context

Although a female born into today's American society will benefit from conveniences, opportunities, and advances that women before her never knew, she will

1 Richard C. Morais, "Porn Goes Public," *Forbes Magazine*, 14 June 1999, 214.

also be introduced into a society that is arguably more sexually coarse, explicit, and risky than that of past eras. While she will have greater access to information, laws, and resources with which to foster sexual health and expression, modern trends in technology and media combine to make her world more sexually complex than ever before. She is also facing these social complexities earlier in her development than ever before.

Although pornography is nothing new, the proximity of the sex industry to the public and private squares is new. In the past, the triple-X bookstore and restricted movie theater were tangible buffers between sexually explicit material and minors, as well as adults who did not want to be exposed to "dirty pictures." Today, anyone with a cable or an internet connection has access to a smorgasbord of sexual content, including obscene content not protected by the First Amendment. Moreover, the sex industry has unprecedented access to those who are technologically connected, and it capitalizes on this contact with stunning effectiveness, not to mention blatant disregard for those who may be harmed (not just offended) in the process.

The rapid growth of internet usage has been identified as the primary reason for the exponential increase in pornography use and production, as well as compulsive sexual behaviors related to pornography use.[2] As one study puts it, "Since its inception, the internet has been associated with sexuality in a kind of synergistic dance, each fueling the transformation of the other. The influence of the internet on sexuality is likely to be so significant that it will ultimately be recognized as the cause of the next 'sexual revolution.'"[3]

This synergistic dance has made pornography and online sexual pursuits "a hidden public health hazard exploding, in part, because very few are recognizing

---

2 Jennifer P. Schneider, "Effects of Cybersex Addiction on the Family: Results of a Survey," *Sexual Addiction & Compulsivity* 7, nos. 1 and 2 (2000): 31–58; Jennifer P. Schneider, "A Qualitative Study of Cybersex Participants: Gender Differences, Recovery Issues, and Implications for Therapists," *Sexual Addiction & Compulsivity* 7, no. 4 (2000): 249–78; Al Cooper and Eric Griffin-Shelley, "A Quick Tour of Online Sexuality: Part 1," *American Psychotherapy* 5, no. 6 (November–December 2002): 11–13.

3 Al Cooper et al., "Sexuality and the Internet: The Next Sexual Revolution," in *The Psychological Science of Sexuality: A Research Based Approach*, eds. Frank Muscarella and Lenore T. Szuchman (New York: Wiley, 1999), 519–45.

it as such or taking it seriously."[4] My own clinical observations and research have caused me to align with this line of thinking. Over the last decade, I have noticed that often those who claim pornography to be harmless entertainment, benign sexual expression, part of developing one's sexual potential, or a marital aid, have either never seriously explored the social science data on pornography's risk potential, or minimize the data because it is incongruent with their own lived experiences, values, or sexual worldview. Public policies, psychological treatments, educational curricula, and legal processes need more substantive backing.

The influential interplay between the internet and sexuality has been fueled to a large extent by what has been called the internet's "Triple-A Engine" effect of *accessibility, affordability,* and perceived *anonymity.*[5] Additionally, the "Cyberhex of the Internet"—that the internet is *intoxicating, isolating, integral, inexpensive, imposing,* and *interactive*—makes it a unique and powerful medium, and helps explain why it has had such an influential role in altering the American sexual landscape.[6]

According to current internet traffic statistics, there are approximately 246 million internet users in North America (17.5% of internet users worldwide).[7] Since 2000, internet usage has increased 127.9%, with 73.1% of the North American population now having access.[8] Approximately 20% to 33% of those using the internet do so primarily for sexual purposes,[9] and online measurement services

---

4 Al Cooper, David L. Delmonico, and Ron Burg, "Cybersex Users, Abusers, and Compulsives: New Findings and Implications," *Sexual Addiction & Compulsivity* 7, nos. 1 and 2 (2000): 5–29.

5 Al Cooper, "Sexuality and the Internet: Surfing into the New Millennium," *CyberPsychology & Behavior* 1, no. 2 (1998): 181–87; Cooper, Delmonico, and Burg, "Cybersex Users, Abusers, and Compulsives"; Barry W. McCarthy, "The Wife's Role in Facilitating Recovery from Male Compulsive Sexual Behavior," *Sexual Addiction & Compulsivity* 9, no. 4 (2002): 275–84; Schneider, "Effects of Cybersex Addiction on the Family"; Schneider, "A Qualitative Study of Cybersex Participants."

6 David L. Delmonico, Elizabeth Griffin, and Joseph Moriarty, *Cybersex Unhooked: A Workbook for Breaking Free from Compulsive Online Sexual Behavior* (Center City, Minn.: Hazelden Educational Press, 2001).

7 Miniwatts Marketing Group, "Internet World Stats: Usage and Population Statistics," http://www.internetworldstats.com/stats.htm (accessed 16 June 2008).

8 Ibid.

9 Al Cooper, "Online Sexual Activity in the New Millennium," *Contemporary Sexuality* 38, no. 3 (2004): i–vii.

indicate that 42.7% of internet users view pornography online.[10] Online measurements also indicate that one out of every four search engine requests is related to pornography.[11]

Furthermore, the larger social context has troubling implications for the social, emotional, spiritual, physical, and intellectual lives of women, as the sex industry and pornography are gaining greater acceptance and presence in our culture, and around the world. For example:

- In 2006, worldwide pornography revenue was estimated to be $97.06 billion, with $13.3 billion of that being generated in the United States.[12]
- Approximately 30% of online pornography is consumed by females.[13]
- In 2005, 13,585 hard-core pornographic video/DVD titles were released in the United States. This was up from 1,300 titles in 1988.[14]
- 22% of teen girls (ages thirteen to nineteen) and 36% of young adult women (ages twenty to twenty-six) have electronically sent nude or semi-nude pictures or video of themselves.[15]
- 37% of teen girls and 56% of young adult women have sent or posted a sexually suggestive message to someone.[16]
- 47% of teen girls and 38% of young adult women say "pressure from guys" is a reason why they have sent or posted sexually suggestive images or messages.[17]
- At the November 2002 meeting of the American Academy of Matrimonial Lawyers, 62% of the 350 attendees said the internet had been a significant factor in divorces they had handled during that year. Sixty-eight percent of the divorce cases involved one party meeting a new love interest over the internet, 56% involved

---

10 Jerry Ropelato, "Top Ten Internet Pornography Statistics," http://internet-filter-review.toptenreviews.com/internet-pornography-statistics.html (accessed 16 June 2008).

11 Ibid.

12 Ibid.

13 Ibid.

14 Ibid.

15 National Campaign to Prevent Teen and Unplanned Pregnancy, *Sex & Tech: Results from a Survey of Teens and Young Adults*, 2008, http://www.thenationalcampaign.org/sextech/PDF/SexTech_Summary.pdf (accessed June 2008).

16 Ibid.

17 Ibid.

one party having an obsessive interest in pornographic websites, and 33% cited excessive time communicating in chat rooms (a commonly sexualized forum).[18]

- The number of sex scenes on American television nearly doubled between 1998 and 2005.[19]
- Between October 2004 and April 2005, 70% of the twenty television shows most commonly watched by American teens included sexual content, and 45% contained sexual behavior.[20]
- Every two minutes, someone in the United States is sexually assaulted (including rape, attempted rape, and other sexually violent felonies), and every eight minutes someone is raped.[21]
- In the United States, one in four adolescent females (ages fourteen to nineteen) is infected with at least one sexually transmitted disease, and 15% have more than one.[22]

There are many ways to interpret this data, as well as a plethora of other data that could be listed. Because many of these trends are relatively new, it will take time to clarify how these factors influence female development and lived experiences. In the meantime, my clinical work with women is teaching me that an increasing number of women are seeking out mental health practitioners for issues related to these trends and the manner in which these phenomena affect their relationships; their home, work, and school environments; their sexuality; their self-esteem; and their identity as women.

---

18 Jonathan Dedmon, "Is the Internet Bad for Your Marriage? Online Affairs, Pornographic Sites Playing Greater Role in Divorces," press release from the Dilenschneider Group, Inc., November 2002, http://www.expertclick.com/NewsReleaseWire/ReleaseDetails.aspx?ID=3051&CFID=1696313&CFTOKEN=23726003.

19 Dale Kunkel et al., *Sex on TV 4* (Menlo Park, Calif.: The Henry J. Kaiser Family Foundation, 2005).

20 Jochen Peter and Patti M. Valkenburg, "Adolescents' Exposure to a Sexualized Media Environment and Their Notions of Women as Sex Objects," *Sex Roles* 56, nos. 5 and 6 (2007): 381–95.

21 Rape, Abuse & Incest National Network, "How Often Does Sexual Assault Occur?," June 2008, http://www.rainn.org/print/287 (accessed 17 June 2008).

22 Lawrence K. Altman, "Sex Infections Found in Quarter of Teenage Girls," *New York Times*, 12 March 2008, http://www.nytimes.com/2008/03/12/science/12std.html (accessed 17 June 2008).

Female adolescents and pornography

Despite the illegality of exposing minors to sexually explicit material, and regardless of the lip service it gives to the contrary, the pornography industry does not discriminate against young consumers. Sexually explicit material on the internet, for example, is "very intrusive" and can be inadvertently stumbled upon while searching for other material or when opening e-mail.[23] Thirty-four percent of adolescents report being exposed to *unwanted* sexual content online.[24] Furthermore, a different study showed that 70% of youth ages fifteen to seventeen report accidentally coming across pornography online, and 23% of them said this happens "very" or "somewhat" often.[25] In a nationally representative sample of youth ages ten to seventeen, 19% reported unwanted sexual solicitation, and 6% had been harassed online.[26]

Another startling indicator of this indiscriminate accessibility is that Nielsen NetRatings, a reputable and well-recognized source for online audience measurement, includes children beginning at two years of age in their demographic statistics for online "adult" traffic.[27] It is troubling to consider the long-term impact of increasing numbers of youth being exposed to sexual content when they lack the risk attenuation and maturity to process and navigate these experiences in safe and healthy ways.[28]

Filters and active parenting are frequently touted as solutions, but the pornography industry and even our own justice system fall unacceptably short in supporting parents in the difficult task of safeguarding the choice not to have sexually explicit content in their home, never mind honoring existing laws by protecting children from obscenity. For example, only 3% of pornographic websites require

---

23 Kimberley Mitchell, David Finkelhor, and Janis Wolak, "The Exposure of Youth to Unwanted Sexual Material on the Internet: A National Survey of Risk, Impact, and Prevention," *Youth and Society* 34, no. 3 (2003): 330–58.

24 Janis Wolak, Kimberley Mitchell, and David Finkelhor, "Unwanted and Wanted Exposure to Online Pornography in a National Sample of Youth Internet Users," *Pediatrics* 119, no. 2 (2007): 247–57.

25 The Henry J. Kaiser Family Foundation, "Key Facts: Teens Online," Fall 2002, http://www.kff.org/entmedia/loader.cfm?url=/commonspot/security/getfile.cfm&PageID=14095 (accessed 24 May 2005).

26 Mitchell, "The Exposure of Youth to Unwanted Sexual Material."

27 See "Nielsen Netratings," http://en-us.nielsen.com/tab/product_families/nielsen_netratings (accessed 25 May 2005).

28 Delmonico and Griffin, "Cybersex and the E-Teen."

proof of age before granting access to sexually explicit material, and two-thirds of pornographic websites do not include any adult content warnings; approximately 75% of pornographic websites display visual teasers on their homepages before asking if viewers are of legal age.[29]

Effective age verification systems are available, so why is the industry not employing them, and why are they not required to do so by society? It is strange how the virtual world has escaped the societal standards accepted in various public squares. Even more troubling is the fact that there are currently no effective filtering systems in place for cell phones with internet access or iPods that can transmit "podnography," despite the growing popularity of those media amongst youth.[30]

A number of studies and surveys have shown that one of the initial impacts pornography has on a developing, adolescent mind is that it evokes upset and distress when one is not psychologically able to process the images.[31] Youth ages eleven to seventeen in an Australian survey used the words "sick," "yuck," "disgusted," "repulsed," and "upset" to describe how they felt about exposure to online sexual material.[32] If the upset or distress was fleeting, it might not be as concerning, but we know

29 Dick Thornburg and Herbert S. Lin, *Youth, Pornography, and the Internet* (Washington, D.C.: National Research Council, National Academy Press, 2002), quoted in "The Porn Standard: Children and Pornography on the Internet," July 2005, http://www.thirdway.org/publications/14 (accessed 3 August 2005).

30 Delmonico and Griffin, "Cybersex and the E-Teen," 433.

31 Mitchell, "The Exposure of Youth to Unwanted Sexual Material"; Kimberley Mitchell, David Finkelhor, and Janis Wolak, "Victimization of Youths on the Internet," in *The Victimization of Children: Emerging Issues*, eds. Janet Mullings, James Marquart, and Deborah Hartley (Binghamton, N.Y.: Haworth Maltreatment and Trauma Press, 2003); eds. Cecilia von Feilitzen and Ula Carlsson, *Children in the New Media Landscape: Games, Pornography, Perceptions* (Goteburg: UNESCO-Nordicom, 2000); Media Awareness Network, "Canada's Children in a Wired World: The Parent's View," *Media Awareness* 20, no. 2 (2000): 17–18, quoted in Sonia Livingstone, "Children's Use of the Internet: Reflections on the Emerging Research Agenda," *New Media and Society* 5, no. 2 (2003): 147–66.

32 Michael Flood and Clive Hamilton, *Youth and Pornography in Australia: Evidence on the Extent of Exposure and Likely Effects* (The Australia Institute Discussion Paper Number 52, 2003, https://www.tai.org.au/documents/dp_fulltext/DP52.pdf).

that early exposures to pornography leave a lasting and mostly negative impression,[33] and that females report more negative memories of sexually explicit content than do males.[34]

We are beginning to understand how pornography influences attitudes and behavior in adolescents, in addition to its leaving vivid memories and negative associations. For example, when male and female adolescents are exposed to a sexualized media environment, they are more likely to have stronger notions of women as sex objects,[35] and this association is particularly strong when they consume audiovisual formats such as television shows or internet movies.[36] As cable television and the internet are the most common ways adolescents access sexual content, the influence of these media on beliefs about women are of significant concern.[37]

Research conducted with first-year college students has brought forth insights into how adolescents and young adults are affected and even harmed by exposure to sexually explicit material. One study found that frequent exposure to pornography is associated with the following attitudes and dynamics:

- Normalization of adverse reactions to offensive material;
- Increased tolerance toward sexually explicit material, thereby requiring more novel or bizarre material to achieve the same level of arousal or interest;

---

33 Joanne Cantor, Marie-Louise Mares, and Janet S. Hyde, "Autobiographical Memories of Exposure to Sexual Media Content," *Media Psychology* 5, no. 1 (2003): 1–31, quoted in Patricia M. Greenfield, "Inadvertent Exposure to Pornography on the Internet: Implications for Peer-to-Peer File Sharing Networks for Child Development and Families," *Applied Developmental Psychology* 25 (2004): 741–50.

34 Patricia M. Greenfield, "Inadvertent Exposure to Pornography on the Internet: Implications for Peer-to-Peer File Sharing Networks for Child Development and Families," *Applied Developmental Psychology* 25 (2004): 741–50.

35 L. Monique Ward, "Does Television Exposure Affect Emerging Adults' Attitudes and Assumptions About Sexual Relationships? Correlational and Experimental Confirmation," *Journal of Youth and Adolescence* 31, no. 1 (2002): 1–15; L. Monique Ward and Kimberley Friedman, "Using TV as a Guide: Associations Between Television Viewing and Adolescents' Sexual Attitudes and Behavior," *Journal of Research on Adolescents* 16, no. 1 (2006): 133–56; Peter and Valkenburg, "Adolescents' Exposure to a Sexualized Media Environment."

36 Peter and Valkenburg, "Adolescents' Exposure to a Sexualized Media Environment."

37 Elisabet Häggström-Nordin, Tanja Tydén, and Ulf Hanson, "Associations Between Pornography Consumption and Sexual Practices Among Adolescents in Sweden," *International Journal of STD & AIDS* 16, no. 2 (2005): 102–7.

- Misperceptions about the extent of sexual activity in the general populace and the prevalence of less common sexual practices (e.g., group sex, bestiality, and sado-masochistic activity);
- Diminished trust in intimate partners;
- Decreased desire to achieve sexual exclusivity with a partner;
- Increased risk of developing a negative body image, especially for women (Siegel, 1997);
- Acceptance of promiscuity as a normal state of interaction;
- Assuming that sexual inactivity or abstinence constitutes a health risk;
- Beginning to view love in a cynical manner;
- Belief that superior sexual satisfaction is attainable without having affection for one's partner;
- Belief that marriage is sexually confining; and
- Belief that raising children and having a family is an unattractive prospect.[38]

The effects of these attitudes and behaviors can be especially dangerous to adolescents in light of the fact that young people are reaching puberty and engaging in sexual intercourse earlier than previous generations.[39] Exactly how these beliefs and dynamics will play out in the lives of young women is unclear, but these research findings are consistent with what I am witnessing with young clients.

Through my clients, I have learned that pornography has become a major socializing agent and the primary sexual educator of today's adolescents. If, through pornography, an adolescent stood a good chance of acquiring accurate, respectful, and helpful information about sexuality and had the developmental capacity to decipher it and avoid illegal, demeaning, fraudulent, or violent material, I would be less concerned. However, my clinical observations have taught me that internet pornography is handicapping youth from being able to develop a healthy sexual self, and affecting their attitudes and behavior on multiple levels. Pornography influences everything from how teens speak of and frame sexuality, to why and how they pierce certain body parts, to what they expect to give and receive in intimate relationships.

---

38 Dolf Zillmann, "Influence of Unrestrained Access to Erotica on Adolescents' and Young Adults' Dispositions Toward Sexuality," *Journal of Adolescent Health* 27, no. 2 (2000): 41–44.

39 Robert E. Longo, Steven M. Brown, and Deborah Price Orcutt, "Effects of Internet Sexuality on Children and Adolescents," in *Sex and the Internet: A Guidebook for Clinicians*, ed. Al Cooper (New York: Brunner-Routledge, 2002), 87–105.

I am also witnessing more female adolescents tolerating emotional, physical, and sexual abuse in dating relationships, feeling pressure to make out with females as a way to arouse young men, looking at or producing pornography so that their boyfriends will think they are "open-minded" and "hot," and normalizing sexual abuse done to them because they see the same acts eroticized in pornography—after all, how bad can it be if the larger culture around you finds abusive and demeaning acts a turn-on? Moreover, it concerns me as a woman, a mother, a clinician, and a citizen that an increasing number of young females have come to view sex as a spectator sport, and a form of entertainment totally detached from consequences, relationships, and (heaven forbid) a procreative or sacred role.

When female adolescents share with me some version of "my body and my sexuality are the most important things I have to offer the world," I am struck at how ignorant this generation has become of the feminist ideals of preceding generations. Ironically, feminism has become a foreign, off-putting, rarely uttered word, while pornography and whorish behavior have become mainstream. How did so many young women become gullible to pornographic scripts, excruciatingly narrow definitions of 'sexy,' pseudo-intimacy, and eroticized violence toward women? Why are they selling themselves so short? Feminist writer and thinker Naomi Wolf provides an interesting insight:

> Does all this sexual imagery in the air mean that sex has been liberated—or is it the case that the relationship between the multi-billion-dollar porn industry, compulsiveness, and sexual appetite has become like the relationship between agribusiness, processed foods, supersize portions, and obesity? If your appetite is stimulated and fed by poor-quality material, it takes more junk to fill you up.[40]

Wolf's statement begs the question: How can society provide nourishing and ennobling messages to our youth regarding sexuality?

Exactly how exposure to pornography affects the beliefs and actions of today's young women, if it does at all, is uncertain, but research indicates that it is affecting sexual behavior in young adults. Research has shown that adolescents themselves

---

40 Naomi Wolf, "The Porn Myth," *New York*, 2 October 2003, http://nymag.com/nymetro/news/trends/n_9437/index1.html (accessed 14 December 2009).

recognize that pornography influences their own sexual behavior, even though they tend to believe it influences others to a larger degree.[41]

For example, three separate studies that focused on adolescents and pornography use found that for males and females there was a strong association between pornography consumption and engaging in oral and anal sex,[42] even though the majority of females described anal intercourse as a negative experience.[43] Because condom use has been found to be low (40%) for those engaging in anal intercourse,[44] and the number of sexually transmitted diseases being contracted through genital-oral contact has risen, the implications for the transmission of disease and other health risks need to be considered.

Young women are also facing increasingly complex interactions with young men as a result of the pornographic undercurrents in social and dating relations. Many young women I have worked with dislike the fact that young men consume pornography, but they are conflicted about how to reject their behavior while at the same time trying to garner and compete for their romantic attention. Young women used to have allure and mystery on their side. Now, young men are inundated with airbrushed images of naked and sexually engaged females that dramatically alter the flirtatious dance between the sexes. Culturally, we have forgotten that a big part of what made "Victoria" magnetic in the first place was that she had a "Secret."

Women as consumers of pornography

It used to be that men were the primary consumers of pornography, while adult women were the staple of pornographic images. The internet era, however, has fostered a level playing field of sorts. More and more women are producing and viewing pornography than ever before. Some greet this cultural shift enthusiastically, claiming that it helps women "own" and "express" their sexuality. In my office, and the

---

41 Christina Rogala and Tanja Tydén, "Does Pornography Influence Young Women's Sexual Behavior?" *Women's Health Issues* 13, no. 1 (2003): 39–43; Häggström-Nordin, Tydén, and Hanson, "Associations."

42 Rogala and Tydén, "Does Pornography Influence Young Women's Sexual Behavior?"; Tanja Tydén and Christina Rogala, "Sexual Behavior Among Young Men in Sweden and the Impact of Pornography," *International Journal of STD & AIDS* 15, no. 9 (2004): 590–93; Häggström-Nordin, Tydén, and Hanson, "Associations."

43 Rogala and Tydén, "Does Pornography Influence Young Women's Sexual Behavior?"

44 Ibid.

offices of many of my colleagues, however, we see female consumers of pornography regularly dealing with increased insecurity, poor self-image, deficient social skills, body-image issues, addictions, eating disorders, sexual anxieties, and relationship difficulties. It is not uncommon for a history of sexual abuse or trauma to be entangled in their pornography consumption, consistent with the finding that women who had suffered sexual trauma were more accepting of pornography than women who had not suffered sexual trauma.[45]

Although men are 6.43 times more likely to use internet pornography than women,[46] current research indicates a growing number of women are consuming it. In a recent study of college-age students, 31% of the women reported using pornography (compared with 87% of the men), and almost half (49%) agreed that viewing pornography is acceptable (compared with 67% of the men).[47] The women surveyed were more accepting of pornography than their fathers were just one generation ago.[48]

Female patterns of usage, however, are markedly different from those of their male peers.[49] For men, "pornography use is as common as drinking is among college-age men," and a significant number report "bingeing" on pornography with a frequency and intensity similar to those who binge-drink.[50] Women who consume, on the other hand, are more likely to view pornography once a month or less, and only 3.2% report using it weekly or more often. Other gender differences in pornography consumption: Women are exposed to pornography at a later age than male peers, consume less hard-core and more soft-core material than men, are more likely to consume pornography with a regular sexual partner than by themselves, masturbate to pornography significantly less than men, and watch significantly more group sex (one woman with multiple men) than men.[51]

---

45 Clifford L. Broman, "Sexuality Attitudes: The Impact of Trauma," *Journal of Sex Research* 40, no. 4 (2003): 351–57.

46 Steven Stack, Ira Wasserman, and Roger Kern, "Adult Social Bonds and Use of Internet Pornography," *Social Science Quarterly* 85, no. 1 (2004): 75–88.

47 Jason S. Carroll et al., "Generation XXX: Pornography Acceptance and Use Among Emerging Adults," *Journal of Adolescent Research* 23, no. 1 (2008): 6–30.

48 Ibid.

49 Ibid.

50 Ibid., 23.

51 Gert Martin Hald, "Gender Differences in Pornography Consumption Among Young Heterosexual Danish Adults," *Archives of Sexual Behavior* 35, no. 5 (2006): 577–85.

A key finding in the research is that the intellectual acceptance of pornography is as strongly correlated to women's attitudes and behaviors as is their actual consumption. As the researchers state:

> Pornography should be regarded as much as a value stance or a personal sexual ethic as it is a behavioral pattern. This may be a particularly salient finding for emerging adult women who report higher levels of acceptance than actual use of pornography. Furthermore, pornography acceptance among women was a stronger correlate with permissive sexuality, alcohol use, binge-drinking, and cigarette smoking than was actual pornography use.[52]

It is unclear what the long-term implications for changes in female pornography consumption and acceptance will be, or how those changes will affect society. The body of research that documents a wide range of effects on male consumers needs to be reexamined with a female population in mind.

As a clinician, however, I have observed in female users many of the same effects associated with male consumption. For example, many of the female consumers I have worked with experience increased difficulty in developing long-term, intimate relationships; have become desensitized to graphic material and sexual content; have less-sensitive attitudes toward males; are more willing to use a male for sexual gratification while not being emotionally committed to him; and take greater risks with their sexual health. Although some would like to think that female consumption of pornography is helping women be more sexually confident and secure, my clinical observations inform me differently. As pornography has become mainstream, we have forgotten that pornography is dispensable; it is not needed for human development, sexual maturation, happiness, or relational success. If anything, pornography is an impediment to such goals.

---

52 Carroll et al., "Generation XXX," 24.

Wives of pornography users

Many of those using pornography are married men. Married men outnumber single men in internet use,[53] and the majority of people struggling with sexual addictions and compulsivities involving the internet are married, heterosexual males.[54] Consequently, examining the impact of pornography on wives of consumers is a logical focal point when exploring the impact of pornography on women.

Generally speaking, North American women are socialized to seek, if not to expect, marital and intimate relationships that foster equality between partners and that are founded on mutual respect, honesty, shared power, and romantic love. In stark contrast, pornography promotes and eroticizes the antitheses of these relational and marital ideals: power imbalances, discrimination, disrespect, abuse, violence, voyeurism, objectification, and detachment.

Consequently, when a North American, married woman discovers that her husband has been secretly consuming pornography, the discovery not only devastates her sense of self and trust, but often threatens the foundation upon which she has constructed and framed her relational world. She is suddenly confronted with how psychologically, spiritually, and sexually split her supposedly "modern man" really is. It's not uncommon for women in this situation to say things such as, "I have no idea who he is anymore," "I now feel like I've lived a lie the entire time I've been married," or "I thought we had a good marriage until this was revealed."

To add insult to injury, many wives are directly or indirectly blamed for their husband's pornography use by her spouse, family, or confidant. Many women I have worked with clinically describe stinging insinuations that the marriage must be unsatisfying, that she has "let herself go" and is no longer as physically attractive as she once was, that she is closed-minded to new sexual experiences, or that she is overly focused on her children and not attending to her husband's needs. Too often the woman's experience of the marital relationship and the historical context of his pornography habit become conveniently dismissed as irrelevant by those seeking to assign blame to her. Consequently, the husband's pornography use is justified, and the effects of pornography use are unchallenged. When wives are scapegoated,

---

53 Enid Burns, "The Online Battle of the Sexes," *ClickZ*, 29 December 2005, http://www.clickz.com/3574176 (accessed 7 July 2008); Cooper, Delmonico, and Burg, "Cybersex Users, Abusers, and Compulsives."

54 Cooper, Delmonico, and Burg, "Cybersex Users, Abusers, and Compulsives."

pornography problems are enabled, and the cultural chime of boys-will-be-boys is reinforced and everyone loses.

Several researchers have found that women commonly report feelings of betrayal, loss, mistrust, devastation, and anger as responses to the discovery or disclosure of a husband's consumption of pornography and/or online sexual activity.[55] Some researchers have even suggested that individuals in committed relationships who discover that their partner is engaged in compulsive pornography use or other sexually addictive behaviors can manifest symptoms of post-traumatic stress disorder.[56] Additionally, many women experience physiological effects such as fatigue, increases or decreases in appetite and libido, and other signs and symptoms of anxiety and depression, including suicidal tendencies.[57]

It is also common for women to report dramatic changes in personal conduct in the wake of this kind of marital crisis. For instance, I have worked with women who, upon learning of their husband's pornography use, began viewing pornography themselves, started drinking or using drugs, engaged in infidelity, or participated in sexual acts they previously found degrading and contrary to their values. These abrupt changes in behavior usually represent maladaptive attempts to cope with the sense of threat and competition evoked by a spouse's betrayal, or desperate efforts to reclaim a sense of control and stability.

Increased risk of marital distress, separation, and divorce. Over and above their intense emotional distress, women who are married to a pornography consumer can experience a range of very serious risks and effects that often get dismissed with the minimizing, cultural mantra of "porn is harmless entertainment." Some of the most significant impacts on women include increased risk of marital distress, separation, and divorce; increased isolation; and increased risk of abuse.

---

55 Ana J. Bridges, R. M. Bergner, and M. Hesson-McInnis, "Romantic Partners' Use of Pornography: Its Significance for Women," *Journal of Sex and Marital Therapy* 29, no. 1 (2003): 1–14; Jill C. Manning, "A Qualitative Study of the Supports Women Find Most Beneficial When Dealing with a Spouse's Sexually Addictive or Compulsive Behaviors," unpublished doctoral dissertation (Provo, Utah: Brigham Young University, 2006); Schneider, "Effects of Cybersex Addiction on the Family."

56 Barbara A. Steffens and Robyn L. Rennie, "The Traumatic Nature of Disclosure for Wives of Sexual Addicts," *Sexual Addiction & Compulsivity* 13, nos. 2 and 3 (2006): 247–67.

57 Jill C. Manning, "A Qualitative Study of the Supports Women Find Most Beneficial"; M. Lynn Wildmon-White, and J. Scott Young, "Family-of-Origin Characteristics Among Women Married to Sexually Addicted Men," *Sexual Addiction & Compulsivity* 9, no. 4 (2002): 263–73.

Although women in various kinds of relationships can experience intense and adverse reactions to a partner's or a husband's pornography use, there is a significant difference between women who are dating or cohabiting and those whom are married. According to research, married women are significantly more distressed by a partner's online pornography consumption than women in dating or cohabiting relationships, and they view internet pornography consumption as a significant threat to the marital bond.[58] As might be expected, the distress they reported increased according to the perceived frequency of their husband's online sexual activities, and was not significantly influenced by their religious beliefs.

Another study found that cybersex addiction was a major contributing factor to separation and divorce for affected couples.[59] Although a range of online sexual activities were listed, viewing and/or downloading pornography accompanied by masturbation was present in every case.

As cited previously, at the November 2002 meeting of the American Academy of Matrimonial Lawyers, a professional organization comprising the nation's top divorce and matrimonial law attorneys, 62% of the 350 attendees said that the internet had played a role in divorces they had handled during the last year, and 56% of the divorce cases involved one party having an obsessive interest in pornographic websites.[60]

Increased risk for contracting a sexually transmitted disease from one's partner. An increasing number of women I have worked with clinically have learned about a partner's involvement with pornography and related infidelity through the discovery that they had contracted a sexually transmitted disease. It is particularly traumatic and life-changing for a woman who has been faithful in her marriage to learn she has a sexually transmitted disease.

This discovery is not surprising. Individuals who used the internet and had had an extramarital affair were 3.18 times more likely to have used internet pornography than were individuals who used the internet but did not engage in affairs, according to survey data.[61] People who have paid for sex (i.e., prostitution) were 3.7 times more apt to use internet pornography than were those who had not engaged

---

58 Bridges et al., "Romantic Partners' Use of Pornography."
59 Schneider, "Effects of Cybersex Addiction on the Family."
60 Dedmon, "Is the Internet Bad for Your Marriage?"
61 Ibid.

in paid sex.[62] These statistics indicate that internet pornography is often associated with activities that can undermine marital exclusivity and fidelity, and subsequently increase the risk of contracting and transmitting sexual diseases.

Increased isolation. Marriages in which a pornography problem or sexual compulsion exists are commonly pervaded not only with diminished intimacy and sensitivity, but with anxiety, secrecy, isolation, relationship dysfunction, and decreased temporal security due to the risk of job loss or related debts.[63]

In addition, these wives tend to feel lonely and isolated because they are vulnerable to getting entangled in keeping their husband's secret in an effort to cope with the problem.[64] Additionally, women commonly fear they will not be understood if they do speak out, or fear the potential risks, ridicule, and consequences of sharing the information.[65] As a result, most women withdraw from their typical sources of social support.[66] Given the insinuations and types of blame I have witnessed female clients encounter, it is not surprising that most withdraw or remain silent for long periods of time.

In my research with wives of sex addicts who had reported pornography being an issue in their marriage, the majority (68.18%) had experienced some form of isolation (emotional, spiritual, physical, or social) while dealing with this problem.[67] What was interesting was that many of the women reported having strong networks of support and family ties, but still described being isolated due to the shameful nature of this particular problem. This suggests women who are high-functioning and well-supported in other areas of life may still be at risk for isolation, delayed help-seeking behavior, and/or prolonged psychological struggle because the problem is so shaming and public awareness of it is in its infancy.

---

62 Stack et al., "Adult Social Bonds and Use of Internet Pornography."

63 Patrick J. Carnes, *Don't Call It Love* (New York: Bantam Books, 1991); Schneider, "Effects of Cybersex Addiction on the Family"; Wildmon-White and Young, "Family-of-Origin Characteristics Among Women Married to Sexually Addicted Men."

64 Judith C. Heaton Matheny, "Strategies for Assessment and Early Treatment with Sexually Addicted Families," *Sexual Addiction & Compulsivity* 5, no. 1 (1998): 27–48.

65 Wildmon-White and Young, "Family-of-Origin Characteristics Among Women Married to Sexually Addicted Men."

66 Manning, "A Qualitative Study of the Supports Women Find Most Beneficial."

67 Ibid.

In addition, isolation can put women at risk for heightened psychological stress and turmoil if they are used to receiving support in other areas of life, thereby making this population more vulnerable overall. The common pattern of isolation underscores the need for increased public awareness and ways to connect these women to resources and supports that can help them heal.

Increased risk of sexual and physical abuse. A growing number of researchers and clinicians are beginning to recognize a connection between pornography use and abuse in marriage.[68] It is not uncommon for wives of pornography users to report being asked to reenact pornographic scenes, consume pornography with their partner, or being pressured or coerced into sexual acts they find uncomfortable or demeaning.[69]

While conducting my own research, I was surprised to learn how many women had experienced marital rape when asked about how pornography had affected their marriage. Unfortunately, my experience as a researcher was not unique. For example, another researcher found that one third of the females in her sample reported that their partner consumed pornography, and that there was a correlation between pornography use and the most sadistic rapes.[70]

Sadly, these findings are not surprising when we consider that men exposed to violent pornography are six times more likely to report rape behavior than those not exposed,[71] and pornography use is the strongest correlate of sexual aggression.[72]

---

68 Mark Laaser, *Faithful and True: Sexual Integrity in a Fallen World* (Grand Rapids, Mich.: Zondervan, 1996); Wildmon-White and Young, "Family-of-Origin Characteristics Among Women Married to Sexually Addicted Men"; Eunjung Ryu, "Spousal Use of Pornography and Its Clinical Significance for Asian-American Women: Korean Women as an Illustration," *Journal of Feminist Family Therapy* 16, no. 4 (2004): 75–89; Janet Hinson Shope, "When Words Are Not Enough: The Search for the Effect of Pornography on Abused Women," *Violence Against Women* 10, no. 1 (2004): 56–72.

69 Laaser, "Faithful and True"; Ryu, "Spousal Use of Pornography"; Hinson Shope, "When Words Are Not Enough."

70 Rachel Kennedy Bergen, "The Reality of Wife Rape: Women's Experiences of Sexual Violence in Marriage," in *Issues in Intimate Violence*, ed. Rachel Kennedy Bergen (Thousand Oaks, Calif.: Sage, 1998), 237–50.

71 S. B. Boeringer, "Pornography and Sexual Aggression: Associations of Violent and Nonviolent Depictions with Rape and Rape Proclivity," *Deviant Behavior* 15, no. 3 (1994): 289–304.

72 Leslie L. Crossman, *Date Rape and Sexual Aggression by College Males: Incidence and the Involvement of Impulsivity, Anger, Hostility, Psychopathology, Peer Influence, and Pornography Use*, unpublished doctoral dissertation (College Station: Texas A&M University, 1994).

Furthermore, a survey of women who had been battered found that: 75% of the women had been shown pornography and had been asked or forced to perform similar sex acts; 64% had had pornography described to them and had been asked or forced to perform similar sex acts; 31% had been asked to participate in pornographic photographs; and 81% had reported rape.[73]

While definitive causal ties cannot be determined, it is important to recognize the correlation between pornography use and abuse in marriage for many women. As we get better at asking the right questions, I am confident that the impact of pornography on spousal abuse and oppression will come into focus. In the meantime, however, countless women are suffering.

Conclusion

Several years ago I would have considered myself complacent, if not downright indifferent about the issue of pornography. Today, I feel an urgency that often surprises me. As a woman, I have a deep, foreboding sense of concern over the impact pornography is having on our society, and on women in particular. As a clinician, I am troubled by the sharp rise in individuals who are seeking treatment because their mental health has been affected. As a mother, I am passionate about doing all that I can to protect youth from sexualized media that hijack some of the best parts of being a child, and distort some of the best parts of being an adult. As a citizen, I fear the cultural tide of political correctness, sexual permissiveness, and egocentric hedonism will pollute the values and principles upon which this country was founded. As with any cultural shift, it can be frustrating to wait for the research and societal mindset to catch up with what is happening in the trenches and in individual lives.

I trust, however, that through further research, the sharing of personal narratives, and the persistent efforts of concerned citizens, we will effect change. Just as women are influencing the spread of pornography, they also play an indispensible role in fighting it.

---

73 Elizabeth Cramer and Judith McFarlane, "Pornography and Abuse of Women," *Public Health Nursing* 11, no. 4 (1994): 268–72.

PORNOGRAPHY'S EFFECTS ON INTERPERSONAL RELATIONSHIPS

Ana J. Bridges

An as intern at an adult psychiatric hospital, my first client was a woman who had a partner she described as "addicted" to pornography. For some time, she had been struggling to change his behavior—through cajoling, pleading, threats and ultimatums, tears, and tantrums. Although at times effective for a little while, she continually found a restocked stash of pornographic materials, despite his promises to stop. Her distress and his inability to hear her distress reached such high levels that she had attempted suicide: thus her admission into the hospital and our meeting.

I had studied depression, anxiety, trauma, and psychosis, but I was wholly unprepared for this. Was this a cognitive distortion? Did she just need to "lighten up," to stop interpreting his behavior in unhealthy and unhelpful ways and just accept it? Did she have a right to demand that his sexuality be limited to what she found acceptable? Was there such a thing as pornography addiction? Was there something else going on she was unable to talk about directly? Could she actually be that upset over something so normal? Didn't all men look at pictures of naked women and masturbate?

As a neophyte clinician and conscientious graduate student, I immediately consulted the professional and scientific literature. I found an array of articles examining how short-term exposure to pornography in a laboratory setting affected male viewers. I found not one single empirical study of pornography use from the romantic partner's perspective. My research area was born.

Fortunately, in the past decade, research on the interpersonal effects of pornography use has risen considerably. This paper will begin by describing theoretical models that help explain how pornography affects interpersonal relationships and then review research that helps systematically disentangle the full spectrum of effects that pornography may exert in interpersonal relationships. Although I will be focusing primarily on romantic relationships, these results often extend to parental, work, and peer relations.

Several theories exist for how pornography affects consumers and others. We will look at the imitation, social learning, sexual script, permission-giving beliefs, perception of social norms, and cultural climate models.

Models of pornography's effects

Imitation model. The simplest is the *imitation model.* It theorizes that consumers imitate what they have seen. There is some indirect and qualitative support for such a theory,[1] but it is grossly inadequate. Most users do not commit the abuses they see in the pornography. This model ignores the complexities of the relationship between media and individual behavior and suggests that consumers of pornography are uncritical automatons. Critics of anti-pornography efforts have repeatedly focused on this model for their attacks, stating that consumers are aware of the difference between fantasy and reality.[2]

This has implications for public policy. If this model was the only or even the primary mechanism by which pornography affected users, limiting access or even banning pornography would clearly be indicated. However, the evidence does not support such a simplistic mechanism.

Social learning model. A slightly more complex theory, this model posits that people learn through observation, but that only behaviors that are rewarded are likely to be imitated.[3] Thus, if a pornographic depiction shows a man overpowering a woman sexually, when she initially refuses such advances but eventually invites them and derives pleasure from them (a script for what is called the "rape myth"[4]), the viewer learns that overpowering women sexually leads to sexual rewards both for himself and for his partner, and he is then more likely to imitate the behavior. Research has continually demonstrated that the combination of sexual arousal and violence results in more misogynist attitudes and behaviors than depictions of

---

1 Mimi H. Silbert and Ayala M. Pines, "Pornography and Sexual Abuse of Women," *Sex Roles* 10, nos. 11–12 (June 1984): 857.

2 David Loftus, *Watching Sex: How Men Really Respond to Pornography* (New York: Da Capo Press, 2003).

3 Albert Bandura, "Behavioral Psychotherapy," *Scientific American* 216, no. 3 (March 1967): 78–86.

4 Robert Bauserman, "Sexual Aggression and Pornography: A Review of Correlational Research," *Basic and Applied Social Psychology* 18, no. 4 (December 1996): 405–27.

violence against women or sexually explicitness alone.[5] However, as with the imitation model, this model is limited in its ability to explain the discrepancy between widespread and common use of pornographic materials and relatively low rates of overt sexual violence.[6]

This implication for public policy of the social learning model rests on both individual media consumers and media producers. Individuals, such as parents, may need to monitor the media they or their children consume to avoid depictions wedding violence and sexuality. On the other hand, regulatory bodies such as the Federal Communications Commission (FCC) may seek to ban such media from public sale. In fact, countries such as England and Australia have made it illegal to sell or possess violent pornography.[7]

Sexual scripts

Sexual script model. A more general version of both models is *sexual script theory.* Scripts are memory structures that provide information and rules for behaving. They evolve over time and with repeated exposure to a set of stimuli or with repetition of particular behaviors.[8] For example, people develop scripts for how to behave in a public library, a football game, or when stopped by a police officer for speeding.

Pornography's scripts emphasize culturally accepted beauty standards, the idea of the constant sexual availability and insatiable sexual appetites of men and women, the excitement of sexual novelty, and sex outside of a primary romantic relationship.[9] It rarely includes affection, intimate relationships, or expressions of love, and it often involves men ejaculating outside of a woman's body while she expresses

---

5 Neil M. Malamuth, "Aggression Against Women: Cultural and Individual Causes," in *Pornography and Sexual Aggression*, eds. Neil M. Malamuth and Edward Donnerstein (New York: Academic Press, 1984).

6 Michael S. Kimmel and Annulla Linders, "Does Censorship Make a Difference? An Aggregate Empirical Analysis of Pornography and Rape," *Journal of Psychology and Human Sexuality* 8, no. 3 (August 1996): 1–20.

7 BBC News, 26 January 2009, "Mother's Violent Porn Ban Now Law," http://news.bbc.co.uk/2/hi/uk_news/england/berkshire/7851346.stm; Alan McKee (2005). "The Objectification of Women in Mainstream Porn Videos in Australia," *Journal of Sex Research*, 42, 277–90.

8 Ramesh Lakshmi-Ratan and Easwar Iyer, "Similarity Analysis of Cognitive Scripts," *Journal of the Academy of Marketing Science* 16, no. 2 (1988): 36–42.

9 Hans-Bernd Brosius et al., "Exploring the Social and Sexual 'Reality' of Contemporary Pornography," *Journal of Sex Research* 30, no. 2 (1993): 161–70.

orgasmic pleasure. Frequently, pornography lacks foreplay and afterplay: The focus on sexual penetration is so pervasive that caressing, kissing, or cuddling are minimized or eliminated.[10]

As scripts for sexual intimacy with a real life partner, these nearly always fall short. Sometimes a partner is too tired or too ill to desire sex. Sometimes the comforts of a routine sexual encounter are precisely what one desires. Sometimes we feel unattractive. And sometimes, although one hates to admit it, we prefer hurried sex, before the kids' Saturday morning cartoon finishes. Furthermore, real life requires the capacity to switch mental gears so that we desire sex despite last night's argument over hanging up wet towels and having seen one another pass gas. Unlike a movie, these awkward moments are not edited out of life. They are the very fabric that creates intimacy. It is not surprising, then, that learning about gender roles through pornography's unrealistic portrayals leads to reduced sexual and relational satisfaction.[11]

But this is not pornography's most disturbing script. A recent content analysis of fifty best-selling adult videos revealed a grim "reality" characterized by inequality and violence.[12] Nearly half of the 304 scenes analyzed contained verbal aggression, while over 88% showed physical aggression. Seventy percent of aggressive acts were perpetrated by men, and 87% of the acts were committed against women. By far the victims' most common responses were pleasure or neutrality. Fewer than 5% of the aggressive acts provoked a negative response from the victim, including flinching and requests to stop. This pornographic "reality" was further highlighted by the relative infrequency of more positive behaviors, such as verbal compliments, embracing, kissing, or laughter.

---

10 Donald L. Mosher and Paula MacIan, "College Men and Women Respond to X-Rated Videos Intended for Male or Female Audiences: Gender and Sexual Scripts," *Journal of Sex Research* 31, no. 2 (1994): 99–112.

11 Joan Shapiro and Lee Kroeger, "Is Life Just a Romantic Novel? The Relationship Between Attitudes About Intimate Relationships and the Popular Media," *American Journal of Family Therapy* 19, no. 3 (September 1991): 226–36.

12 Robert Wosnitzer and Ana J. Bridges, "Aggression and Sexual Behavior in Best-Selling Pornography: A Content Analysis Update" (paper presented at the annual meeting of the International Communication Association, San Francisco, 2007).

The importance of the sexual scripts usually seen in pornography may explain why women are more likely to respond negatively to "conventional" pornography compared with men.[13] Women consumers are likely to react negatively to the scripts just described. If this is the case, pornography that better adheres to women's romantic and sexual scripts ought to be better-received, and "femme pornography" (made by women for women) should produce greater sexual arousal and more positive effect in women, since it focuses less on the genitals and male pleasure, and more on slower, more sensual sexual pleasures and relationships.

One study found that men liked both types and that both increased their post-viewing sexual activity (both solitary and otherwise), while women were more disgusted by conventional pornography but more aroused and less negative about femme pornography.[14] They engaged in higher levels of sexual intercourse, though not of masturbation, following exposure to femme videos.

These two models also have implications for policy. If they help explain how pornography exerts its effects on users, efforts should be aimed at limiting production and consumption of pornographic materials that reward aggression and violence against others. Sexually explicit materials that promote egalitarian depictions of erotic encounters would be preferred.

Two other models

Two other cognitive models of pornography's effects on users, both drawn from the alcohol and substance abuse literature,[15] merit discussion. Cognitive models focus on internal thoughts and beliefs or interpretations of stimuli that then drive behavior. They explain why the same event can have very different meanings for different people—why, for example, one woman may encourage her partner's pornography use while another is completely devastated.[16]

---

13 Pornography of the sort analyzed by Brosius et al., "Exploring the Social and Sexual," and Wosnitzer and Bridges, "Aggression and Sexual Behavior."

14 Mosher and MacIan, "College Men and Women Respond to X-Rated Videos."

15 Cory Newman and Christine L. Ratto, "Cognitive Therapy of Substance Abuse," in *Comparative Treatments of Substance Abuse*, eds. E. Thomas Dowd and Loreen G. Rugle (New York: Springer, 1999), 96–126.

16 Ana J. Bridges, Raymond M. Bergner, and Matthew Hesson-McInnis, "Romantic Partners' Use of Pornography: Its Significance for Women," *Journal of Sex and Marital Therapy* 29, no. 1 (January–February 2003): 1–14.

Permission-giving beliefs model. The first of these models refers to thoughts that rationalize behavior.[17] Pornography users may tell themselves that the women clearly enjoy what they are doing and are not harmed by it (many pornographic DVDs include bloopers and deleted scenes that reinforce this belief), or that using pornography is much better than seeking out women for affairs.

Interestingly, my own research suggests that female partners of male pornography users utilize similar permission-giving beliefs. For example, many women report thinking that their partner's behavior is preferable to his having a real-life affair, that all men view pornography, and that it is a relief at times that her partner does not turn solely to her to fulfill his frequent sexual demands.[18]

Perceptions of social norms model. This model describes how the heavy use of pornography skews the users' perception of what is normal (that is, what the average person does), so that they are unable to recognize just how uncommon their own behavior is. Heavy use normalizes this perception and leads to overestimation of how frequently certain sexual activities are actually practiced. Adolescent boys with higher consumption rates of pornography are more likely than others to engage in anal and group sex and to report "hook-ups" (having sexual relations with a friend who is not a romantic partner).[19]

In using cognitive models to decide policy, the downside is that they place the problem, and therefore its solution, firmly inside the individual. Although community-wide campaigns with corrective educational information may attempt to change social norms, the proposed mechanism of change remains at the level of the individual's thoughts.[20]

---

17 Mary Anne Layden, "Use of Pornography, Including Internet Pornography, Nonconsensual Sex, Use of Prostitutes, Acceptance of the Rape Myth, and Permission-Giving Beliefs" (paper presented at the annual meeting of the Association for Behavioral and Cognitive Therapies, Orlando, Fla., 2008); Loftus, *Watching Sex.*

18 Bridges, Bergner, and Hesson-McInnis, "Romantic Partners' Use of Pornography."

19 Elisabet Häggström-Nordin, Tanja Tydén, and Ulf Hanson, "Associations Between Pornography Consumption and Sexual Practices Among Adolescents in Sweden," *International Journal of STD & AIDS* 16, no. 2 (2005): 102–7.

20 H. Wesley Perkins, "Social Norms and the Prevention of Alcohol Misuse in Collegiate Contexts," *Journal of Studies on Alcohol,* supplement 14 (2002): 164–72; Schultz et al., "The Constructive, Destructive, and Reconstructive Power of Social Norms," *Journal of Psychological Science* 18, no. 5 (2007): 429–34.

Cold and hot states

One important implication of the cognitive models is that each relies on the rational choice of the consumer: The viewer chooses to behave in a way that has been previously modeled and reinforced by adult films, or provides permission-giving thoughts that serve to neutralize other thoughts that may turn him away from pornography. The user may be following a scripted cognitive map of how to behave in sexual situations, or rationally be considering how normative his behavior may be. Treatment relies on appeals to a more rational mind: one that asks the pornography user to weigh carefully his values and possible long-term consequences for behavior, and then make a choice.

However, in a clever study, behavioral economists at MIT demonstrated that these "cold," rational choices are different from those we may make while in a "hot" or aroused state.[21] College men were asked to answer questions about sexual interests and behaviors while in a "cold" state of mind (simply reading the questions) or in a "hot" state of mind (while masturbating to pornographic pictures). They were asked about risky sexual behavior; sexual arousal, including whether they found elderly women, young girls, or shoes sexually arousing; sexual behavior, including their interest in slapping someone during sex, bondage, or in engaging in anal sex or bestiality; and sexual violence, including their willingness to coerce someone in order to have sex.

During the aroused state, they were significantly more likely to report behaviors, people, and objects as sexually arousing and increased willingness to both engage in the behaviors and to use coercive methods to obtain sex. The only two items arousal did not affect were their willingness to have sex with other men and their interest in having sex with the lights on.

This study points to an important consideration when planning interventions for pornography users: what is wholeheartedly and earnestly promised in a cold state will not readily translate into real behavior change while in an aroused state. It may be preferable to have people practice behaviors in the same physiological state that they will be experiencing when expected to perform them.

---

21 Dan Ariely and George Loewenstein, "The Heat of the Moment: The Effect of Sexual Arousal on Sexual Decision Making," *Journal of Behavioral Decision Making* 19 (2006): 87–98.

A more comprehensive model

Cultural climate model. A more comprehensive model for understanding the effects of pornography on interpersonal relationships considers larger contextual and societal factors rather than the way individuals interact with pornographic media. The *cultural climate model* states that pornography contributes to an environment in which violence toward women becomes acceptable, but that the broader environment itself contains what can be called "pornography norms."[22] These effects are seen not only in men's perceptions of women, but in women's own perceptions of themselves.

Theoretically, for women exposure to pornography results in reduced self-esteem and body-image satisfaction, increased sense of vulnerability to violence, and an increased sense of defenselessness; for men it results in reward for displays of hyper-masculinity and trivializing or excusing violence against women. Partial support for this has been found in the psychological literature,[23] but pornographic norms for gender relationships and sexuality infuse many other forms of media, such as music videos, reality television shows, even children's toys. Thus, it becomes difficult to distinguish pornography's specific effects from those of the general climate of gender inequality in a pornified culture.[24]

Interestingly, some research suggests that whatever relationship may appear to exist between consumption of pornography and violence against women is better thought of as a relationship that is supported by general social acceptability of violence as a whole, with sexual violence being but one of many types. One study of circulation rates of pornographic magazines and incidents of sexual assault found that an initial positive relationship was made nonsignificant with the inclusion of a measure of approval of violence in general.[25] Such findings support the cultural climate theory.

---

22 Carol Krafka et al., "Women's Reactions to Sexually Aggressive Mass Media Depictions," *Violence Against Women* 3, no. 2 (1997): 149–81.

23 Ibid.

24 Pamela Paul, *Pornified: How Pornography is Damaging Our Lives, Our Relationships, and Our Families* (New York: Henry Holt and Co., 2005).

25 Larry Baron and Murray Straus, "Sexual Stratification, Pornography, and Rape in the United States," in *Pornography and Sexual Aggression*, eds. Neil M. Malamuth and Edward Donnerstein (New York: Academic Press, 1984), 185–209.

The American Psychological Association has already spoken of the negative effects of a more sexualized culture on girls.[26] Studies have repeatedly demonstrated that higher exposure to sexualized imagery and pornography is associated with earlier initiation of sexual activity, increased sexual risk-taking behavior, and increasingly tolerant attitudes toward sexual promiscuity.[27] Similarly, more frequent viewing of pornographic videos is associated with higher engagement in anal sex, group sex, and hook-ups.[28]

Third person effects. An important consideration when speaking with the public about the effects of pornography is the empirical finding that people are significantly more likely to perceive others as being susceptible to media influences while simultaneously believing that they are immune.[29] Thus, public education must include both information about how pornography exerts its effects and information about this perceptual bias so that people are not so quick to dismiss the educational message.

This model is akin to the radical feminist sociopolitical position: It advocates for widespread cultural change in how sexuality is constructed. A simple ban on certain materials would be insufficient, since pornography norms are infused throughout the culture. Instead, new models of healthy sex and gender relationships are required, models that do not view sex appeal as narrowly defined by physical looks, where a person's worth is determined by more than just sexual behavior, where sexuality is expressed between consenting beings. In these new models of healthy sex, people are not reduced to sexual objects, valued only insofar as they can sexually service one another.

The interpersonal effects of exposure

Having described the theoretical models that help explain how pornography affects interpersonal relationships, I now turn to the research that helps us understand

---

26 American Psychological Association, *Report of the APA Task Force on the Sexualization of Girls* (Washington, D.C., 2007), http://www.apa.org/pi/wpo/sexualization.html (accessed 5 December 2008).

27 Gina M. Wingood et al., "Exposure to X-Rated Movies and Adolescents' Sexual and Contraceptive-Related Attitudes and Behaviors," *Pediatrics* 107, no. 5 (5 May 2001): 1116–19.

28 Häggström-Nordin, Tydén, and Hanson, "Associations Between Pornography Consumption and Sexual Practices."

29 Ibid., 9.

pornography's effects on interpersonal relationships. Among the effects of the use of pornography are an increased negative attitude toward women, decreased empathy for victims of sexual violence, a blunted affect, and an increase in dominating and sexually imposing behavior.

Pornography increases negative attitudes toward women. Media depicting women as objects existing for male sexual pleasure and as subordinates negatively affect the users' attitudes and behaviors toward women. Studies have examined the impact of pornography on attitudes of gender roles. One study of male college students found that their use of erotic material (sexually explicit materials that were non-violent and non-degrading) did not affect their attitudes toward women.[30] However, their use of pornographic materials (sexually explicit materials that included coercion or violence) was (though the effect was small) positively correlated with beliefs that women should occupy more gender-defined, traditional roles, should be less independent than men, drink and swear less, exhibit less interest in sexual behaviors, and maintain more traditional roles in marriages.

The results have direct implications for romantic relationships. Men who consume pornography may expect their partners to occupy traditional female roles and be less assertive. This restriction could lead to increased dissatisfaction among their partners.

Decreased empathy, blunted affect

Pornography decreases empathy for victims of sexual violence. Another study of college men found that after repeated exposure to one of three film types (graphically violent sexual films, degrading but non-violent pornographic films, or degrading but non-violent and nonsexual films), those who had seen the violent sexual film showed significantly less sympathy for a rape victim during a mock trial than did the others.[31] Interestingly, those who saw the nonsexual but degrading film generally did not differ significantly from control subjects (who had not seen any film) in their empathy for

---

30 Luis T. Garcia, "Exposure to Pornography and Attitudes About Women and Rape: A Correlational Study," *Journal of Sex Research* 22, no. 3 (August 1986): 378–85.

31 Daniel G. Linz, Steven Penrod, and Edward Donnerstein, "Effects of Long-Term Exposure to Violent and Sexually Degrading Depictions of Women," *Journal of Personality and Social Psychology* 55, no. 5 (1988): 758–68.

the victim. The authors concluded that the combination of degradation and sexually explicit material seems particularly detrimental.

In a similar study of college women the subjects were assigned to view sexually explicit but non-violent films, sexually explicit and violent films, or mildly explicit but graphically violent films for four consecutive days. On the fifth day, they were told the last film had not arrived and were invited to participate in an experiment on jury selection for a rape trial through the university's law school. Women who had seen the graphically violent films showed reduced empathy for the victim and a decreased sense of personal vulnerability to crimes compared with the other two groups. However, they did not change in their level of endorsement of the rape myth.

A review of studies of attitudes toward rape found that six of the seven studies of people who had viewed pornography for less than one hour found that exposure to violent pornography had significant negative effects (reduced sympathy for victims, increased sense of the woman's responsibility for the rape, and decreased punishments for the perpetrator).[32] Of the seven studies of people who had viewed sexually explicit films for more than one hour, five found negative effects (more lenient sentences for the rapist, less empathy for the victim, less support for women's equality, and greater endorsement of their own likelihood of raping were they assured they would not be caught). The two studies that did not find such effects had shown only non-violent erotica.

Attitudes such as these can affect romantic relationships, both directly and indirectly. Directly, legitimizing violence in male-female interactions may put more women at risk (this will be discussed in greater detail later on). Indirectly, a relationship in which the man holds such demeaning attitudes is likely to result in diminished relationship satisfaction.

Pornography leads to blunted affect. Anxiety-provoking stimuli lose their ability to evoke strong reactions with repeated exposure.[33] Researchers have argued that this occurs with violent and degrading pornographic material.[34]

---

32 Daniel Linz, "Exposure to Sexually Explicit Materials and Attitudes Toward Rape: A Comparison of Study Results," *Journal of Sex Research* 26, no. 1 (February 1989): 50–84.

33 Isaac Marks and Reuven Dar, "Fear Reduction by Psychotherapies: Recent Findings, Future Directions," *British Journal of Psychiatry* 176 (2000): 507–11.

34 Diana E. H. Russell, *Against Pornography: The Evidence of Harm* (Berkeley, Calif.: Russell Publications, 1993).

A study of college men demonstrated that repeated exposure to violent, sexually suggestive material leads to declines in the negative emotions they feel when viewing such material.[35] Participants were repeatedly exposed to overtly violent, mildly sexually explicit films ("slasher" films), sexually explicit, non-violent but degrading films, or nonsexual but degrading films. The first group became habituated to the slasher films, so that by the last day they reported significantly less anxiety and depression than they had at the beginning of the study. The feelings of the other two groups did not change. Each group, however, perceived the materials to be less violent, negative, and degrading on the last day than they had on the first.

This blunting of strong affect is not limited to men.[36] In the study of college women described above, women who had watched violent films responded to these disturbing films with less anger, anxiety, or upset on the last day of viewing than they did initially. Those women who had watched sexually explicit but non-violent films over the course of the experiment responded to a subsequent violent film with more distress than those who had been exposed to multiple violent films. This desensitization to the degradation and violence of women has negative implications for interpersonal violence in romantic relationships. Unlike the male subjects in the previous study, the women did not change from the first to the last day their perceptions of how violent or degrading the films were. While women still recognized violence after repeated exposure to these films, they demonstrated less of a strong, negative emotional response to the violence.

Dominance and imposition

Pornography increases dominating behaviors. Exposure to pornography also results in more dominating, degrading, and sexualizing behaviors in men. In one study using male and female college students, the males were told that they were participating in a study of the perceptions of media communications and randomly assigned to one of three films: erotica, nonsexual news coverage of war, or pornography.[37] Following the films, they were invited to attend a short, ostensibly separate experiment

---

35 Linz, Penrod, and Donnerstein, "Effects of Long-Term Exposure."

36 Krafka et al., "Women's Reactions to Sexually Aggressive Mass Media Depictions."

37 Anthony Mulac, Laura Jansma, and Daniel Linz, "Men's Behavior Toward Women After Viewing Sexually Explicit Films: Degradation Makes a Difference," *Communication Monographs* 69, no. 4 (December 2002): 311–28.

in which each was paired with a female participant in a problem-solving task. They were filmed while completing the task, and trained raters coded the videotapes to determine behaviors for each participant, including eye gaze, interruptions, touch, unwanted sexual remarks, and disregard of a partner's suggestions. The men who viewed the sexually explicit films (both erotica and pornography) showed more dominant behaviors, touched their female partners for longer periods of time, and ignored their partner's contributions more often than males who viewed the news clips. Furthermore, men who had watched the pornography interrupted their partners more and showed more anxious behaviors than those in the other two groups.

The authors were interested in seeing whether the *women's* behaviors varied as a function of the film their partner had watched. The women did not know that their partners had watched these movies, but their behavior correlated highly with their male partner's. Women whose partners had viewed sexually explicit materials showed similar levels of anxiety, physical proximity, partner touch, and gazing at their partners. This behavioral matching, argue the researchers, suggests that women can be negatively affected by a partner's use of sexually explicit material, *even when they are unaware of such use.*

Pornography increases sexually imposing behaviors. Studies of aggression in the laboratory must use proxy tasks, as one obviously cannot ethically put participants in danger.[38] To deal with this problem, the authors of one study investigated a more subtle form of sexual aggression: exposing a woman with known negative attitudes toward sexually explicit material to erotica or pornography.[39] The female was a confederate supposedly engaged in a memory task, and the participants (both men and women) were instructed to attempt to distract her by showing her a series of slides. They could choose from pictures of sports, autopsies, nudes, partners engaging in sexual acts, or sexual deviance (including bondage). They knew the woman disliked sexually explicit material, and they also knew that all categories of slides were equally distracting to her.

---

38 Edward Donnerstein and Gary Barrett, "Effects of Erotic Stimuli on Male Aggression Toward Females," *Journal of Personality and Social Psychology* 36, no. 2 (February 1978): 180–88.

39 Gordon C. Nagayama Hall, Richard Hirschman, and Lori L. Oliver, "Ignoring a Woman's Dislike of Sexual Material: Sexually Impositional Behavior in the Laboratory," *Journal of Sex Research* 31, no. 1 (1994): 3–10.

Of the males, 72% ignored the woman's stated dislike of sexually explicit materials and showed her slides from one of the three explicit categories, while 44% of the females did so. The authors replicated the experiment, but this time the participants were told that the female was neutral about sexually explicit materials. Female use of the sexually explicit slides was similar to that of the previous experiment (41%), but significantly fewer males (54%) showed the sexual material. The authors suggest that this type of disrespect toward a woman's stated preferences has implications both in the workplace for sexual harassment, and in the home for romantic relationships. Specifically, men may use sexual media or locker-room talk in an instrumental way—to distract, impose, or subtly aggress against women (especially women with a known dislike for such media). In relationships, perhaps this means that men may use sexual media to "get back" at a partner when angry.

Pornography's effects within romantic relationships

There are numerous ways in which sexually explicit materials can be incorporated into romantic relationships. For example, couples may choose to view such materials together, as an enhancement to their sex lives. Many couples who have done so have felt positively about such shared use.[40] Sexually explicit materials may be acceptable alternatives to sexual intercourse when a partner is absent or simply too tired for sexual relations. In such instances, the use is usually perceived as benign by both partners.[41] Sexually explicit materials have been used successfully by numerous marital and sex therapists to enhance lovemaking in romantic relationships.[42]

However, more often than not pornographic materials are used outside of the relationship, in private, and often without the knowledge of the romantic partner.[43] The combination of secrecy, sexual activity outside the relationship, and

---

40 Bridges, Bergner, and Hesson-McInnis, "Romantic Partners' Use of Pornography."

41 Christina A. Clark and Michael W. Wiederman, "Gender and Reactions to a Hypothetical Relationship Partner's Masturbation and Use of Sexually Explicit Media," *Journal of Sex Research* 37, no. 2 (2000): 133–41; C. Moll and Ana J. Bridges, "Women's Perceptions of How Partner Pornography Use Affects Self-Esteem: Empirical Test of Three Variables," in progress.

42 Beatrice E. Robinson et al., "Therapeutic Uses of Sexually Explicit Materials in the United States and the Czech and Slovak Republics," *Journal of Sex and Marital Therapy* 25, no. 2 (April 1999): 103–19.

43 Alvin Cooper et al., "Sexuality on the Internet: From Sexual Exploration to Pathological Expression," *Professional Psychology* 30, no. 2 (April 1999): 154–64.

the user's perceptions of the alternative "reality" portrayed in pornography have led significant numbers of women to find their partners' use disturbing.[44] Studies of the effects of pornography on romantic relationships show that they have reasons for concern.

Pornography use can be addictive. A clear, negative consequence of pornography use is that it may escalate to the level of addiction.[45] The negative effects of compulsive use—use that occurred despite negative consequences to the person's occupational or relationship functioning—may be obvious, such as the loss of a job due to surfing adult websites on the company computer, but may be more insidious, such as role disruption that occurs when a husband spends significant portions of his evenings online masturbating to explicit images rather than being with his family.[46] In fact, increasingly, pornography use is becoming implicated in marital ruptures.[47] Depression and stress are risk factors for compulsory use.[48]

Women are reluctant to enter into relationships with frequent pornography users. The discovery of a partner's use of pornography can be a traumatic event.[49] Some women report feeling shocked, hurt, and confused when they learn of the nature and extent of their partner's sexual activities. One study investigating whether foreknowledge of a potential romantic mate's use of pornography would affect intentions

---

44 Bridges, Bergner, and Hesson-McInnis, "Romantic Partners' Use of Pornography."

45 Patrick Carnes, *Out of the Shadows: Understanding Sexual Addiction* (Center City, Minn.: Hazelden, Pa., 1983); Alvin Cooper, David Delmonico, and Ron Burg, "Cybersex Users, Abusers, and Compulsives: New Findings and Implications," *Sexual Addiction & Compulsivity* 7, nos. 1 and 2 (2000): 5–29; Natasha Petty Levert, "A Comparison of Christian and Non-Christian Males, Authoritarianism, and Their Relation to Internet Pornography Addiction/Compulsion," *Sexual Addiction & Compulsivity* 14, no. 2 (2007): 145–66.

46 Jennifer P. Schneider, "Effects of Cybersex Addiction on the Family: Results of a Survey," *Sexual Addiction & Compulsivity* 7, nos. 1 and 2 (2000): 31–58.

47 Andrea Coombes, "Computer Infidelity: Online Chat, Porn Increasing Factors in Divorce," *CBS MarketWatch*, 2002, http://www.marketwatch.com/News/Story/Story.aspx?guid=%7BE69E5888-614A-4327-8917 (accessed 5 December 2008).

48 Cooper et al., "Sexuality on the Internet"; Martin P. Kafka, "The Paraphilia-Related Disorders: Nonparaphilic Hypersexuality and Sexual Compulsivity/Addiction," in *Principles and Practice of Sex Therapy*, 3rd ed., eds. Sandra R. Leiblum and Raymond C. Rosen (New York: Guilford Press, 2000), 471–503.

49 Raymond Bergner and Ana J. Bridges, "The Significance of Heavy Pornography Involvement for Romantic Partners: Research and Clinical Implications," *Sex and Marital Therapy* 28, no. 3 (May 2002): 193–206.

to enter into a serious, long-term relationship asked college men and women to view numerous mock online dating website-like profiles of individuals and to rate their interest in pursuing a long-term romantic relationship with each person.[50] Women had significantly lower intentions to pursue a relationship with a potential mate who frequently used pornography. In contrast, men's knowledge of a potential female partner's pornography use was completely unrelated to their pursuit intentions.

Decreased satisfaction

Pornography leads to decreased satisfaction with a romantic partner. The association between use of pornography and dissatisfaction in romantic relationships has been shown. Even short, experimental situations involving a one-time exposure to popular pornographic depictions create negative consequences for males' evaluations of their romantic partner's attractiveness and how in love with them they feel. Compared with men who watched a neutral film, men who watched a pornographic film subsequently rated themselves as less in love with their romantic partner.

In a sample of internet users, happily married people were 61% less likely to report having visited a pornographic website in the prior thirty days.[51] Similarly, a survey of heterosexual couples found differences in sexual satisfaction associated with men's pornography use. Specifically, couples where men reported high use of pornography reported significantly lower sexual satisfaction than couples where men viewed less pornography.

In a two-part study, researchers first found that exposure to pictures of female centerfold models from *Playboy* or *Penthouse* significantly lowered both men's and women's judgments about the attractiveness of "average" attractive persons. This occurred regardless of whether or not they found the pictures to be pleasant.

In the second part of the study, centerfolds from *Playgirl* were used along with the *Playboy* and *Penthouse* centerfolds. After viewing the opposite sex models, participants were asked to rate how sexually attractive they felt their mate was. Men who had looked at the centerfolds rated their female partner's attractiveness and scores on Rubin's Love Scale significantly lower compared with the males who had

---

50 Tara McGahan and Ana J. Bridges, "What Traits Do Men and Women Want in a Romantic Partner? Stated Preferences Versus Actual Behavior," in progress.

51 Steven Stack, Ira Wasserman, and Roger Kern, "Adult Social Bonds and Use of Internet Pornography," *Social Science Quarterly* 85, no. 1 (March 2004): 75–88.

not seen the centerfolds, but women's ratings did not show this effect. This supports the notion that in this culture men find physical attractiveness to be more central to their sexual response than women, and that consumption of popular pornographic magazines may adversely affect males' commitments to monogamous relationships. It also validates women's experiences that they are being unfavorably compared with the impossible ideal portrayed in pornography and erotica.[52]

Very strong experimental evidence demonstrates that pornography can negatively impact sexual satisfaction within a current, heterosexual relationship. Similarly, over a six-week period, participants in one study viewed either common, non-violent pornographic videotapes or sexually innocuous comedic acts taken from prime time television.[53] Following repeated exposure to pornography, sexual satisfaction significantly decreased for both men and women in their partner's displays of affection, physical appearance, sexual curiosity, and actual sexual performance. More general items of satisfaction (e.g., general life happiness, satisfaction in non-romantic relationships, and so forth) remained unchanged, showing that the reduction in satisfaction was specific to the sexual partner of the participant, not a decline in satisfaction overall.

Although men's use of pornography has a demonstrated negative relationship to satisfaction with a romantic partner, women's use is more complex. In one study of heterosexual couples, women's use of pornography was positively associated with their male partner's relationship and sexual satisfaction.[54] The researcher suggests that this difference may be explained by the primary reason for use of pornography: For men, it was a masturbatory aid, but for women, it was part of lovemaking with their partner.

To explore further the relationship between shared versus solitary use of pornography, another study examined survey data for men and women who reported being in a romantic relationship.[55] Approximately half of survey participants

---

52 Bergner and Bridges, "The Significance of Heavy Pornography Involvement."

53 Dolf Zillmann and Jennings Bryant, "Pornography's Impact on Sexual Satisfaction," *Journal of Applied Social Psychology* 18, no. 5 (1988): 438–53.

54 Ana J. Bridges and Patricia Morokoff, "Sexual Media Use and Relational Satisfaction in Heterosexual Couples. Personal Relationships," in press.

55 Ana J. Bridges, Tara McGahan, and Patricia Morokoff, "The Association Between Shared Use of Sexually Explicit Materials and Satisfaction in Romantic Couples" (poster presented at the annual meeting of the Association for Behavioral and Cognitive Therapies, Orlando, Fla., 2008).

reported viewing explicit materials with their partners, and they reported higher relationship and sexual satisfaction. These results were particularly strong for men. The researchers believe that this may be due to the different sorts of explicit materials that tend to be marketed toward individual male users versus couples. Sexually explicit videos marketed to couples tend to emphasize story lines and foreplay and afterplay, use softer lighting, and include less focus on genitalia and fewer close-up shots of coital activity.[56] (Currently, I am exploring this further in a study of forty romantic couples.)

Problematic usage

Pornography users may not see their use as problematic ... A survey of 9,177 internet users found that 70% kept secret from their romantic partner how much time they spent online in their sexual pursuits.[57] While most (68%) felt their online sexual pursuits did not interfere with any area of their lives, follow-up analyses found that 93% of males and 84% of females admitted that others in their lives had complained about their online sexual activities.[58] Another study of web users found that participants without internet sexual experiences were significantly more likely to rate the use of pornography as an act of infidelity compared with users.[59]

... *However, partners of users are affected.* The use of pornography not only affects the attitudes and behaviors of the consumer, it affects his or her partner's well-being. In the most extreme example, a study of women entering a program for battered women in a large metropolitan city showed that a partner's pornography use nearly *doubled* the odds that a woman reported being sexually assaulted by her partner.[60] Forty-six percent reported being sexually abused, and 30% reported their partners used pornography. Fifty-eight percent identified their partner's pornography use as having played a part in their sexual assault. Although alcohol reduces inhi-

---

56 Sara E. Pearson and Robert H. Pollack, "Female Response to Sexually Explicit Films," *Journal of Psychology and Human Sexuality* 9, no. 2 (June 1997): 73–88.

57 Cooper et al., "Sexuality on the Internet."

58 Alvin Cooper et al., "Toward an Increased Understanding of User Demographics in Online Sexual Activities," *Journal of Sex and Marital Therapy* 28, no. 2 (March 2002): 105–29.

59 Monica Therese Whitty, "Pushing the Wrong Buttons: Men's and Women's Attitudes Toward Online and Offline Infidelity," *CyberPsychology and Behavior* 6, no. 6 (2003): 569–79.

60 Janet Hinson Shope, "When Words Are Not Enough: The Search for the Effect of Pornography on Abused Women," *Violence Against Women* 10, no. 1 (2004) 56–72.

bitions, alcohol use did not significantly increase prediction of sexual assault above and beyond that of pornography use alone.

Partners of identified "sexual addicts" (ninety-one females, three males) were interviewed in one study to determine the effects their partner's cybersex use had on their romantic relationships.[61] The effects they reported included feelings of hurt and betrayal, lowered self-esteem, mistrust, decreased intimacy, anger, feelings of being unattractive and objectified, feeling their partners had less interest in sexual contact, pressure from the partner to enact things from the online fantasy, and a feeling that they could not measure up to the women online.

Interestingly, women who had had frequent, repeated exposure to pornography and found it difficult to avoid in their daily lives are the most negative about such materials (29% of the sample).[62] These women disliked pornography immensely because of its negative images of women and unrealistic standards of physical attractiveness. They tended to see women as being victimized or violated in such materials.

Over half of these women were involved with male consumers of pornography, and most felt negatively about this. They identified with the females portrayed in such materials. They had argued with their partners about their use, had felt rejected by it, reported that it had a negative impact on their relationship, and believed part of how they were being treated by their partners was a result of the pornography use.

Also noteworthy, women who held neutral to mildly positive views on pornography (7% of the sample) were nonetheless conflicted about its impact on their personal romantic relationships.[63] They did not feel pornography showed violence and victimization of women, nor did they believe it was related to violence against women. They viewed themselves as very distinct from the women in the pornography. However, they did feel that it created unrealistic standards of physical attractiveness and sexual prowess, and that this had hurt their self-esteem or made a partner's use of pornography emotionally painful to them.

When asked to imagine a scenario where their partner used sexually explicit materials to engage in solitary sexual stimulation, women had fewer positive reactions

---

61 Schneider, "Effects of Cybersex Addiction on the Family."

62 Charlene Y. Senn, "Women's Multiple Perspectives and Experiences with Pornography," *Psychology of Women Quarterly* 17, no. 3 (1993): 319–41.

63 Ibid.

and more negative reactions, while men were more likely to view a partner's use of sexually explicit materials as an attempt to enhance the couple's sexual experience.[64] Both men and women disagreed slightly that solitary sexual stimulation was due to problems in the romantic relationship, particularly when no use of pornographic materials accompanied the masturbation. Participants did not react negatively to this sort of sexual activity, perhaps because the scenarios were hypothetical and described as taking place when the partner was out of town. Reactions might have been considerably more negative if the partner was described as available at the time of the behavior, since that would more clearly show the partner *choosing* the sexually explicit material and/or masturbation over sexual relations with their partner.

To explore this possibility, a similar study asked college women to read a series of descriptions of romantic couples in which the male partner used pornography, some when his partner was in town, some when his partner was out of town.[65] The study participants rated the women in the stories as being less satisfied with their bodies and their relationships when the partner was a heavy user of pornography, and as even less satisfied when the partner was in town and presumably available for sexual relations.

When how partners feel about the use of pornography in a real-world context rather than a hypothetical scenario is examined, the results are clearer. One study examined conversations with women who identified their partners as pornography "addicts," were quite upset over this use, and were seeking help from an online, anonymous, public forum. The study found that the woman's partner's use of pornography was associated with her having numerous devastating interpretations of her role in his use, his moral character, and the state of their romantic relationship.[66] Themes of the women's self-descriptions included seeing herself as the reason for her partner's use ("I am not attractive enough," "I should be more available"), seeing the partner as uncaring or selfish ("If he loved me, he wouldn't hurt me this way," "I've told him it bothers me and he still uses pornography; he must not care about me"), and viewing the relationship as a farce ("We pretend like everything is fine, but really our relationship is sick and unhealthy").

---

64 Clark and Wiederman, "Gender and Reactions."

65 Moll and Bridges, "Women's Perceptions."

66 Bergner and Bridges, "The Significance of Heavy Pornography Involvement."

Another study conducted a web-based survey of 100 women whose partners used pornography. Nearly one-third reported moderate to high levels of distress about their partner's use of such material.[67] They reported feeling as though their partners were not interested in making love to them, but during sexual intercourse were instead picturing the women they had seen in the pornography. They also felt their partners were less trustworthy, usually because they would keep the use of pornography a secret (even when they did not object to it).

Nearly three-quarters reported feeling that the partner's use negatively affected their own self-esteem. Some felt they had failed their partners sexually; if they had been better sexual partners, their partners never would have had to turn to such material for sexual satisfaction.

An intriguing finding

These studies show that, for a significant minority of women in heterosexual romantic relationships, their partner's use of pornography negatively impacts their perceptions of themselves, their partners, and their relationship, but that a majority express either neutral or positive attitudes toward it. While the distressed and broken marriage merits our clinical attention, this intriguing and consistent finding merits our scientific attention. Why do some women report interpersonal difficulties stemming from a partner's use of pornography while others do not? What characterizes couples who are able to accommodate such use successfully, perhaps even in a manner that enhances the self-reported quality of their relationship, while others become so distraught that they consider divorce or even suicide?

This phenomenon remains a mystery, but its solution may provide us with insight regarding the mechanisms by which pornography exerts its negative effects. Currently, I am exploring this question in a study of forty heterosexual couples. Although these data are not yet available, I am certain that they will generate numerous fruitful pathways for future research that will continue to enhance our understanding of this important area of study.

---

67 Bridges, Bergner, and Hesson-McInnis, "Romantic Partners' Use of Pornography."

Summary

As pornography has become increasingly accessible, it has played a more prominent role in romantic relationships and in shaping sexual norms. The experimental and survey data reviewed above suggest that there is cause for concern: Young men and women who report higher pornography use, and from earlier ages, engage in more risky sexual behaviors. Compulsive pornography use is hurting some marriages and increasingly is playing a role in divorce. Although there is growing recognition of its potential for harm, therapists are largely untrained in the many ways pornography use can impact individuals, couples, and families. An important first step is acknowledging the role pornography plays in these negative life events. However, we must continue to research *how,* for *whom,* and *why,* so that we can help those who have been hurt and help prevent future harm.

PART TWO:
MORAL PERSPECTIVE

THE ABUSE OF SEX

Roger Scruton

We are a long way from the days when homosexuality was described as a perversion, pornography as an offense against public morals, and masturbation as "self-abuse." The old morality that condemned sex outside marriage and saw nothing wrong with treating homosexuality as a criminal offense, even if it has a following in the Muslim world, has few adherents in the West. We have moved on at such a pace in the last half-century that to many people any talk of sexual morality at all appears quaint. If there is sexual misconduct, it is only a special case of the more general sin of forcing, defrauding, or manipulating other people into doing something they do not really want to do. If they really *do* want to do it, and the feeling is mutual, then what on earth is wrong?

That is the view I wish to challenge. What I say may not persuade everyone; indeed, it may not persuade anyone. But I will have achieved half of my purpose if I convince you that the argument is not about consent but about the very nature of the sexual act and the desire expressed in it.

Some modern myths

This way of describing and in consequence experiencing sexual phenomena I believe to be founded in five myths. Some of the myths originate in wishful thinking, and some in scientific and pseudoscientific theories.

The first myth is that sexual desire is desire for a particular kind of pleasure, located in the sexual organs. On this view all sex is like masturbation—a manipulation of the sexual organs for the sake of pleasure. The other person is a stimulus to the desire, but not an object of it. The desire is not for him or her but for a pleasure that could be obtained in other ways. The effect of this myth is to remove sexual desire and sexual pleasure from the realm of interpersonal responses, and reconstitute them as purely sensory appetites, like the desire to scratch and the pleasure of scratching.

Why should people believe that? There are two dominant reasons, I think. One is that it simplifies the phenomena of sex in a way that makes them intellectually manageable. Sex becomes like eating and drinking: the desire is for sensory gratification, and is part of the general pleasure-seeking character of the animal organism. The instinct on which this pleasure depends is aroused by the sight of or contact with another person: and that explains the function of sexual pleasure in the life of the human organism, and why it is usually aroused by a member of the opposite sex. This pleasure helps the reproductive process, in just the way that the pleasure of eating helps to keep the organism fed.

The other reason for believing this myth is that it simplifies the phenomena of sex in ways that make them *morally* manageable. If sex is just like eating, then personal relationships, commitment, and the rest can be discounted from the moral point of view. As long as the other person sits down with you voluntarily to enjoy the meal, the elementary requirements of morality are satisfied. Maybe you should be careful about the diet, but only for health reasons. All those old reasons for care, such as shame, honor, marital duty, and the rest, are as irrational as the Jewish dietary laws and a mere survival from an era in which "safe sex" was difficult to guarantee.

The second myth is that sexual satisfaction depends upon such factors as the intensity and duration of sensory pleasure, culminating in orgasm, and that "good sex" is a matter of getting those things right. This is what lovers should aim at, and what ultimately cements the bond between them. Around the myth of "good sex" has grown an enormous literature, both popular and "scientific."

Like the previous myth, this one serves to simplify the phenomena of sex, both factually and morally. It reduces to a technique what is more properly described as an art, and represents as a means what is understandable only as an end. In short, it "instrumentalizes" the sexual act.

The third myth is of a different kind, since it involves an attempt at, or at any rate a pretense of, science. This is the myth that sexual urges need to be expressed, and that the attempt to "repress" them is psychologically harmful. The origins of this myth lie in the theories of Freud, who did not, however, endorse the view that repression is harmful. What Freud did do was to introduce the "hydraulic" imagery with which sexual desire is now so often understood. The urge welling up inside can be kept down for a while, but eventually will seek a channel to escape, and if not allowed to escape through one channel may escape through another. The longer it is kept down, the more dangerous might its inevitable eruption be, if it finds release in activities such as sadism or child abuse. The great apostle of this view was Wilhelm Reich, who saw orgasm as a kind of release, sex as the technique for securing it, and repression as the path to insanity.

Associated with this third myth is a fourth, which is that sexual desire is the same kind of thing, whatever the nature of the partner who arouses it. The urge welling within me might be stimulated by a woman, or a man, or an animal, or an imaginary being. Convention and decency set limits to how a human being should satisfy his sexual urges. But nothing in the urge itself demands any particular kind of partner. Sexual "orientation," as it is now called, is simply an ingrained habit of arousal, trained on a particular object.

This myth goes naturally with the other three, but the motive for adopting it is rather different, namely the desire to revise and perhaps even abolish the traditional idea of sexual normality. For the fourth myth offers an easy path to the conclusion that there is no such thing as sexual normality, and that homosexuality (for example) is not in itself a perversion. Homosexual and heterosexual conduct use different *instruments*, but to the same end, and any argument for distinguishing right from wrong applies equally to both. There should be no coercion, no fraud, no trickery; and each partner must be open and honest with the other, but the sex of the partner is irrelevant to the morality of the act.

Finally, the fifth and in many ways most important of the modern myths about sex tells us that attitudes such as shame, guilt, and disgust are unhealthy. What makes people feel bad is the "judgmental" attitude prevalent in the surrounding culture, which people interiorize, so that they accuse themselves in the very moment of sexual release. Hence we should strive to free ourselves from these hangovers from an old and discredited ethic of "pollution and taboo," and learn to engage in sexual activity in full awareness that it is in essence no more guilty an activity than eating or drinking—a psychological benefit that need have no psychological cost. Much modern sex education is designed as a therapy for guilt and shame, a way of getting young people to accept their sexual urges and to find ways to express them without feeling bad about doing so. Moral progress means freeing ourselves from this internal judgment, learning to express our sexuality freely, and to overcome the irrational guilt that stems from others and not from our true inner selves.

Now, I agree with the view that we must find ways to express our sexual desires without feeling guilt and shame. But I also think that guilt and shame are often justified, and that what they demand of us is not therapy, in order to remove them, but right conduct, in order to avoid them.

Some consequences of the myths

Not everyone adheres to these myths, and there are of course more and less subtle ways of upholding them. But they define a pattern of thinking in our society, which affects every aspect of the culture. Whenever people write of the "recreational" use of sex; whenever they suggest that there is no basis to sexual morality other than the rule that force and fraud are forbidden; whenever they describe "gay" sex as though it were a mere variation of an activity that exists also in a "straight" variety—they are usually leaning on those myths.

Perhaps the greatest evidence of the triumph of these myths is the growing indifference in our society toward the glut of pornography. For if these myths are true, it is impossible to condemn pornography or the practice of those who use it as a sexual stimulant. Indeed, pornography might even be regarded as the best form of sexual recreation, in that it is free from the dangers—medical, psychological, and personal—of sex with a partner. As Oscar Wilde said of masturbation: "It is cleaner, more efficient, and you meet a better class of person," by which he meant himself.

Now, I am one of those who think of pornography as something we should avoid ourselves and do everything we can to forbid to our children. But nothing in the modern myths justifies that attitude, and therefore I must search for the error these myths involve, and replace them with a rival picture of human sexual desire.

This is what I wish to sketch in the remainder of this paper. But first, let me make some disclaimers. First, these myths involve an "instrumentalized" view of sexual conduct—the view that the sexual act, in whatever form it takes, is a means to something else, be it sensory pleasure, orgasm, or relief from internal pressure. It does not follow from this that the act does not have some other value. Just as eating is a means to gustatory pleasure and also to nourishment, so does it have another value—especially eating in company, a form of companionship that brings with it both intimacy and comfort.

Second, someone could adhere to the instrumentalized view of sexual desire and still argue that when we take this pleasure in company there is a social payoff, in the form of an intimacy and mutual enjoyment, and go on to build a picture of "good sex" which reconstructs some of the moral values we associate with loving relations in general and marriage in particular. However these moral values will not be intrinsic to the sexual act. They will be by-products of the act, and will have no intrinsic bearing on the morality of the act itself, any more than the social value of dinner à deux has any bearing on the rightness or wrongness of eating the particular thing that is eaten (and which may in fact be forbidden by some dietary code).

Finally, in opposing these myths, I am not insisting that the only alternative to them is the old morality that regards heterosexual relations within marriage as the only legitimate form of sexual expression, and which, for example, dismisses homosexuality as a perversion. Exactly what moral code is the right one, or whether there is any single right one, is not a matter that concerns me directly in this paper. I am concerned only with the more fundamental question, which is a question of philosophical psychology rather than morality—the question of what to put in place of the instrumentalized view of sex. If I go on to draw moral conclusions, they will be tentative, and based in a sense of what is at risk in our sexual encounters.

Persons and animals

The first point to make is that sexual desire belongs to that aspect of the human being which we summarize in the concept of the person. Many of the things that we experience we experience as animals, and what we feel does not normally depend upon thought, intention, or personality. We feel the same pain from a wound that a dog might feel if wounded in the same way. But there are other states of mind that only persons can experience. While a dog can experience aggression, he cannot experience remorse or shame, cannot wonder about the laws of nature, cannot judge another dog morally, and so on.

There are some states of mind that are rooted in our animal nature, but are transformed by our involvement as persons. Soldiers in the front line respond to an attack on their comrades by joining with them in the fight, and this response belongs to those collective reactions exhibited by pack animals. However, the soldier who rushes to share the danger of his comrades is not just obeying an instinct. He has risen above that instinct and judged acting on it to be right and honorable. He has not just an urge to join the battle but a motive, and that motive is honor and duty toward his fellows, and shame at letting them down. The soldier is acting for *others*, and from a conception of *himself*, and of how he looks in others' eyes. Such a motive can prevail over the animal instincts of fear and dread only because the soldier also has the virtue that enables him to act on it—the virtue that we know as fortitude or courage. In short, he acts from a full, free, personal involvement in his predicament, conscious that he is judged for what he does, and aiming at a good that he understands in personal terms.

Exactly similar things should be said of sexual desire. Sexual desire is rooted in instincts we share with the other animals, and the pursuit of one person by another may not look so very different from the encounter of horse and mare in a field. However, just as in the case of the soldier, the person who responds to these instincts also stands in judgment upon them. Is it right or wrong to respond? When he responds, he responds from a judgment that this is the right person, that in doing this thing he is in her eyes not demeaning himself but gaining her acceptance, just as she is in his. They share a reciprocity of glances, a gradual accommodation in which their consent is woven into their desire, so that the desire becomes an expression of something other than instinct. Of what?

To answer that question we must look a little more closely at the concept of the person. Most animals are not persons, and some persons are not animals. We, however, are both. Hence there are features of our mental life that non-personal animals do not share. We have rights and duties; we make judgments, reflect on past and future, on the possible and the impossible; we are self-conscious, distinguishing self and other, and attributing our mental states to ourselves on no basis; we relate to each other not as animals but as persons, through dialogue, judgment, and moral expectations. Indeed, there are arguments for saying that the concept of the person is essentially tied to interpersonal relations: To explain what a person *is*, we must explain how persons relate to each other. One vital feature of interpersonal relations is their emotional content. My stance toward self and other is reflected in my emotional life. Emotions such as shame, guilt, anger, remorse, gratitude, forgiveness, and rejoicing are essentially directed toward persons—whether self or other—and learning to feel these things is part of what it means to grow up, i.e., to pass from the animal to the personal condition.

Fundamental to all these emotions, and to the life of persons generally, are our beliefs about freedom and responsibility. No two philosophers agree as to what freedom and responsibility presuppose, but for our present purposes we can leave the philosophical controversies to one side; my sole concern is to examine how we actually envisage ourselves in our lives as persons. In all our conduct toward each other we treat both self and other as free. My responsibility is revealed in my shame, and my freedom in my forgiveness. The belief in freedom and responsibility is presupposed in anger and resentment, in gratitude and love. Take that belief away and little would remain of our emotional life and its rewards.

The heart of freedom is the self. Kant suggested, in his lectures on anthropology, that the distinctiveness of the human condition is contained in the fact that human beings can say "I." Self-consciousness brings with it the condition of freedom, and the knowledge of both self and other as responsible. But there is a yet more remarkable fact about the use of "I." By my use of this word I create a new center of being: I set my body aside, as it were, and replace the organism with the self, and present to others another target of their interest and response. To know my mind, and also to change it, they do not examine my body: They look to my words, my opinions, my thoughts. They enter into dialogue with this thing called "I," and see it as standing in the arena of freedom, both part of the physical world and situated on its very edge.

Something like this is assumed in our ordinary human relations. Just think of your response, when your friend betrays your secrets. You don't think of him as you would of a computer, in which you stored information that somehow got out. You don't ask yourself about who hacked into his brain. You go to him and you address him in the second person, I to I: "You promised," you say, and your words are addressed to that very center of being where his "I" resides. In accusing him you are not trying to provoke some physical reaction. You are expecting a response from that I—a response from the center of freedom where he resides, one self-conscious subject among others. You expect him, in other words, to take responsibility for what he did, to say "I am sorry," and maybe to show how he is going to atone for his fault, to make amends, and in this way re-establish your relations in such a way that you will forgive him. There is a process here, in which one "I" faces another, both of them exercising their freedom, taking responsibility for their choices, and acting as the sovereign of the human animal.

This does not mean that there are two things here—person and animal. There is one thing—an organism, organized as a person. That is how we treat each other in all our free relations.

Persons and desire

Now for sexual desire. It is rooted in animal instincts, but in a person desire is re-centered, self-attributed to the I, so as to become part of the interpersonal dialogue. It is an interpersonal emotion, in which subject and object confront each other I to I. Hence sexual desire, as we know it, is peculiar to human beings. In describing sexual desire, we are describing *John's* desire for *Mary*, or *Jane's* desire for *Bill*. And the people themselves will not merely describe their desires, but also experience them, as *my* desire for *you.* "I want you" is not a figure of speech but the true expression of what I feel. And here the pronouns identify that very center of free and responsible choice that constitutes the interpersonal reality of each of us. I want you as the free being who you are, and your freedom is wrapped up in the thing that I want.

You can easily verify this, as I show in my book *Sexual Desire,* by studying sexual arousal. This is not a state of the body, even though it involves certain bodily changes. It is a process in the soul, a steady awakening of one person to another, through touches, glances, and caresses. The exchange of glances is particularly important, and illustrates a general feature of personal relations. People look *at* each other, as animals do. But they also look *into* each other, and do this in particular when mutually aroused. The look of desire is like a summons, a call to the other self to show itself in the eyes, to weave its own freedom and selfhood into the beam that calls to it. There is a famous description of this phenomenon by John Donne, who writes in "The Ecstasy":

> *Our eye-beams twisted, and did thread*
> *Our eyes upon one double string.*
> *So to engraft our hands, as yet*
> *Was all the means to make us one;*
> *And pictures in our eyes to get*
> *Was all our propagation.*

The experience described by Donne is known to every sighted person who has ever been aroused. Likewise the caress and the touch of desire have an *epistemic* character: they are an exploration, not of a body, but of a free being in his or her embodiment. They too call to the other in his freedom, and are asking him to show himself.

All the phenomena of desire can be understood in that way, as parts of a mutual negotiation between free and responsible beings, who want each other as persons. And this has an important metaphysical consequence, which in turn has important moral consequences. Persons are individuals in the strong sense of being *identified,* both by themselves and by others, as unique, irreplaceable, *not admitting of substitutes.* This is something Kant tried to capture in his theory of persons as "ends in themselves."

Somehow the free being is, in his own eyes and in the eyes of all those in a personal relation with him, the being who he is. He is never merely an instance of some useful attribute. To treat him merely instrumentally is always in a measure to abuse him; and while I can employ you for a job and in doing so recognize that someone else might have served my purpose just as well, I must, in employing you, respect your individuality, and not treat you as a tool or a slave. You are for me, even in this functional relation, the free being who meets me I to I.

It follows from this that, in those relations between persons in which self and other relate as subject and object, each views the other as unique, without a substitute. This has an immediate impact on sexual desire. John, frustrated in his desire for Mary, cannot be offered Jane as a substitute. Someone who says "Take Jane, she will do just as well" does not understand *what* John wants, in wanting Mary.

It follows also that desire requires complex, compromising, and potentially embarrassing negotiations, and that without these negotiations sexual intimacy is liable to induce self-disgust. When girls complain of date-rape, it is this kind of thing they have in mind. It is not necessarily that they didn't consent to what happened. Outwardly maybe they did. But inwardly they did not, and didn't realize, until too late, that this was so. Consent has to be prepared by elaborate games and intimacies, in which freedom and responsibility are alertly deployed by both parties to the transaction.

What I have said points at every juncture to difficult philosophical issues concerning the nature of persons, of freedom, of responsibility and self-awareness. I am consciously refusing to address those issues, because my task is simply to remind you of what you all know and what you all have experienced in moments of desire. Arousal and desire are not bodily states or even states of individual persons: they form one pole of an I to I encounter, and involve a *going out* to the other, in which his or her freedom and responsibility are intimately involved in what is wanted. It is only in this way that we can explain some of our most immovable intuitions about sex.

Consider rape. On the instrumentalized view of sex surveyed earlier, rape is a crime of the same order as leaning on a woman without asking her permission and at the worst like spitting on her, doing something that disgusts her without caring what she feels. It involves using someone for a purpose that could have been achieved with any other instrument, but without troubling to seek her consent and even by ignoring her resistance. As we know, however, rape is next in line to murder, by way of an assault. It is a violation of the other person in the very depths of her being. The view that I have offered immediately explains this. The rapist is not merely prepared to use his victim as a means: He steals her most precious possession, the thing that she wishes to offer only as a gift and in a condition of mutual surrender. He does not merely disregard her freedom: He poisons it, removes from it the most important thing for which it was made, which is the mutual self giving of desire. And that is why rape is experienced as an annihilation and not just an abuse.

This account of desire explains why we feel disgust at pedophilia, impose a taboo on incest, and regard bestiality and necrophilia as perversions. It explains the role of modesty as an invitation to correct behavior, and shame as a protection against abuse—a point vividly made by Max Scheler in his long paper on shame. I do not think I need to spell these things out, since anyone who recognizes the core of truth in what I have said will be able to spell them out for himself.

Disowning the myths

My purpose now is to sweep away the myths I began by enunciating. All of them, it seems to me, arise from a fundamental mistake about the *intentionality* of sexual arousal and sexual desire. These states of mind are not directed toward pleasure, orgasm, or any similar thing. They are directed toward one free being by another.

That last point is worth lingering over. You might think that the rapist is indifferent to the freedom of his victim. On the contrary, however. It is precisely her freedom that he wishes to seize, to overcome, to force to bow before him. For this reason you cannot rape an animal, even if you can sexually abuse it. The victim of rape is a free being, compelled to accept what she does not consent to.

The myths depend upon removing from the picture of sexual activity both the self-conception of the subject and the other-conception of the object. The subject regards the other as a tool with which to induce excitement and pleasure, and conceives himself as a sensory organism. The myths remove from the picture of desire both the person who feels it and the person toward whom it is felt. The myths, in other words, do not describe desire at all, but something else—something that we might observe in animals or children, or, as Socrates put it (according to Xenophon) in pigs rubbing against a post.

One thing that tempts people to endorse the myths is the very obvious fact that sexual activity involves bodily changes and bodily sensations, leading (though not always) to orgasm. This has made the caricature of desire believable, in the minds of those who take an accountant's view of human satisfactions. It looks as though you could enumerate the benefits of sexual activity in terms of pleasure, and the costs in terms of the time and energy needed to find the person willing to stimulate you, and on that basis proceed to give a utilitarian morality of sexual behavior. If that sounds ridiculous, do not be deceived. It is ridiculous, so ridiculous that Judge Richard Posner has written a whole book, called *Sex and Reason,* devoted to treating the phenomena in this way.

There is a downside to such books, and to the myths they reinforce. Myths can work on reality in such a way that they cease to be myths and become true descriptions instead. Thinking of sex in the instrumentalized way that Judge Posner exemplifies you actually prepare yourself to *experience* it in this way. Henry James had an inkling of this when he wrote, in the Preface to *The Bostonians,* of "the decline in the sentiment of sex," meaning the loss of that full-hearted, self-committing form of sexual desire which animates the heroines of Jane Austen, and its replacement by short-lived, titillating forms of seduction. And the more people think of sex as a means to the production of pleasure or a means for obtaining orgasm (as was famously believed by the madman Wilhelm Reich, who even invented a machine to help the orgasm-seeker to reach his goal), the more the other drops out of consideration as irrelevant, and the more sex ceases to be a form of interpersonal relation and retreats into narcissistic solitude.

Pornography and self-abuse

In conclusion I want to touch on the relation of pornography to a highly unfashionable idea, that of self-abuse, a term originally applied to all forms of masturbation, in ways that led to much ridicule and scorn of our ancestors and their puritan hang-ups. It is surely obvious from my account that sex, in what I would wish to describe as its normal form, involves a moving out from the self toward the other—an attempt to know and unite with the other in her body. It involves treating the other as a free subject, and enjoying the mutual arousal which is possible only through the reciprocal interest in each other as conscious and free.

The self is at risk in this: The other may refuse to cooperate, may turn away in disgust, may act in ways that elicit shame and humiliation. That is why you have to be ready for it, and one reason why it is such an injustice to inflict sexual relations on children. In the face of this risk people are tempted to retreat from the direct forms of sexual desire, and take refuge in fantasy objects—objects that cannot damage or threaten you, that cannot withhold consent since they cannot give it, that are without the capacity to embarrass or shame the one who watches them.

Such objects are provided by pornography. The people displayed in the pornographic film have no relation to the viewer, nor are they displayed as being in any other relation to each other than that of each using the other's body as a *machine à frotter*. It is impossible to know what they are feeling, and in any case their feelings are in no way directed to the person who is using them and at the same time abusing himself. The viewer's pleasure is not the pleasure of desire, since there is no one he is desiring. Nor is he really aroused except in the purely physiological sense, since there is no mutual arousal of which he is a party. Everything is cold, bleak, objective, and also free of cost and personal risk.

Pornography exactly conforms to the myths about desire that I have rejected: it is a *realization* of those myths, a form of sexual pleasure from which the interpersonal intentionality has been surgically excised. Pornography takes hold of sexual desire and cuts away the desire. There is no real object, but only a fantasy, and no real subject, since there is nothing ventured of the self. To say that this is an abuse of the self is to express a literal truth—so it seems to me.

Like all cost-free forms of pleasure, pornography is habit-forming. It short-circuits that roundabout route to sexual satisfaction which passes through the streams and valleys of arousal, in which the self is always at risk from the other, and always motivated to give itself freely in desire. The short-circuiting mechanism here is in all probability not different from that researched by Mihaly Csikszentmihalyi and Robert Kubey in their studies of gambling and TV addiction.

It exhibits in addition, however, a depersonalizing habit—a habit of viewing sex as something external to the human personality, to relationship, and to the arena of free encounters. Sex is reduced to the sexual organs, which are stuck on, in the imagination, like cutouts in a child's picture. To think that this can be done, and the habit of doing it fully established, without damage to a person's capacity to be a person, and to relate to other persons as one sexual being to others, is to make a large and naïve assumption about the ability of the mind to compartmentalize.

Indeed, psychologists and psychotherapists are increasingly encountering the damage done by pornography, not to marriages and relationships only, but to the very capacity to engage in them. Sex, portrayed in the porno-image, is an affair of attractive people with every technical accomplishment. Most people are not attractive, and have only second-class equipment. Once they are led by their porn addiction to see sex in the instrumentalized way that pornography encourages, they begin to lose confidence in their capacity to enjoy sex in any other way than through fantasy. People who lose confidence in their ability to attract soon become unattractive.

And then the fear of desire arises, and from that fear the fear of love. This, it seems to me, is the real risk attached to pornography. Those who become addicted to this risk-free form of sex run a risk of another and greater kind. They risk the loss of love, in a world where only love brings happiness.

PORNOGRAPHY: SETTLING THE QUESTION IN PRINCIPLE

Hadley Arkes

I would like to draw the strands of my argument by beginning with two vignettes or cases I recalled in a book of mine with Princeton University Press called *The Philosopher in the City* (1981). One ran back to the spring of 1977, with Dr. Judith Densen-Gerber testifying on Capitol Hill in hearings on child pornography and showing the only X-rated film going in the halls of Congress.

There are congressmen whose lives could make X-rated movies resemble Disney films, but this showing of child pornography was quite unusual as a screening. In the course of her remarks, Dr. Densen-Gerber referred to situations as grotesque as the discovery of gonorrhea of the throat in infants as young as nine months and eighteen months.

I was in the audience that day, and I was curious as to how she understood the *wrong* of pornography. When I posed the question, she remarked that the children involved in these productions were more likely to be drawn into prostitution later in life. I pressed the question one step further: Did she herself regard prostitution as morally wrong, in fact as a wrong that could be barred in the law? That question fired the reflexes I had sensed were there, and she quickly responded that she did not think prostitution should be regarded as morally wrong, and legally actionable, for consenting adults.[1]

The "problem," then, for Dr. Densen-Gerber, was that children drawn into pornography were likely, in their mature years, to be drawn to occupations she regarded as quite legitimate. If the children were likely to be drawn into careers as lawyers or interior decorators, would the indictment have been the same? Some parents have been anxious to hire out their children for work as models or as actors in Disney films, and those engagements often have been the source of experience quite corrosive of character. Still we have permitted parents to tender their consent for their own children here as in other places. And yet when it came to child

---

1 The account of the encounter with Dr. Densen-Gerber is set down in Hadley Arkes, *The Philosopher in the City* (Princeton, N.J.: Princeton University Press, 1981), 414–15.

pornography, the consent of the parents would not be taken as sufficient to make these engagements legitimate. Apparently the wrong ran so deep that the consent of the responsible adults was not sufficient here to dissolve the moral problem. There must have been something notably different then between pornography and the productions of Disney.

There is of course a link between pornography and prostitution. "Pornography" is drawn from the Greek *pornographos,* writing about prostitutes. And it is telling, I think, that feminists in our own day have found themselves divided over whether it is legitimate to cast an adverse moral judgment on prostitution. That erosion of moral conviction about prostitution has to be bound up with the things that induce many feminists to recede from an adverse judgment on pornography as well.

The two must be connected in principle—or so I would argue—and that late uncertainty about the moral ground for judging prostitution and pornography may account for why so many feminist writers seem to be affected by one of the false lures of social science or the more implausible formulas of the law, which converge in offering this seduction: They offer a rationale for condemning and barring pornography, while avoiding the vexing business of actually casting a moral judgment—and then taking up the discipline of supplying a moral justification for the use of the law in closing off this domain of freedom.

As part of those converging strands, I would take my second case, and this one involves the audacity and imagination of the Mexican-American Anti-Defamation Committee. In the early seventies there was a rather entertaining ad for FRITOS® Corn Chips, involving the appealing animated figure of a small fellow, with a sombrero, mustache, and a rather caricatured Spanish accent, who was given the name of Frito Bandito. The Defamation Committee did not find the ad as fetching as did others in the country. The Committee argued that the ad offered a stereotyped version of the Mexican, and it went into court in an action for defamation.

In a curious turn, the Committee brought the complaint as an action for personal damages, and it sought $100 in punitive damages for every Chicano in the United States.[2] The concern here was long known in the law as the defamation of racial or ethnic groups, but the action brought out what was so singularly inapt in treat-

---

2 United Press International, "Damage Suit Scores 'Frito Bandito' Ads," *New York Times,* 1 January 1971, final edition, p. 31.

ing that concern as a tort, seeking personal damages. There is nothing unreal about nurturing a climate of hostility to certain racial or ethnic groups. Nor are the injuries always intangible that spring from wounding words, from the inciting of hatred directed at these groups, and from the occasional outburst into racial rioting. But it is virtually impossible that every member of the group will suffer an injury, or that one could establish a connection between the diffusion of ethnic stereotypes and the decision of any employer or landlord to turn away from Mexican-Americans.

I have argued myself that there is a distinct wrong of defaming whole racial groups, a wrong that may manifest itself in material injuries.[3] But the law cannot hinge on the showing of material injuries in any case. It has to involve recognition of what is wrong with that kind of defamation *in principle,* and the matter is more aptly treated by a law that simply forbids that kind of defamation as defamation *per se.* It would be a matter of recognizing things that we could judge as libelous or hurtful in themselves, even if we cannot demonstrate quite yet that a material injury has been done.

The law on the defamation of racial groups works properly through the criminal law, say in assigning a fine, perhaps of a couple of hundred dollars, or by issuing an injunction to stop the broadcast of the defamation. But it hinges, not on a measurement of the injuries to any person, as much as on the ground of our judgment that certain words or expressions are clearly fixed, in ordinary language, as terms that carried the function of insulting or denigrating. Of course there would be nothing wrong with denigrating rapists, murderers, and arsonists. The wrong in principle came with casting an adverse judgment on whole racial groups, as though race or ethnicity "determined" or controlled the character of people—as though, if we knew solely a person's race or ethnicity, we would know whether we were dealing with a good or a bad person, whose presence should be welcomed or shunned.[4] I will forbear running through the complete argument here, but I would contend that the wrong of this kind of defamation is rooted in the logic of moral judgment itself: that if our conduct were determined by our race or ethnicity, none of us would be responsible for his own acts, and the whole language of morality and law, in assigning responsibility and blame, would dissolve in its meaning.

---

3 Arkes, *The Philosopher in the City*.

4 Ibid., 46–50; Hadley Arkes, *First Things* (Princeton, N.J.: Princeton University Press, 1986).

I raise the matter because we have seen some notable feminist writers arguing against pornography in this way: that pornography teaches a degraded view of women, and that it incites all sorts of injuries to women, ranging from rape to demeaning gestures that humiliate. But once again, we find it exceedingly difficult or impossible to map a causal link between any version of pornography and particular harms suffered by particular women.

My own pitch is that it would make far better sense to recognize that pornography may indeed be deeply wrong, but that it would be a wrong in principle. And in justifying that judgment to regard it as a "wrong," and repress it through the law, we would need to explain that wrong in principle much in the way that we have to explain other things that are wrong in principle. The wrong of pornography may of course involve a denigrating view of women, and more than that: a denigrating, debased view of sex itself and the kind of love that rightly envelops sex between those creatures we can recognize as "moral agents." They are those beings, "composed of eros and of dust," who alone can give reasons in matters of right and wrong, and who may bring some exacting tests to the persons they would admit to this unparalleled intimacy. But whether that intimacy is unparalleled and rare, or whether it is frequently paralleled and offered widely, without a discrimination strenuously exacting, are matters at the heart of the question.

And yet it has been the hallmark of our modern approaches in the law—indeed a matter eliciting high genius and no small measure of self-congratulation—to address these kinds of questions by cleverly avoiding any kind of moral judgment at all. In this respect, the leading voice of modernity in the law is the voice of Justice Oliver Wendell Holmes. Holmes thought it would be a decided gain "if every word of moral significance could be banished from the law altogether, and other words adopted which should convey legal ideas uncolored by anything outside the law."[5] And distinctly "outside the law," in this construal, would be any judgments of a distinctly moral character.

Tutored in this way, we would find legislators flexing their genius by dealing with prostitution and pornography with measures that carefully avoided any mention of those notions of right and wrong that have underlain the law in the first

---

5 See Oliver Wendell Holmes, "The Path of the Law," *Collected Legal Papers* (New York: Harcourt Brace and Company, 1920), 179. By way of contrast, see Roscoe Pound, *Law and Morals* (Chapel Hill: University of North Carolina Press, 1926), 74–75.

place. A notable case in point came in New York City years ago as the authorities sought to deal with those bogus massage parlors that were really brothels in disguise. How did urbane New Yorkers deal with that ruse? By insisting that "real" massage parlors establish their authenticity by appearing either in hotels with more than two hundred rooms, or in centers that contain facilities for sports, such as swimming pools (with a minimum of 1500 square feet), squash courts (which must be 25 feet wide, 45 feet long, and 20 feet high), or other kinds of courts whose dimensions may be specified with equal precision.[6] The extraordinary precision reflects what I've called the ritual of empty exactitude, which the law is forced to undertake in defining the surface features of a problem when the authorities are either unable or unwilling to define the essence of the moral offense itself.

In our own day the example of a judge exemplifying the state of mind we are seeking to describe has been furnished with excruciating faithfulness by Justice David Souter. Souter wrote his undergraduate thesis on Holmes, and so it should not have been a surprise that when he confronts matters of prostitution or topless dancing, he insists that the law reach the matter, not by offering a moral judgment on the act itself, but a concern for the "secondary effects" of the acts.[7]

And so, for example, a neighborhood marked by prostitution and pornographic stores and tawdry entertainments is more likely to attract pickpockets and muggers than a concert featuring Mozart quartets. A Holmes or a Souter might argue that these "secondary effects" are reasons enough for restricting prostitution and pornography. But of course pickpockets and muggers are likely to be attracted to many happenings that draw a dense crowd —they are highly likely to be drawn to Grand Central Station on a Friday during rush hour, or to Yankee Stadium on the occasion of a game filling the park. And yet nothing in the array of these thefts or assaults would establish in any way that there is something unwholesome or illegitimate about Yankee games or Grand Central Station.

The puzzle that afflicts some commentators in dealing with these moral problems recalls to me that time, years ago, when I was invited by my late friend, Nachman Greenberg, to a meeting at the Illinois Masonic Hospital in Chicago. Greenberg and his staff of psychologists were dealing with the problems of incest

---

6 Arkes, *The Philosopher in the City*, 403.

7 See, as the most notable example, Justice David Souter's dissenting opinion in the "topless dancing case," *Barnes v. Glen Theatre*, 501 U.S. 560 (1991).

and the abuse of children. I asked which of those maladies did they think I exemplified—that is to say, why call on me? The reason I soon learned: The clinicians were persuaded that anything they regarded as psychologically disturbing or undesirable would manifest itself in a material hurt of some kind. And so they were rather perplexed by the father who observed that, since he and his teenage daughter had been having sex, her grades had improved, her acne had cleared up, and she had stopped stuttering. She was flourishing.

What came as a kind of revelation to them was that something could indeed be wrong in principle even if the people involved were not suffering any material harm, and indeed even if they were apparently flourishing, with rosy cheeks and an upbeat sense of self-esteem. But the perplexity was amplified for the clinicians by the fact that the discipline would change: There was now a need to explain what was wrong in principle, and that task was not in their department, within the reach of their skills; it was the work of philosophers.

The sociologist Lynn Chancer, in her book *Reconcilable Differences*,[8] rather reflected the moral ambivalence of feminist writers in facing that main, philosophic question. "To negatively judge any prostitute who undertakes sex work"—as Professor Chancer calls it, shading the moral question—"is exactly as foolish" as "hastily condemn[ing] young males" who use cocaine or participate in gangs "for their techniques of survival."[9] And yet she does want to hold back from saying that this "sex work" is no different from nursing or working as a professor or a lawyer.

But she regards this "sex work" as something women do as part of their "techniques of survival." They are techniques cast upon them either by necessity, springing from their poverty; or from the patriarchal manipulation of men acting as pimps; or from the dangers of incarceration coming from its illegality; or from the want of health insurance in an occupation not usually covered with insurance plans provided by employers; or from the dangers posed by their "johns" or customers.[10] In other words, if this work is less than desirable, it is so mainly because

---

8 Lynn S. Chancer, *Reconcilable Differences: Confronting Beauty, Pornography, and the Future of Feminism* (Berkeley: University of California Press, 1998).

9 Ibid., 194.

10 Ibid., 196.

of causes beyond the control of the prostitute—by her poverty or her gendered powerlessness in relation to men—or because of the conventions that keep her occupation illegal and vulnerable to the rapine of the police. Nothing in the act of selling sex to strangers marks any wrong that might involve the act of sex itself under these conditions—sex removed from a relation of love and commitment and from its natural telos in the begetting of offspring. There is no hint that she thinks anything in this sale of sex with strangers may mark a corrupted form of love and sex.

Professor Chancer is a sociologist, and finding the ground of moral judgments does not happen to lie within her field as she understands it, though that is not a stance necessarily implied in sociology as a field seeking to understand things human. But her perspective has been shared by writers who do take philosophy as their profession. Her argument was probably approximated fairly well by Professor Alan Goldman years ago in his essay, "Plain Sex."[11] He conceded that sex enveloped by love would be handsomely amplified. That tuna casserole served up by a loving wife may have a significance well beyond its culinary virtues. But he insisted that sex could be taken as plain sex, savored for its own delights, savored quite detached from any of those attributes of love and commitment and the children who embody that merging of the partners in sex. What is central, he said, is "the immersion in the physical aspect of one's own existence and attention to the physical embodiment of the other."[12] Goldman recognized that sex can be part of a means-ends chain leading to a harm. Sex can be used to injure, not only in rape, but in many other subtle forms of wounding. But he held to the possibility that sex could be undertaken by people in evanescent relations, with eyes open, so to speak, with no expectation of commitment, and undertaken then with full innocence. What he rejected is the notion that sex has any moral implications at all. As he argued:

> [T]here are no moral implications whatever [in sex]. Any analysis of sex which imputes a moral character to sex acts in themselves is wrong for that reason. There is no morality intrinsic to sex, although

---

11 Alan H. Goldman, "Plain Sex," *Philosophy & Public Affairs* 6, no. 3 (Spring 1977): 267–87.

12 Ibid., p. 268.

> general moral rules apply to the treatment of others in sex acts as they apply to all human relations.[13]

There stands the case for "plain sex," plainly made. If we have reservations about that position, we repair to an understanding nourished by generations, and consecrated in song: that there is, after all, something notably different about sex. Something that makes it virtually impossible to detach sex in this way from any trace of moral significance. It is not that this understanding cannot be ignored or conveniently overlooked by the obtuse, but that it is no more possible to purge moral significance from sex than it is to follow Holmes in purging moral significance from the very notion of law.

I think that the entry into the problem was disclosed years ago when a group of undergraduate women at Yale demanded that rape should be regarded, in the code of student conduct, as a crime apart from others. Presumably, assaults were regarded as an offense under the statutes at Yale. If rape were nothing more than another assault—an unwarranted setting upon the body of another person—it would have been no more necessary to make any further specifications for rape than to distinguish assaults directed at the arms, say, from assaults directed at the legs. The undergraduate women must have been aware of rape as not merely a striking of the body, but an act of larger arrogance and violation. There *is* something different, after all, about the penetration, the forceful access to an intimacy reserved for someone with whom the woman has a special connection.

It may be hard to put the matter artfully, but it must be said also that this is an assault in which the assailant presumes to engage the reproductive capacity of the woman. This assault, unlike other assaults, may actually generate new life, and one does not typically engage in anything as grave as that with anyone who just happens along on the street.

It is hard to account for the revulsion that marks rape as a crime apart from others without recognizing what is different about the intimacy of sex and the portentousness of begetting new life. At the same time the revulsion would not be diminished in any way by the news that the assailant or the victim was sterile. Our understanding of the crime is formed by our awareness of the special significance and the moral import that invests the act of sex, this coupling of the bodies, even if

---

13 Ibid., p. 280.

it cannot beget offspring. That is why the moral outrage that the crime elicits is virtually indifferent to any showing that the probability of conception in rape is very slight (which it is) or that the rapist and the victim were incapable of generating children.[14] But the very same reason may also inform the traditional objections to casual sexual encounters by people who may not seem impressed with the significance that envelops the act of sex, or who are conspicuously less than awed by an inventory of consequences that truly merits their awe.

The popular understanding here is probably a more accurate guide to the nature of the problem than the ingenious offerings of social scientists. The wrong of prostitution, for example, cannot be found in any contingent reckonings about venereal disease, the stimulation of crime, or the breakup of families. It must be found in principle—in a principle, we might say, that begins with the awareness of principle itself and of beings that alone have access to the understanding of principles. The aversion to prostitution finds its proper ground in the recognition that there is something of inescapable moral significance about sex in creatures who have moral reasons for extending or withdrawing their love. This is a point curiously overlooked—the distinct nature of love in beings who are moral agents. To speak of a love that merits commitment is to speak of a love that may endure even as looks wither with age. But that is to say, this is a love that finds something enduringly admirable, enduringly worthy of respect in one's partner. And when we speak in those terms we are speaking of an enduring good, not reducible to material things; we are speaking of something of distinctly moral significance.

With that sense of things, the conceiving of children may be enveloped with a far more complicated understanding and purpose than the motives that inspire procreation in animals. In sum, we find creatures who treat as profoundly serious the terms of principle upon which sexual franchises are tendered, and that sense is shared, ironically, even by the people who seek their sexual freedom by denying

---

14 That point also works to counter the most important argument put forth in defense of same-sex marriage: That marriage cannot find its principal rationale as a framework for the begetting of children, for many married couples are incapable of bringing forth children. There is a significance that still attaches to the union of bodies between men and women, paired in nature for reproduction; a significance that cannot be replicated in the relations of two men or two women. There is, in the case of men and women, a correspondence between the uniting of the bodies and that *telos*, or purpose, of sexuality in bringing forth new life, embodying the marriage or merging of the man and the woman, united in the sexual embrace. But on that, more at another time.

any grounds for judging acts of sex. For something seems to make this matter, for everyone, a matter of central, not peripheral, importance.

The notion of a "commitment" marks another nexus between the law and moral judgment. I find my students speaking loosely about being in a "committed" relationship with their girlfriends or boyfriends, when all they mean is that they are "going steady" with each other. But that is quite different from a commitment made serious in the law. That sense of a commitment may be grasped even by the child, who somehow has an awareness that his parents have foregone the freedom to quit their association with him—or with each other—as it suits their convenience. There is only one kind of creature who can understand the notion of a commitment, or the idea of a principle or a "law," that may compel his respect and obedience even when It runs counter to his interests and inclinations. As Maggie Gallagher said, in a line I've often quoted, "it is not free love but the vow that is daring. To dare to pledge our whole selves to a single love is the most remarkable thing most of us will ever do."[15] Only human beings, beings with a moral judgment, can do such a thing; only human beings can understand a love woven with those moral meanings. Prostitution distinctly mocks that kind of love, or the kind of love and commitment that provides the distinct and necessary setting for sex—if sex is understood with its full seriousness, and not made trivial by being reduced to another form of recreation, such as tennis or bridge.

Alan Goldman conceded that there was something about love that made a logical claim to monogamy or exclusiveness, but he argued that no such meaning attached to sex. Roger Scruton has pointed out that there is something about love that demands exclusivity and removes it from relations that are fungible—but he has not seen a division in that respect between love and sex. And so, for example, we could imagine someone saying to a friend, "I had a date to play tennis with Fred this week, or bridge with the Johnsons, but I can't go. Would you take my place playing tennis with Fred or bridge with the Johnsons?" But we would react differently, I think, if someone said, "Look, I was supposed to have sex with Louise this weekend—could you go in my place?" The fact that the laugh comes from liberals as well as conservatives may suggest that there is something in the *nature of the thing* that strikes us instantly as inapt, not merely our conventions and political alignments.

---

15 Maggie Gallagher, *The Abolition of Marriage: How We Destroy Lasting Love* (Washington, D.C.: Regnery Publishing, Inc., 1996), 265.

I know rather sophisticated men who will speak about brothels they've known in Asia, and insist that men can visit brothels as they visit barbers, without undermining in any way their love for their wives and families. But nothing in that affectation of "realism" alters the point that prostitution mocks the kind of sex that is enveloped with love and commitment; the kind of sex and commitment that mark the character of "the family." I have found that a sophisticated fellow, so flippant about the matter of Asian brothels, will not show any enthusiasm, or even a worldly openness to the matter, when he is asked how he would feel if his daughter, now at Yale, decided to make her career in prostitution.

Prostitution has elicited contempt over the years because it has been understood to run counter to that nature of sex and its moral meanings that seems to be understood by ordinary people as a matter of common sense. Or understood, as we might say, naturally. It is at odds in principle with that understanding of sexuality bound up with love and the family. Pornography, as writing about prostitutes, teaches the same idea, mocks the same institutions, and draws on the same wrong in principle.

It was one of Kant's insights that for every kind of activity, there is a class of those activities that we ought not choose. To put it another way, anything we could name—any thing, any activity—could be part of a means-ends chain leading in a wrongful direction. The knowledge of driving a car could be used to drive an ambulance or a getaway car for the Mafia. A pen could be used to defraud or to sign a donation to a charity. As Alan Goldman recognized, sex too can be a vehicle for harms inflicted without justification: rape, incest, adultery.

Now is it conceivable that, among all of the things in this world, only the arts—whether writing, painting, film, theater—only the arts can be entirely free of this moral significance? Every artist I know is convinced that art is freighted with moral and cultural significance—that a society with a vibrant artistic life is a better society. They seem to be convinced that the arts can elevate the tone and character of a society. But if the arts can elevate, it must follow that they can also degrade or debase; they can injure and diminish. Several years ago, a group of black aldermen in Chicago invaded an art gallery in order to remove from its walls a portrait of the late Mayor Harold Washington, pictured wearing women's underwear. It was merely paint on a canvas, and yet these aldermen apparently felt stung by that portrait. They regarded it not only as an insult to the late mayor but an insult to the black community.

The arts do convey moral meanings, and as we've long understood, the arts teach. Films, plays, and books have themes; they hold up models of behavior; they are frequently imitated in ordinary life; and so, in one way or another, they are engaged in moral instruction. If that is the case, the community can hardly be unconcerned about the things that are taught or the sensibility that is cultivated through entertainments. As Walter Berns put it, "the laws cannot remain indifferent to the manner in which men amuse themselves, or to the kinds of amusements offered them."[16] We could hardly be faulted for worrying that the spectacle of gladiators being disemboweled in a matinee in Rome may not help to cultivate a people sensitive to the hurts suffered by those around them. Several years back a reporter in the *New York Times* recalled seeing a movie in which a man with a chain saw dismembered a woman. Behind him he heard a fellow savoring the moment deeply with moans of "yeah, yeah." The reporter felt a pang of fear that he might meet this same man on the street when they left the theater. Then he recognized that this man could also be a fellow voter, someone who shares power with us over our lives together. Do we think that the pleasure offered by the entertainment helped to shape the moral sensibility of this spectator in a wholesome or less-than-wholesome way?

The judgment seems to have settled a long while ago that executions generally ought not be treated as public spectacles, and that decision cannot be explained by a simple aversion to taking the life of the prisoner. It is quite possible to support capital punishment while holding that executions should not become a new form of public entertainment. The concern, I think, is that even if an execution is justified, people should not be encouraged to cultivate a certain sadistic pleasure in watching the suffering of others.

The question, then, is just what does pornography teach, and how does it shape sensibilities? When shorn of its larger pretensions, the purpose of pornography is probably nothing more than to arouse the appetite for sex by depicting sexual acts with great variety and explicitness. It may not even be inconsistent with the character of pornography to arouse the appetite for sex in situations confined

---

16 I refer here to Walter Berns's classic essay, "Pornography vs. Democracy: The Case for Censorship," *Public Interest* no. 22 (Winter 1971): 10.

to marriage. And yet that is not the life it seeks to depict or the lessons it seeks to teach. As anyone would instantly understand, pornography conveys an ethic of liberating sex from the constraints of commitment, marriage, and even love. It does not really seek, as part of its art, to bring out with any authenticity the relations of love that add meaning to sexual intercourse. Something in its own character and dynamic push it to the portrayal and endorsement of a radically different ethic.

What is distinct to pornography is the portrayal of sexual intercourse with uncommon frequency and variety, without the restrictions of marriage, the tethers of commitment, or the ties of love. What pornography finally teaches is an eroticism detached from any love that is distinctly human—which is to say, a love that is affected by the bonds of loyalty and moral understanding that are uniquely possible in human beings. Should it then really come as a surprise that pornography so often subverts or corrodes that kind of love, turns men away from their wives and their marriages?

Well, one could argue in response, many things in the arts do not exactly bring out what is most distinct and ennobling in human love, or in anything else. And clearly, not everyone will absorb and act out the ethic conveyed in pornography. But the matter has sharpened in concern for us precisely because of the evidence that large numbers of people are getting absorbed in this culture of pornography, with some devastating effects for real people. By one recent count, pornography has become a billion-dollar business in this country—one writer put it at $20 billion. I learned recently, from a friend who is a priest, that the Catholic bishops finally delivered themselves of a statement on this problem because priests, in the confessionals, were hearing more and more about the wreckage wrought by pornography. They heard of husbands so addicted to pornography that they would stay up well into the night viewing the videos. So much so that they would be short on sleep, become laggard at work the next day, and even lose their jobs.[17] They would also make demands on their wives for a kind of performance their wives regarded as

17 These impressions have been borne out, with the addition of some precise figures, in Pamela Paul, *Pornified: How Pornography Is Damaging Our Lives, Our Relationships, and Our Families* (New York: Henry Holt and Co., 2005). Paul draws on that study in her contribution in this volume.

bizarre or demeaning. They were turning their wives into the whores who really drew their sharpest erotic interest now.[18]

Of course people have been affected by other addictions, which also have distracted them from their families and wrecked their marriages. I've heard, in that vein, of serious computer addictions, which have alienated spouses and brought on divorces. For that matter, people have been addicted to Beethoven or football (think of the "weekend widows"), or to stocks, investments, and yes, their businesses. We remind ourselves simply of an old truth, that even the most innocent of things can generate compulsions, destructive of relations in the family, if people lose a sense of scale or temperance, or the proper ordering of things. But that is strikingly different from an activity that lures people into absorbing an ethic that is in principle inimical to the understanding of that wedding of love and sex that is the defining key of marriage; an ethic that subverts the family that springs from that marriage.

It is that principle, again, that stands at the heart of the thing. In that respect, it is useful to return to the comparison to things libelous or defamatory per se. It may be impossible to establish a precise empirical connection between libelous utterances and the harms suffered by the targets of those libels. And yet the destruction of lives and reputations by libelous speech is a serious concern of the law. In the same way, it may be impossible to establish firm empirical connections between pornography and the breakup of any particular marriage. And yet none of that would establish that pornography has become any less of a proper concern of the law.

In the same vein, if we can recognize that the arts do have a moral dimension, it must be legitimate and even necessary to judge the things offered in the name of entertainment to a decent people. With the same understanding, there is nothing inscrutable about the notion that certain entertainments strike at marriage by teaching a corrupted version of human love and sexuality. When we bring these points together, we would remind ourselves of understandings settled long ago: that

---

18 We have been told now that the women in pornography view themselves as actors, not as whores, for they are not selling their sex to a customer. See Theresa Reed, "Private Acts Versus Public Art," in *Prostitution and Pornography*, ed. Jessica Spector (Stanford: Stanford University Press, 2006), 249–57. But they are willing to have sex with men they've just met, with a public viewing by strangers, outside any confines of intimacy. It is an arguable point, however: that a prostitute is willing to be recorded at work does not itself make her an actress, or make her any less a prostitute.

it is eminently reasonable to have restrictions on entertainments laced with sexuality, as it is in any other domain touched by the restraints of the law.

I saw, years go, the advertisement for one X-rated film proclaiming that "Nothing can be bad if it feels good." Blurbs may be no more than blurbs, but this particular aphorism did convey, in its root simplicity, the premises of many who have sought to defend pornography. The defenders of pornography have had to take the line that all forms of expression in the arts and politics stand essentially on the same plane of legitimacy, that there are no grounds on which to say with any truth that any one publication is more decent or noxious than another. In this view, the only principle acceptable in a democratic society is *that there are no principles* on which to say that certain interests and ideas are any more legitimate than others. But by this logic it cannot even be said that a government of law is preferable to a despotism, or that this regime of wide freedom, including sexual freedom, is in principle any better than a regime that would repress that freedom altogether. There is a rejection, in other words, of those necessary truths that a free people would be obliged to respect because they establish the premises upon which their own freedom rests.

I return in closing to the sociologist Lynn Chancer, who urged us to free ourselves from these vexing and pretentious moral judgments. She was making the case for academics to study their subjects from the inside, by working in factories, living with gangs, or working as topless dancers or prostitutes. She found herself running up against the hesitations even of other sociologists, who had long absorbed an unwillingness to cast moral judgments on others. She recalled putting out the draft of one of her chapters, and being jarred by the reactions of her colleagues in sociology and feminist studies. For they were still affected by a deep hesitancy about women acting as "sex workers" in order to give a firsthand account of the women doing this "sex work."

Professor Chancer was especially taken aback when one of her colleagues asked her whether her writing here indicated that . . . well, that she herself had worked as a prostitute. She took the question as marking a kind of unlovely schizophrenia in her colleagues. They are sophisticated people, and yet the subject of sex elicits, she says, a "defensive laugh, a nervous titter," and she encountered among these supposedly liberated people a combination of "titillation and attraction" on the one hand, and what seemed to her an indecorous desire for "distance" on the other. In other words, she found among them a certain lingering aversion to studying prostitution by working as a prostitute.

What she affected not to notice—but in affecting not to notice, drew to our notice—was that her own recoil from their reactions was triggered by that question of whether she herself had worked as a prostitute. Her own reaction may be far more telling than the nervous laugh and titters of her colleagues. The truth that dare not speak its name is that she was unsettled, slightly stung, and, it looks to me, offended by the question.

And in that instant recoil she revealed something deeply planted. My own hunch is that it was not a matter merely of conventions long absorbed. It was quite arguably a reaction springing from a natural understanding, an understanding about the rightful and wrongful character of sex, an understanding she was likely to find, not only in the academy, but in the common sense of ordinary folk, wherever she would find them, even in places more exotic, on the other side of the world. For the moral reactions are not dependent solely on conventions; they are planted more deeply, in a nature that will ever remain the same.

DESIRE AND THE TAINTED SOUL: ISLAMIC INSIGHTS INTO LUST, CHASTITY, AND LOVE

Hamza Yusuf

What is desire? In Plato's dialogue, *Philebus*, Socrates provides one answer, stating that hunger, thirst, and such appetites fall under the realm of desire. "When one becomes empty then, apparently he desires the opposite of what he is experiencing; being emptied, he longs to be filled." Desire is an attempt at filling an emptiness within us. The desire may be profound, such as a desire to know why we are here. It also may be less than profound, such as the desire to own objects that preoccupy and entertain us so that we do not have to confront that void.

The thirteenth-century poet, jurist, and theologian Rumi begins his *Mathnawi* by describing the sounds of the reed flute as mournful because they are cut off from the source. He explains that being severed from his source, man enters a mournful state, and his hollowness and emptiness sets him to find his heart's desire. The English word "desire" hints at this celestial meaning of humanity's need to reconnect with its source. "Desire" is derived from the Latin word, meaning "to long for, wish for," but it originally meant "to await what the heavens would bring." "We are star-dust / We are golden / And we've got to get ourselves / Back to the garden," sings Joni Mitchell. This essential desire to get ourselves back to the Garden of Eden is a sacred perspective of desire.

However, the world dazzles. Its myriad forms entice men and women who are seduced by its resplendent ornaments, and their pursuits and desires fragment. Some seek power, some wealth, some love, and some set their sights no higher than seeking physical pleasure. Each of these pursuits, however, is rooted in our desire for the ephemeral, which can become insatiable and destructive.

Can desires be considered right or wrong? From a modern perspective, few desires are categorized as wrong per se. In our individualistic Western societies, people are encouraged to pursue their "heart's desire," as long as they do not exploit or hurt others. Both rational ethics and religious ethics, however, distinguish quite clearly between right and wrong desires, and posit that wrong desires may result in damaging and destructive pursuits that shatter one's psychological well-being and wreak havoc on human relationships.

In wrong desire, what is desired is a partial good, yet it is desired excessively as a sole good, or it is a means to a good, but it is taken as an end in itself, or it is only an illusory good. This last reason is most pernicious and particularly pronounced in carnal desire. Shakespeare describes the state of one under the influence of illusive destructive desire in Sonnet 129:

> The expense of spirit in a waste of shame
> Is lust in action; and till action, lust
> Is perjured, murderous, bloody, full of blame,
> Savage, extreme, rude, cruel, not to trust,
> Enjoy'd no sooner but despised straight,
> Past reason hunted, and no sooner had
> Past reason hated, as a swallow'd bait
> On purpose laid to make the taker mad;
> Mad in pursuit and in possession so;
> Had, having, and in quest to have, extreme;
> A bliss in proof, and proved, a very woe;
> Before, a joy proposed; behind, a dream.
> All this the world well knows; yet none knows well
> To shun the heaven that leads men to this hell.

While Shakespeare refers to sensual lust, his words hold true for other types of lust—such as the lusts for blood, power, and wealth. For once lustful craving takes hold of one's heart, one indeed becomes "mad in pursuit and in possession so." The depths of human depravity are startling, and once we lose our balance, the fall can be long and hard, causing pain for those who witness it, and despair—even death—for the one falling.

The tainted soul

In the Islamic tradition, the root of such destructive tendencies in the pursuit of desire is the *nafs*, an Arabic word which can loosely be defined as the ego, but more appropriately as the tainted soul. This tainted soul resembles a wild animal. The untamed *nafs* is both the single most destructive force in our world and the source of our special nature and distinction among other creatures, for when refined and tempered, it can soar with the angels.

According to the Qur'an, the *nafs* has three stages: the compulsive or commanding self, the reproachful self, and the self at peace. The compulsive self is the infantile self that demands and compels one to act in pursuit of the self's desires. This lowest aspect of the self is aided by three other destructive elements: the passions, the illusory nature of the world, and an obsessive and compulsive force referred to as Satan, which according to the Prophet Muhammad, flows in the very arteries of men and women. All these poisons can be controlled and overcome by sincere human struggle, which is easier when aided by divine grace but can be achieved by anyone who engages in that struggle, regardless of faith or belief.

The most stereotypical pursuits of the *nafs* involve pleasure, wealth, fame, and power. The quest for pleasure preoccupies most of us, and the most base of pleasures are the sensual pleasures, including eating, drinking, resting, and recreation, but culminating for most people in the greatest of bodily pleasures: sex. Both moral philosophy and religion prescribe temperance as the key virtue that can contain pleasure so it remains a beneficial good and not a cause for destructive behavior.

Moral philosophers, working within the ethos of the secular, have recognized that man without virtue is worse than a brute. In *Politics*, Aristotle writes: "If he have not virtue, man is the most unholy and the most savage of all animals, and the most full of lust and gluttony."[1] Virtue, for Aristotle, was not predicated upon a belief in some divine order, but rather in the compelling argument that reason presents to the reflective person of how one should order one's life.

Religious tradition, however, is not merely concerned with a person's psychological or rational well-being, but more importantly, with the supernatural element of man, otherwise known as the soul. In the Catholic tradition, it is the soul that is at risk when a person commits a sin. Deadly sins are those that "kill the life of the soul, leaving the sinner without sanctifying grace."[2] Interestingly, in the Catholic

---

1 Aristotle, *Politics*, tr. Benjamin Jowett (1253a35-36), in Richard McKeon, ed., *The Basic Works of Aristotle* (New York: Random House, 1941), p. 1130.

2 *Modern Catholic Encyclopedia*, eds. Michael Glazier and Monika K. Hellwig (Collegeville, Minn.: Liturgical Press, 2004), 779.

formulation, the seven deadly or mortal sins are states, not actions. They relate to the will of a person, and not to any one act.

In the Catholic doctrine of purgatory, souls not sanctified in this world must be purged of their wrongs before entering Paradise; the souls are not purged of the act of sin, but rather of the stain of sin. The seven deadly sins are understood to be the matrices from which all individual acts of sin emanate. The sins themselves are distortions of the human being's desire, perversions of the direction of one's love and its ultimate object. Thus, paradoxical as it may seem, love is at the root of sinfulness.

The last sin

In Dante's *Purgatorio,* there are seven cornices (ledges or shelves) on Mount Purgatory, corresponding to the seven deadly sins. The lower part of purgatory consists of the cornices wherein the sins of love perverted (pride, envy, wrath, and sloth) are purged, the upper part of those wherein the sins of excess (avarice, gluttony, and lust) are purged. In Dante's schema, lust—the excessive love of the animal kingdom as embodied in carnality—is the last sin to be purged before one can enter the earthly paradise, symbolizing the tenacious hold that lust has on the individual. The lustful sinners are found marching through a wall of flame to purge them of the fires of their misdirected passions.

In the *Inferno,* however, lust is the least of the sins punished. Sins are divided into three categories, and the one including lust is that of incontinence, which also includes gluttony. Those lost souls condemned as a result of their lust are described as being blown about by a violent gust of wind that symbolizes the violent force of the desires that caused them to go astray. (The Arabic word for passionate desire, *hawaa,* is a direct cognate of the word for wind, '*hawa*', meaning "to fall down.")

To understand the sin of lust, one must first understand the concept of sin in the Abrahamic faiths. The English word "sin" is possibly related to a Saxon word that meant "to wander" and is an English translation of the Hebrew term *het,* which like both its Arabic and Greek counterparts—*khati'ah* in Arabic and *hamartia* in the New Testament—is originally an archery term that meant "to miss the mark," and "sin" was used in archaic English as an archery term for a miss. Sin originates in a sound attempt at achieving a good but "misses the mark" by mistaking an apparent good for a real one. Repentance is, in essence, redressing the miss and realigning one's spiritual sights for the next attempt.

The goods to which human beings, and men in particular, aim are referred to in the Qur'an as pleasure, wealth, and power. "Made to seem pleasing to humanity is love of desires for mates [pleasure] and children [power], and heaps and hoards of gold and silver [wealth], domesticated horses, and cattle, and fields [wealth and power]. Those are the conveniences and enjoyments for the life of the world, while the finest resort is the presence of God" (3:14).

In other words, pleasure, wealth, and power are means, not ends. The true end is ultimate concern. The pursuit of these attractive goods as ends can lead to despair for those who attempt to create meaning out of their pursuit. Shakespeare's *Macbeth*, whose blind pursuit of power leads him to the abyss of despair, ends his life concluding that he is a mere shadow, without substance, trapped in a "tale told by an idiot, full of sound and fury, signifying nothing."

Like Macbeth's pursuit of power, revealed to him in the end as empty, the lust-driven pursuit of bodily pleasures is another attempt at sustaining one's meaning for the time being. Lust was referred to as the sin of *luxuria* in Latin. From it, comes our English word "luxury," but the Latin meaning is closer to exuberance, or superfluous abundance. Lust is only possible with animal spirits and with vitality.

In her essay on the deadly sins, Dorothy Sayers identifies two main reasons people are susceptible to the sin of *luxuria*: "It may be through sheer exuberance of animal spirits: in which case a sharp application of the curb may be all that is needed to bring the body into subjection and remind it of its proper place in the scheme of man's twofold nature. Or—and this commonly happens in periods of disillusionment like our own, when philosophies are bankrupt and life appears without hope—men and women may turn to lust in sheer boredom and discontent, trying to find in it some stimulus which is not provided by the drab discomfort of their mental and physical surroundings."

When this is the cause of lust, she continues,

> stern rebukes and restrictions are worse than useless. It is as though one were to endeavor to cure anemia by bleeding; it only reduces further an already impoverished vitality. The mournful and medical aspect of twentieth century pornography and promiscuity strongly suggests that we have reached one of these periods of spiritual depression, where people go to bed because they have nothing better to do. In other words, the "regrettable moral laxity" of which

> respectable people complain may have its root cause not in *Luxuria* at all, but in some other of the sins of society, and may automatically begin to cure itself when that root cause is removed.[3]

Is the "root cause" of the sins of incontinence—the "hot sins" like lust and gluttony—simply boredom? Kierkegaard believed that man's inability to find any real meaning in life resulted in an indifference, a cynicism, and a boredom with it. The aesthete, who believes he is leading a life in pursuit of pleasure, exemplifies the nihilistic malaise of the modern age. The aesthete's hedonistic life is rooted in his boredom. The irony is that the things he finds to entertain and distract him from his boredom soon become the very sources of boredom: "The boredom that comes later is usually the fruit of a misguided diversion. It seems doubtful that a remedy against boredom can give rise to boredom, but it can give rise to boredom only insofar as it is used incorrectly."

In *Pornified,* an excellent study on the insidiousness of pornography, Pamela Paul arrives at a similar conclusion: "So many women and all so easy; a man tends to gorge. And once he's seen a thousand bare bottoms—no matter the variety of form and function—they start to look the same. Men pummel through woman after woman, plunging into an inevitable cycle of diminishing returns." She quotes one study of men who were shown pornographic films five days a week for ninety minutes each time, who became less interested in and aroused by the material. "What initially thrills eventually titillates, what excites eventually pleases, what pleases eventually satisfies. And satisfaction sooner or later yields to boredom."[4]

This is the inevitable state of the aesthete who lives for pleasure. He seeks pleasure to remedy his boredom, yet the very thing he seeks as a remedy becomes a source of his spiritual ailment once again.

Consciously or not, the hot sins of gluttony, lust, and avarice are rooted in attempts to address one's spiritual vacuum. Each begins with the pursuit of real goods, but not correctly as the means to real happiness that comes from an integrated ethical life rooted in virtue and responsibility. Rather, they are an end in themselves, the pursuit of pleasure for pleasure's sake. Eating not to live, but living to eat; loving

---

3 Dorothy L. Sayers, *Creed or Chaos* (Manchester, N.H.: Sophia Institute Press, 1949), 121–22.

4 Pamela Paul, *Pornified: How Pornography Is Damaging Our Lives, Our Relationships, and Our Families* (New York: Henry Holt and Co., 2005), 83.

not to give, but lusting to take; accumulating wealth not to support, but to create a false sense of security. In short, they are sins driven by emptiness within, mere distractions to avoid confronting a lack of knowledge of life's purpose and relevance.

Choice, anxiety, and ennui

Ibn Hazm (d. 1064), the great ethicist and theologian of Muslim Andalusia, believed that at the core of the human being was dread, that every action was an attempt to ward off anxiety: "Thus the seeker of wealth in fact seeks to repel through it the anxiety of poverty; the seeker of fame is primarily concerned to repel the anxiety of subordination or subservience; the seeker of pleasure simply wishes to repel the anxiety of missing its enjoyment."[5] We hear an echo in Kierkegaard's observation that the seeker of pleasure is attempting to repel boredom, because boredom seeks to repel the state of ennui in which we face our mortality and irrelevance. "Choosing" the hedonistic life of an aesthete is not a choice, but an abstention of choice.

This is profoundly consistent with Islam's doctrine of freewill, a doctrine embedded in the Arabic language itself. "To choose" in Arabic is *akhtaara,* and "choice" is *ikhtiyaar*. The tri-radical source of the word is *khayr,* which means "good." The verbal form *ikhtaara* literally means "to choose good for oneself." Choice is the act of *choosing what is good.*

Sayyid Naquib al-Attas, the contemporary Malay philosopher, persuasively connects the notion of choice to the idea of freedom. "The choice that is meant in *ikhtiyaar* is the choice of what is good, better, or best between the two alternatives," and thus "A choice of what is bad of two alternatives is therefore not a choice that can be called *ikhtiyaar;* in fact it is not a choice, rather it is an act of injustice done to oneself." Freedom, he writes,

> is to act as one's real and true nature demands—that is, one's *haqq* [truth] and one's *fitrah* [original nature] demands—and so only the exercise of that choice which is of what is good can properly be called a "free choice." A choice for the better is therefore an act of freedom, and it is also an act of justice done to oneself. It presupposes a knowledge of good and evil, of virtues and vices; whereas a choice

---

5 Majid Fakhry, *Ethical Theories in Islam* (New York: Leiden, 1991), 170.

> for the worse is not a choice as it is grounded upon ignorance urged on by the instigation of the soul that inclines toward the blameworthy aspects of the animal powers; it is then also not an exercise of freedom because freedom means precisely being free of domination by the powers of the soul that incites to evil.[6]

This enslavement to the inciting self is entirely ignored in our public discussions about freedom. Moral freedom, the freedom to act prudently and virtuously, is dismissed in any discussion of freedom in the modern context of political and circumstantial freedom. Destructive moral dissolution, which was once rightly termed licentiousness, is now considered a type of freedom. According to the Qur'an, these destructive tendencies are a result of the dominance of the commanding self, infantile and domineering, in its unrestrained state.

The fourteenth-century Egyptian poet, Imam al-Busiri, cautions against letting desire take charge of one's self:

> *Do not attempt to break its appetites through wanton indulgence*
> *Notice how food only strengthens the glutton's craving.*
>
> *The self is like an infant—if you leave it, it will grow up loving to suckle,*
> *But if you wean it, soon it will lose its desire for the breast.*
>
> *Divert the self's desires and avoid empowering it—*
> *Whenever desire takes charge, it either destroys or defiles.*
>
> *Shepherd over it as it grazes freely in the field of actions,*
> *But should it find the pasturage sweet, restrain its casual roaming.*
>
> *How often it has found some deadly pleasure delightful,*
> *Not knowing that poison lies hidden in cream!*
>
> *Be on guard against its traps of hunger and satiety—*
> *An empty stomach can be worse than a full one.*[7]

---

6 Syed Muhammad Naquib Al-Attas, *Prolegomena to the Metaphysics of Islam: An Exposition of the Fundamental Worldview of Islam* (Kaula Lumpur, Malaysia: ISTAC, 1995), 33.

7 *The Burda of Al-Busiri*, trans. Hamza Yusuf (Essex, U.K.: Sandala Ltd., 2002), 6.

The wantonness and self-centered nature of the aesthete prevents him from having any mature relationships; others are merely toys in his pursuit of infantile self-gratification, and he is quite literally a "playboy." Kierkegaard wisely identified the aesthete as being on a continuum of pleasure—from the crude plebian pleasures of the brutish class to the rarified genteel pursuits of the elite, but whether the pleasure is Oprah or the opera, the sundry indulgences of humanity find the matrix of their pursuits in the self and its desires.

Kierkegaard believed that each of us is confronted with a choice—an "Either/Or" choice either to renounce our free will and to choose not to choose in our pursuit of pleasure, or to embrace our true self and pursue not pleasure but the ethical life of virtue, which is rooted in commitment to others.[8]

In choosing the ethical life, one does not renounce pleasure. It simply becomes meaningful in ways unimaginable to the aesthete. Kierkegaard writes, "I am no ethical rigorist, enthusiastic about a formal, abstract freedom. If only the choice is posited, all the esthetic returns, and you will see that only thereby does existence become beautiful and that this is the only way a person can save his soul and win the whole world, can use the world without misusing it."[9]

The pleasure monger can only misuse the world because he takes as means other people who should be seen as ends unto themselves. He exploits them for his pleasure or participates in their exploitation by feeding the machine that is exploiting them. The ethical person, on the other hand, is transparent to himself and hence to others. Kierkegaard states, "The person who lives ethically has seen himself, knows himself, penetrates his whole concretion with his consciousness, does not allow vague thoughts to rustle around inside him or let tempting possibilities distract him with their juggling; he is not like a magic picture that shifts from one thing to another, all depending on how one shifts and turns it."[10] He can now develop in his life "the personal, the civic, the religious virtues, and his life advances through his continually translating himself from one stage to another."[11]

---

8 Søren Kierkegaard, *Either/Or: A Fragment of Life* (London: Penguin Books, 1992), 76.
9 Ibid.
10 Ibid., 81.
11 Ibid., 82.

Moderation and pleasure

This ethical life is the life of the second stage of the soul known in the Qur'an as the reproachful self. It is an introspective self that does not commit wrongs willfully but always strives to do what is right, and if the self gets the better of a person in this stage, he or she feels remorse and redresses the wrong. The ethical person may lust but will struggle against that impulse and, more importantly, will not "love to lust." Commenting on the Qur'anic verse, "Made to appear good to humanity is love of pleasure from spouses, children" (3:14), Fakhr al-Deen al-Raazi distinguishes physical and spiritual desire.

> [O]ne's desire for bodily pleasures is something the self is naturally inclined toward and is a fixed faculty of the human, whereas his inclinations to spiritual delights come as a result of short-lived epiphanies that dissipate with the least of causes. Hence, it is of no surprise that the majority of people have extreme predilections toward bodily pleasures. As for spiritual predilections that only occurs among unusual people and only for periods that are limited in their duration. For this reason, God said, "*Made to appear good to humanity is love of pleasure.*"[12]

While these pleasures are not intrinsically negative, they become so with immoderate indulgence. Moderation is the route to an ethical life that results in happiness. Extremes on either side of the golden mean are physically, emotionally, mentally, and spiritually harmful. Both moral philosophy and religion warn of the dangers of intemperance, as expressed in gluttony, drug abuse, sexuality, and other wanton behavior. Sidi Ahmad Zarruq, the fifteenth-century scholar and Sufi master, says, "The self by its nature is inclined toward extremism in both guidance and deviance."

Admittedly, religion has too often been sexually repressive. Shame-based efforts to restrain licentious behavior end up failing if the behavior can be hidden from public view. The anonymity and privacy afforded by modern technology enables people to pursue their pleasures without fear of exposure and subsequent shame. But

---

12 Fakhr al-Deen al-Raazi, *al-Tafsir al-Kabir* (Beirut, Lebanon: Dar al-Kutub al-'Ilmiyyah, 1990), 7–8, 10.

both religion and a commitment to an ethical life outside of religion can effectively address the problem for many individuals struggling to keep their lust in check.

Commitment is the ground of ethics. It is a daily struggle to be committed, to not succumb to solipsistic egoism. Chastity, which is too often conflated with prudery, is not abstinence from sex but the ethical regulation of it. As St. Thomas Aquinas stated: "It belongs to chastity that man may make a moderate use of bodily members in accordance with the judgment of his reason and the choice of his will."[13] Of profound importance for the well-being of men and women is the move beyond lust into the realm of love, which binds one person to another, as he or she is bound to oneself. Love is the gravitational force that holds families together and sustains even the commonweal.

Lust, on the other hand, is merely self-gratification. It is devoid of ethical responsibilities or a commitment to another. Dante finds the penitents on the seventh cornice recalling the great acts of lust past:

> "Sodom and Gomorrah," the new souls cry.
> And the others: "Pasiphae enters the cow
> to call the young bull to her lechery."

The reference to Pasiphae comes from Greek mythology. The god Poseidon sends Minos a bull as a gift for sacrifice, but Minos adds it to his herd of bulls. In revenge, Poseidon makes Minos' wife Pasiphae fall in love with the bull. She conceals herself inside the effigy of a cow so the bull can mount her. The result is the Minotaur, half bull, half human. Lust gives birth to monsters.[14]

Chastity and commitment

True love—not the bestial "love" of lust—is the desire to give pleasure to the other as well as receive it, the former being generally the stronger desire. But acts of betrayal can destroy love; it is chastity that enables one to ethically commit to another without the destructive element of betrayal. While many traditional cultures are seen as patriarchal cultures in which marital taboos maintain male dominance, the reality is quite

---

13 Thomas Aquinas, *Summa Theologica II-II*, Q.151, Art. 1. 15.

14 Described in John Ciardi's commentary in Dante Alighieri's *Inferno* (New York: The Modern Library, 1996), 279, 284.

the opposite: curtailing men's lust by commitment to the marriage bed is the victory of distinctly female virtue over male nature. In their book *Brain Sex*, Anne Moir and David Jessel argue that:

> While men are turned on by glossily reproduced pubic regions of impersonal pin-ups, women achieve moderate erotic stimulation from something very different—the imagination of a sexual relationship. Just as they are more likely to be aroused by the pornographic depiction of a couple coupling, they find gratification in the bodice-ripping romances of popular fiction, which have an overwhelmingly female readership. . . . Men want sex, and women want relationships. Men want flesh, and women want love. Just as the boys wanted the balloons, toys and carburetors, the girls have always wanted contact, and communion, and company.[15]

While as a result of the women's movement in the past forty years ground has been undeniably gained in the necessary rights of women leading to a more just society, there also has been a downside. The sexual freedom that has accompanied the newfound rights has had a tragic side effect that victimizes women. The predominately male characteristics of sex without love, pleasure without commitment, and desire for women without inhibitions have overturned the more communitarian female virtues of loving commitment, meaningful sex, and modest social proprieties that engender respect of the opposite sex.

Chastity, while far too often perceived as an antiquated "woman's virtue," has been a steadfast guardian of human well-being and an effective restraint from falling into the potentially bottomless pit of lust and wantonness. But human beings ultimately find more satisfaction from ethical, intellectual, and spiritual awakenings than they do from sensual awakenings, especially when they are experienced within the nexus of moderation, virtue, and love. We often associate appetites with base instincts and neglect the very real rational and spiritual appetites of human beings.

---

15 Anne Moir and David Jessel, *Brain Sex: The Real Difference Between Men and Women* (New York: Delta, 1991), 107.

When pure lust is served, the venues for intellectual and spiritual pleasure are often blocked. It is chastity that regulates one's sexual desire, enabling one to explore the other necessary aspects of life that afford a fully human experience.

Chastity in the Islamic tradition is, as in the Hellenistic and Christian tradition, seen as one of the four cardinal virtues, where it is usually called temperance, and one that protected the individual from his own destructive inclinations as well as the community from moral disintegration caused by licentiousness. And while Muslim society was notably far more sensual than European Christian culture, the religious elite was constantly lashing out at the loose morals of many of the Muslim societies throughout their fourteen hundred years.

Imam al-Ghazali, an influence on Aquinas and perhaps the single greatest Muslim religious thinker, says: "The virtue of chastity concerns the control of one's bodily appetites and sexual desires. It is in order to insure the self's subordination to its rational component so that its enjoyment or restraint is in accordance with one's intelligence. It is a moderate position between licentiousness and lack of desire. Wantonness is excessive sexual appetite and extreme pursuits of pleasure that the rational component rejects and forbids." Thus, he continues,

> it is necessary that a man is vigilant about his appetites, as the majority of men err on the side of excessiveness, especially when it comes to the genitals and the stomach, not to mention money, power, and fame. Excess and deficiency are both blameworthy in regards to chastity. . . . The desire for sexual intercourse is natural in order that the species is compelled to procreate and to ensure the survival of the species. Hence it is sought after for two reasons—to have children and to remain chaste in the marital bond—and not simply for pastime and pleasure. And when one does seek enjoyment and sensual pleasure from the act, it is in order to ensure the maintenance of mutual love and affection to keep the bond of marriage strong through sexual pleasure.[16]

16 Abu Hamid al-Ghazali, *Mizaan al-'Amal* (Egypt: Dar al-Ma'arif, n.d.), 269–70.

Al-Ghazali goes on to explain that the inculcation of modesty is essential to a chaste society. Modesty is not the same as an excessive shyness or prudery that prevents people from fully participating in life; rather, it is a sense of shame in relation to blameworthy traits that are rationally discernable and not simply societal norms that pass themselves off as universal morality. Modesty concerning sexual matters is deeply natural to the human being, but it can be stripped off a person, and films and visual media are unprecedented means to that end.

The universal idea that sexuality is something best performed in the dark or behind closed doors is not limited to prudish Puritans or priggish busybodies who, like "Old lady judges watch people in pairs / Limited in sex they dare / To push fake morals, insult and stare,"[17] but is assumed by decent people who recognize the threat that a sexualized culture presents to both children and people committed to marriage. The notion that viewing people in heightened states of pleasure is natural is a view pushed by pornographers and their victims. In reality, it is quite alien to most people around the world—the reason that, until recently, it was limited to the dark recesses of the peep show or the windowless sex shops found in the sleaziest parts of a city. "Voyeurism" is a pejorative word in English, and yet pornography is essentially just that.

The self at peace

It is now worth examining a mystical perspective that celebrates the third and final stage of a human's spiritual development, designated in the Qur'an as the self at peace. This is also Kierkegaard's third and most celestial life, the religious life.

Both Christianity and Islam share the concept of the Beatific Vision: "Blessed are the pure at heart, for they shall see God" (Matthew 5:8). Maintaining the heart's purity is a particular focus of the Abrahamic faiths. The Qur'an says, "On the Day of Judgment, nothing will avail a person, neither wealth nor children, only a pure heart" (26: 88-89). Purity of heart is a birthright. The innocence of children is celebrated everywhere and that is precisely why, of all the heinous and dark crimes of men, none elicits more revulsion than pedophilia, which defiles a child's innocence. We know that children must lose their sexual innocence eventually, but every decent parent's desire is that it takes place in adulthood with mutual love and respect.

---

17 Bob Dylan, "It's Alright, Ma (I'm Only Bleeding)," Columbia Records, 1965.

Lust is a manifestation of the Eros impulse that Sigmund Freud rightly identified as the great force of life that opposes our death instinct. When channeled into the pure love of another, it becomes life-affirming, enabling us to experience that person at the deepest and most intimate level with absolute presence in the moment.

It is in the present that we can love and experience the divine in that love. The purity of that love is sustained by presence and destroyed by desiring something else at the time, whether it be another lover or simply the onanistic self-pleasure provided by an objectified human. Simone Weil wrote:

> Every desire for enjoyment belongs to the future and the world of illusion, whereas if we desire only that a being should exist, he exists: what more is there to desire? The beloved being is then naked and real, not veiled by an imaginary future. . . . Thus in love there is chastity or lack of chastity according to whether the desire is or is not directed towards the future.[18]

Chastity of the Eyes

According to Islamic and Christian tradition, the single most corrupting inroad into the heart is through the "concupiscence of the eye." Not for nothing does the Holy Scripture name it among the three powers which constitute the world that "lieth in the power of evil" (1 John 2, 16; 5, 19). It reaches the extremes of its destructive power when it builds itself a world according to its own image and likeness. The destructiveness of this disorder lies in the fact that it stifles man's primitive power of perceiving reality; it makes man incapable not only of coming to himself but also of reaching reality and truth.

If such an illusory world threatens to overgrow and smother the world of real things, then to restrain the natural wish to see takes on the character of a measure of self-protection and self-defense.[19] The Arabic word for "eye" is "*'ayn,*" which also means "wellspring" and "essence." The word for pupil is "*insaan,*" which also means

---

18 This is quoted in Andre Comte-Sponville, *Small Treatise on the Great Virtues* (New York: Metropolitan Books, 2001), 180.

19 Josef Pieper, *The Four Cardinal Virtues* (Notre Dame, Ind.: University of Notre Dame, 1966), 201–2.

"human being." Hence, the eye is reflective of the essence of the human being, and its center is the pupil, created to witness the beauty of this world and gaze upon the beatific vision of the next. We are creatures designed to witness and reflect. The pupil constricts with worldly light and dilates in darkness and when stimulated by pleasure.

We live in a visual culture; never before has humanity been so threatened by the devastating effects of concupiscence of the eyes. It is an appetite that desires not to perceive, but simply to be excited. "What this seeing strives for is not to attain knowledge and to become cognizant of the truth, but for possibilities of relinquishing oneself to the world," writes Martin Heidegger in *Being and Time*.

Chastity of the eyes is the single most difficult form. Far easier is it for a man to abstain from an illicit physical encounter with a woman than to raise his gaze from her exposed cleavage. Yet according to the teaching of the Prophets, this too is adultery of the heart; its perniciousness is perhaps of a lesser degree, but its effects on the soul are, over time, potentially devastating. Add to natural desire the artificial exposure to images of naked forms on the computer and pictures of semi-clad men and women that bombard us from billboards and magazine covers on checkout-line shelves. Such stimuli are so overwhelming that our culture's capacity to continue to generate real meaning is threatened.

Society's eyes are under assault, and that means our hearts are as well. The Qur'an advises men and women to lower their gaze when exposed to the opposite sex and attraction is felt: "Tell the believing men to lower their gaze and guard their chastity; that is purer for their hearts, and God is aware of what they do. And say to the believing women that they too should lower their gaze and guard their modesty; they should not display their beauty and ornaments except what ordinarily appears" (24:30). Imam al-Ghazali says that lust[20]

> is nothing but a wellspring of excessive sexual desire, and is the disease of an empty and unconcerned heart. One should be on one's guard against its preliminaries by abstaining from repeated glances

---

20 Although Dr. Timothy Winter's translation of the Arabic text "'ishq" is "amorous passion," I prefer to use the word "lust," as that is clearly what al-Ghazali is referring to.

> and thoughts. Otherwise it will take firm hold of one and be difficult to shake off.[21]

The "repeated glances" al-Ghazali speaks of were in eleventh-century Iraq, a society extremely conservative in dress and behavior. The current crisis of image overload far more easily corrodes the spiritual potential of a person. Any serious attempts at meditation, prayer, or even leisurely reading are affected by the images that have been allowed into the heart through the inroad of the eyes.

Woman the apotheosis

In Islamic tradition, women have always been associated with the divine. Women are an apotheosis of divine mercy in the world, particularly embodied in the mother. The Prophet Muhammad said, "No one degrades women except vile and contemptible men." Rumi says in his *Mathnawi*: "God has made [woman] attractive, so how can men escape from her? . . . The Prophet, to whose speech the whole world was enslaved, used to say, 'Speak to me, oh 'Aishah!'" The Prophet said that "women totally dominate men of intellect and possessors of heart, but ignorant men dominate women, for they are shackled by the ferocity of animals. They have no kindness, gentleness, or love, since animality dominates their nature. Love and kindness are human attributes, anger and sensuality belong to the animals. She is the radiance of God, she is not your beloved. She is the Creator—you could say she is not created."[22]

The thirteenth-century Spanish scholar, philosopher, and mystic Ibn Arabi considered the most perfect contemplation of the divine in the world to be women. He writes of women as "the Universal Nature is to God in which He revealed the forms of the Cosmos by directing toward it the divine will and command, which, at the level of elemental forms, is symbolized by copulation." He continues:

---

21 Imam al-Ghazali, *Disciplining the Soul and Breaking the Two Desires*, trans. Dr. Timothy Winter (Cambridge, U.K.: Islamic Texts Society, 1995), 169.

22 William C. Chittick, *The Sufi Path of Love: The Spiritual Teachings of Rumi* (Albany: State University of New York Press, 1983), 169.

> Whoever loves a woman in this way loves with divine love, while he whose love for them is limited to natural lust lacks all true knowledge of that desire. For such a one she is mere form, devoid of spirit, and even though that form is indeed imbued with spirit, it is absent for one who approaches his wife or some other woman solely to have his pleasure with her, without realizing whose the pleasure really is. Thus he does not know himself truly, just as a stranger is not known until he reveals his identity. As they say: They are right in supposing that I am in love, only they know not with whom I am in love. Such a man is really in love with pleasure itself and, in consequence, loves its repository in women, the real truth and meaning of the act being lost on him. If he knew the truth, he would know whom it is he is enjoying and who it is who is the enjoyer; then would he be perfected.[23]

In our Western tradition, William Blake wonderfully expresses a glimpse of this same meaning: "The pride of the peacock is the glory of God/The lust of the goat is the bounty of God/The wrath of the lion is the wisdom of God/The nakedness of woman is the work of God." Chastity and purity always have been the great virtues that come naturally to women but that men must learn. The Qur'an uses Mary, the mother of Christ, as the great paragon of chastity and purity of the heart and describes her as an ideal. "And God has made an example for those who believe of Mary who guarded her chastity, so We breathed some of Our spirit into her, and she confirmed the pronouncements and the scriptures of her Lord, and she was among the devout" (66: 11-12).

It is from women then, that men learn chastity and purity, which in turn protect the sacred nature of women, alluded to in the Arabic word for woman, *hurmah,* which means "what is sacred." Now, the failure of men in imitating women in their natural virtue has resulted in women rejecting the double standard and imitating men in their natural vice. The spiritual power of women is great, but so too is

---

23 I Ibn 'Arabi, *The Bezels of Wisdom,* trans. Ralph W. J. Austin (Lahore, Pakistan: Suhail Academy, 1999), 275–78. I altered some wording based upon my Arabic edition of *Fusus al-Hikam, Ibn 'Arabi. Dar al-Kutub al-'Ilmiyyah* (Beirut, Lebanon: 2004), 515–18.

the power of their physical attraction to men. It is this power that causes vile men to want to dominate women, and virtuous men to honor and protect them.

But that physical power of the female form over men is a sensory power that veils men from her metaphysical meaning. Her sensual form prevents the man lost in carnality from knowing her spiritual reality, that she is the source of mercy in the world. The Arabic and Hebrew word for womb (*rahm*) is derived from the word for mercy (*rahma*) and an expression of the creative power of God in man. In degrading woman, we degrade the highest qualities of our human nature; in elevating her, we elevate our highest nature. When her natural virtues—compassion, kindness, caring, selflessness, and love—predominate in men, men are able to overcome their natural vices and realize their full humanity. When, however, those virtues are absent, men descend to the lowest of the low and are worse than beasts.

In unveiling the outward beauty of a woman, we become veiled from her inward beauty. As a poet from the distant past wrote: "I said to my rose-cheeked lovely, 'O you with bud-like mouth, Why keep hiding your face, like flirting girls?' She laughed and said, 'Unlike the beauties of your world, In the veil I'm seen, but without it I'm hidden.'"

PART THREE: DILEMMAS OF LAW AND POLICY

FREEDOM, VIRTUE, AND THE POLITICS OF REGULATING PORNOGRAPHY

James R. Stoner, Jr.

The politics of regulating pornography in the United States is, like so much else in America, complicated by our constitutionalism. Ours is not a parliamentary democracy where a policy decided upon by the cabinet is made into law, though even that would be complicated to analyze, involving a fluid mix of ideas, interests, politics, and personalities in the formation of the policy, however straightforward its enactment. All of these elements are at play in the American context, too, of course, but the constitutional structure of our institutions and the judicial enforcement of constitutional rights add other dimensions.

In the first place, federalism means that policies that touch upon both state and national interests involve governmental institutions at both levels, often in interlocking ways. The regulation of pornography originally fell within what was known as the police power of the states—that is, the general power of government to regulate society to secure health, safety, and morals, with education sometimes also mentioned—and thus involved the federal government only indirectly, through its power to regulate commerce or to deliver the mail.

But in the second place, since the middle of the twentieth century, the freedom of speech and press clauses of the First Amendment have been interpreted to protect communication that the law once suppressed as obscene or pornographic, so that, thanks to the doctrine of "incorporation" which applies the First Amendment to the states, the federal courts have become in many instances the final arbiters of what is and what is not allowed in the control of pornography throughout the land. As scholars increasingly agree, the role of courts in establishing constitutional limits should be analyzed as involving not their review of abstract doctrine but what is now called constitutional politics.[1] Any account of policymaking in an area that in some way touches constitutional issues has to include the courts as players, but also recognize that, though they often hold the trump, they do not hold all the cards.

In this overview of the politics of pornography and its regulation, I will begin by discussing American policy over the course of the last century and a half, as well as the technological developments that have made pornography a moving target and its regulation a repeated challenge, adding a quick review of First Amendment constitutional law. Then I will outline the various ideas and interests that have influenced the development of pornography regulation in recent years. Next I will turn to examine an innovative but ultimately unsuccessful attempt in the 1980s to develop a new rationale in favor of regulation, a new mode of regulating, and a new coalition of support, drawing on Donald Downs' study, *The New Politics of Pornography*.[2] In conclusion I will consider what lessons might be learned from this experience for the issue of regulating pornography in the age of the internet and in light of advanced scientific understanding of pornography's social costs.

Regulation of pornography

The term "pornography" in English has been dated only to the mid-nineteenth century, when it seems to have been borrowed from the French or coined from the ancient Greek, meaning, literally, "writing (or drawing) about prostitutes."[3] "Obscenity" is an older English word, taken from the Latin, where it meant more or less the same as it did for us, at least before the federal courts seized the word: "offensive, foul, loathsome, disgusting."[4]

Known in the West from the ancient world through the poetry of Ovid and Juvenal among others, as well as access to some ancient Eastern texts, and

---

1 See Robert P. George and Sotirios Barber, *Constitutional Politics: Essays on Constitution Making, Maintenance, and Change* (Princeton, N.J.: Princeton University Press, 2001), which defines constitutional politics as "the normative, conceptual, and empirical study of *constitution making, constitution maintenance*, and deliberate *constitutional change* as aspects of a distinct form of political activity."

2 Donald Alexander Downs, *The New Politics of Pornography* (Chicago: University of Chicago Press, 1989).

3 Walter Kendrick, *The Secret Museum: Pornography in Modern Culture* (Berkeley: University of California Press, 1987), 1–32; *Oxford English Dictionary*, 2nd ed., s.v. "Pornography."

4 *Webster's New International Dictionary*, 2nd ed., s.v. "Obscene."

rediscovered in pictorial form with the excavation of Pompeii, the artistic depiction of human sexuality seems to have been a preserve of the upper classes, controlled, if at all, by Church scrutiny or social disapproval but not subject to temporal law, or at any rate to recorded legal action. The first common law prosecution for obscenity in England appears in the early eighteenth century, and only in 1857 in Lord Campbell's Act (the Obscene Publications Act), did Parliament give magistrates statutory authority to destroy obscenity in print.[5]

Though in the states distribution of obscene materials was contrary to common law and sometimes to statutes since Colonial times, the first federal prohibition came in the Tariff Act of 1842, which forbad importation of "all indecent and obscene prints, paintings, lithographs, engravings, and transparencies." This was broadened in 1856 to include the new technology of photography. As a result of an apparent growth in domestic traffic to meet the demand of the troops in the Civil War and at the request of the Post Office, in 1865 Congress made it a misdemeanor to "knowingly" mail any "publication of a vulgar and indecent character."

Eight years later, at the instigation of Civil War veteran and recent founder of the New York Society for the Suppression of Vice, Anthony Comstock, Congress extended the prohibition to include mailing information about abortion and artificial birth control (activities which were illegal in the states), punished receiving obscene mail as well as sending it, multiplied the maximum fine by a factor of ten to $5,000, added the possibility of imprisonment, allowed penalties to be doubled for repeat offenders, and strengthened the enforcement powers of federal judges. A petition effort to repeal the statute a few years later was rebuffed, and by the 1880s Comstock himself had been appointed special agent in charge of its enforcement by the Postmaster General, though for most of his career he was paid by his Society, itself funded by leading businessmen in New York.[6]

If passage of the Comstock Act can be seen as the result of the rise of the technology of mass printing and efficient dissemination, subsequent legislation responded to new technologies in turn. Motion pictures brought forth numerous state boards responsible for film censorship, whose authority was upheld by the US

---

5 Harford Montgomery Hyde, *A History of Pornography* (London: Heinemann, 1964), 12.

6 Gaines M. Foster, *Moral Reconstruction: Christian Lobbyists and the Federal Legislation of Morality, 1865–1920* (Chapel Hill: University of North Carolina Press, 2002), 13, 48, 52, 54.

Supreme Court against a First Amendment challenge in 1915.[7] The movie industry successfully headed off an outcry for federal regulation in 1922 by hiring Postmaster General William Harrison Hays as their public relations agent. He oversaw the development of a system of self-enforced standards, codified in 1934 and applied to almost every movie distributed in the United States for over twenty years, that renounced nudity and the favorable depiction of immorality in American-made films. The system was gradually eroded in the 1950s and the 1960s and replaced by the current rating system, still a self-imposed industry standard rather than a government regulation or law.[8]

Radio communication was, by contrast, treated thus by the Communications Act of 1934:

> Nothing in this Act shall be understood or construed to give the Commission the power of censorship over the radio communications or signals transmitted by any radio station, and no regulation or condition shall be promulgated or fixed by the Commission which shall interfere with the right of free speech by means of radio communication. No person within the jurisdiction of the United States shall utter any obscene, indecent, or profane language by means of radio communication.[9]

Contradictory as these two clauses might seem to modern ears, the law actually followed the old common law pattern for print media, which forbad prior restraint but allowed subsequent legal prosecution for forbidden publication. In fact, the Federal Communications Commission (FCC) was given explicit power to suspend the licenses of broadcasters who allowed obscene or profane speech on the air.

Television, when it came along, was regulated by the same Commission under the same Act. By the time cable television and later the internet fell under FCC regulation, the Supreme Court had become involved in the definition of obscenity.

---

7 *Mutual Film Corp. v. Industrial Comm'n of Ohio*, 236 U.S. 230 (1915).

8 An excellent compilation of the Hays Code, including its various amendments over the years, can be found at http://productioncode.dhwritings.com/index.php (accessed 18 March 2010).

9 See the Federal Communications Act of 1934, Public Law No. 416, 19 June 1934, 73rd Congress, at http://www.criminalgovernment.com/docs/61StatL101/ComAct34.html.

Congress included in the Federal Communications Act of 1996 an Internet Decency Act, which forbad dissemination of indecent and patently offensive materials to minors, but the act was struck within the year by the Supreme Court as overbroad. The Act, ruled the Court, penalized constitutionally protected expression for fear that it might fall before the unsupervised eyes of the young without considering less restrictive means to protect the young by limiting their online access to inappropriate websites.[10]

The Court's introduction of a constitutional dimension to obscenity law was signaled in 1952 in the case of *Joseph Burstyn, Inc. v. Wilson,* which reversed the exclusion of motion pictures from First Amendment scrutiny, and it began in earnest with the case of *Roth v. United States* in 1957, which introduced a decade and a half of legal upheaval before the settlement of a standard in the 1973 case of *Miller v. California.*[11] *Roth,* which involved a prosecution under the old Comstock Law, reaffirmed the previous doctrine of the Court that the First Amendment did not protect obscenity, but it began a process of reinterpreting the term *obscenity* that soon gave full constitutional protection to materials that had long been forbidden by statute as obscene.

Obvious in the background to *Roth* were changing social practice and public opinion: The phenomenal success of *Playboy* magazine immediately upon its appearance in 1953 and the government's decision not to pursue it as obscene raised the question what the legal standard was, statutory law not having been altered, and the Court decided to clarify the matter by invoking the Constitution. Distinguishing the portrayal of sex from obscenity, as the Comstock Law for mail and the voluntary Hays Code for movies did not, and rejecting the old British standard from an 1868 case that treated as suppressible anything that might corrupt the vulnerable, the *Roth* Court announced the following test: "whether to the average person, applying contemporary community standards, the dominant theme of the material taken as a whole appeals to the prurient interest."

By the time of the *Miller* case, the various elements of this test had been disaggregated, other dicta in the *Roth* opinion had been litigated, and the locus of decision apparently clarified: To qualify as obscene and thus unprotected, the material had to

---

10 *Reno v. American Civil Liberties Union,* 521 U.S. 844 (1997).

11 *Joseph Burstyn, Inc. v. Wilson,* 343 U.S. 495 (1952); *Roth v. United States,* 354 U.S. 476 (1957); *Miller v. California,* 413 U.S. 15 (1973).

appeal to prurience, had to depict "in a patently offensive way, sexual conduct specifically defined by applicable state law," and had to lack "serious literary, artistic, political, or scientific value" when taken as a whole."

While determining what constitutes prurience and patent offensiveness in particular cases was left to juries, states were thus instructed to rewrite their laws to define—usually in language that would itself previously have been suppressible—precisely what body parts in what positions doing what could not be shown. Judges, thanks to the "serious value" prong of the test and the restriction of the prurience prong to the dominant theme of the whole work, not isolated passages or moments, were left as guardians of science and literature against whatever will to "Comstockery" might still remain in the people at large.

Miller seemed at the time to be a compromise opinion. Its "serious value" standard was a retreat from the "utterly without redeeming social value" standard floated in an earlier case, but it was presumed that juries would enforce local mores. In practice, its chief effect was probably to force the precise definition of excludable images. Commentators typically opined that *Miller* left "hard-core" pornography unprotected, while taking "soft-core" under the protective mantle of the Constitution.

The First Amendment having been firmly set as the dominant regulatory limit and so a presumption having been established against suppression of pornography, legislative attention turned to regulating the "time, place, and manner" of its dissemination, something courts had upheld in other contexts even for constitutionally protected speech. One approach to regulating pornography that the Court allowed in the post-*Miller* years involved zoning restrictions and regulations in a gray area of "indecent" expression between the obscene, which was unprotected, and that expression which was fully protected. Jurisdictions could cluster indecent businesses in "red light districts" or alternatively, scatter them apart, while the FCC was permitted to confine "dirty words" on radio or nudity on cable television to late-night hours, to protect children's ears and eyes.[12] But the internet—which, as others have said, puts an "adult bookstore" in every home at any hour of every day—quickly overcame both the physical and the broadcast zoning exception, and as noted above, the Court canceled Congress's first attempt to suppress internet indecency. Concerning child

12 See *Young v. American Mini-Theatres*, 427 U.S. 50 (1976); *City of Renton v. Playtime Theatres, Inc.*, 475 U.S. 41 (1986); *FCC v. Pacifica*, 438 U.S. 726 (1978).

pornography, which had been ruled unprotected in any venue, because its initial production necessarily involved child abuse, technology again outstripped the lawyers: Faced with computer-generated images of children in pornography, the Court found its rationale undercut and disallowed regulation.[13]

Four perspectives on pornography

What are the interests and the ideas that drive the efforts both to regulate and to prevent the regulation of pornography? The interests, I suppose, are at once more immediate and less visible than in most other areas of policymaking.

Obviously, those who profit from making and selling pornography would favor its deregulation and have benefited enormously from that over recent decades. They are hampered politically only to the extent that some shame still attaches to the industry, but some of the most shameless have turned even this to political advantage—think of Larry Flynt, who brought down a Speaker-designate of the House of Representatives. Their customers likewise might be presumed to support deregulation, though again, to the extent that shame still operates, they are likely to want to cover their preference with a principle, or express it only in the privacy of a voting booth.

Those whose interests are most directly on the other side—women and children exploited in the making of pornography, children who deserve a decent environment in which to mature, men addicted to pornography and their wives—will generally need to rely for protection on others whose concern is moral or even moralistic. These will include parents and others who care for the character of a community and its denizens, and maybe also those of aesthetic sensibility who recognize that redefining obscenity in law does not make the "offensive, foul, filthy, and disgusting" inoffensive or clean.

To be sure, there can be all sorts of complexities in the analysis of interests. In antebellum America, for example, attempts at federal regulation of morality were typically rebuffed by defenders of slavery, who feared a precedent for interference with their own domestic practices, while in the aftermath of the Civil War, Abolitionist success propelled Christian moralists of many kinds. Still, whether because

---

13 Cf. *New York v. Ferber*, 458 U.S. 747 (1982) with *Ashcroft v. Free Speech Coalition*, 535 U.S. 234 (2002).

they drive action on their own or mask interests that dare not speak their name, political ideas are critical to understand if one is to grasp what lies behind public policy. In the modern regulation of pornography, there are at least four distinct sets of ideas or perspectives to consider.

Christian moralism. First, there are the Christian moralists, responsible for the traditional suppression of obscenity and, as in the case of Comstock, motive forces behind new statutes and policies. It bears repeating that traditional Christian sexual morality is strict and simple: Sex is licit only within marriage, marriage is intended to be for life, and every act of marital intimacy is to be open to procreation, permitting no artificial contraception and frowning on sexual practices that are not procreative in type.

Although the Protestant Reformation brought an acceptance in some denominations of divorce and remarriage in certain limited circumstances, other deviation in Christian moral doctrine is recent, beginning with the allowance of contraception in hardship cases by the Anglican Communion in 1930. Since Christ himself had said in the Sermon on the Mount that "every one who looks at a woman lustfully has already committed adultery with her in his heart,"[14] it is evident to Christians that pornography is sinful in itself.[15] The poetry of love merits its own book in the Old Testament, *The Song of Solomon,* which is undeniably erotic in its imagery, however allegorical its interpretation, but the Christian is instructed to live chastely, inside marriage and out.

Comstock spent little time elaborating on Christian teaching concerning these fundamentals, but he clearly drew his inspiration from a Christian sensibility. He wrote about obscene publications:

> The effect of this cursed business on our youth and society, no pen can describe. It breeds lust. Lust defiles the body, debauches the imagination, corrupts the mind, deadens the will, destroys the memory, sears the

---

14 Matt. 5:28 (RSV), para. 2354.

15 Here is modern Catholic teaching, from the *Catechism of the Catholic Church*, para. 2354: Pornography "offends against chastity because it perverts the conjugal act, the intimate giving of spouses to each other. It does grave injury to the dignity of its participants (actors, vendors, the public), since each one becomes an object of base pleasure and illicit profit for others. It immerses all who are involved in the illusion of a fantasy world. It is a grave offense. Civil authorities should prevent the production and distribution of pornographic materials."

> conscience, hardens the heart, and damns the soul. It unnerves the arm, and steals away the elastic step. It robs the soul of manly virtues, and imprints upon the mind of the youth, visions that throughout life curse the man or woman. Like a panorama, the imagination seems to keep this hated thing before the mind, until it wears its way deeper and deeper, plunging the victim into practices that he loathes.[16]

He is confident in his knowledge of right and wrong on these matters, indignant at those who engage in wrongdoing and at the "liberals" who apologize for them, and confident in his ability to employ the law and moral force of government to fight sexual vice. Though a reformer, unlike the abolitionists Comstock did not imagine a transformed society; vice might be suppressed, but I don't believe he ever supposed it could be eliminated. His is the language of vigilance, appealing to a consensus among the righteous—and finding it widespread in Protestant America, even in the midst of demographic and social change.

Neither in temperament nor in occupation is there anything Catholic about Anthony Comstock. The Christian reformers with whom he was often associated were all Protestants, and sometimes, especially in their signature campaign against the moral evils associated with drink, not a little anti-Catholicism was implicit or even explicit in their rhetoric, and indeed the Comstock Law passed in "hot haste" thanks to the patronage of House Speaker James G. Blaine, probably the most influential anti-Catholic politician of the age.[17] It is particularly interesting, then, that moral control of motion pictures in the early twentieth century was arranged with important Catholic participation, evident in the clear Catholic influence on the Hays Code itself, prompted by the formation of a Catholic Legion of Decency, and drafted by Fr. Daniel Lord, SJ, professor of dramatics at St. Louis University and editor of a widely circulated publication for Catholic youth.

The Hays Code included not only a list of rules covering numerous matters beyond obscenity, but often a list of reasons underlying them, as can be gleaned from this excerpt:

---

16 Anthony Comstock, *Frauds Exposed, or How the People Are Deceived and Robbed, and Youth Corrupted* (New York: J. H. Brown, c. 1880), 416.

17 Foster, *Moral Reconstruction*, 52–53.

> Law, natural or human, shall not be ridiculed, nor shall sympathy be created for its violation. By *natural law* is understood the law which is written in the hearts of all mankind, the great underlying principles of right and justice dictated by conscience. By *human law* is understood the law written by civilized nations.

Here is the elaboration of one rule about the depiction of sex:

> Out of regard for the sanctity of marriage and the home, the triangle, that is, love of a third party by one already married, needs careful handling. The treatment should not throw sympathy against marriage as an institution. *Scenes of passion* must be treated with an honest acknowledgment of human nature and its normal reactions. Many scenes cannot be presented without arousing dangerous emotions on the part of the immature, the young, or the criminal classes.

There follows a recommendation that even pure love not be shown in all its facts, and as for impure love, "the love which society has always regarded as wrong and which has been banned by divine law," it must not be shown as attractive, laughable, or permissible, nor in a way to arouse "morbid curiosity." As even these brief excerpts make clear, the code did not merely prevent egregious harm but instead attempted positive moral instruction. The basic prohibition of vulgarity, obscenity, and profanity is thought not to even need further reasons beyond the mere statement of the rules forbidding them.[18]

Liberalism. A second group of ideas rightly can be clustered under the name Comstock already gives them, *liberal.* Beginning in earnest in mid-nineteenth-century England and captured in works such as John Stuart Mill's *On Liberty,* liberalism

---

18 Gregory D. Black, *Hollywood Censored: Morality Codes, Catholics, and the Movies* (Cambridge, U.K.: Cambridge University Press, 1994). Numerous recent books detail aspects of the code and the controversy surrounding it, including Thomas Doherty, *Hollywood's Censor: Joseph I. Breen and the Production Code Administration* (New York: Columbia University Press, 2007), and Laura Wittern-Keller, *Freedom of the Screen: Legal Challenges to State Film Censorship, 1915–1981* (Lexington: University Press of Kentucky, 2008).

would limit government regulation to "other-regarding" actions and leave individuals the masters of their personal moral opinions and behavior.

While their precise claims were often expressed in muted form in environments where Christian moralism was widely and deeply influential, liberals held sexual morality to be a private matter and thus called into question social and legal practices that restricted sex to marriage. Moreover, as in Mill's celebrated tract, they made freedom of speech an independent value and thus found censorship of sexual material doubly offensive: for imposing upon free expression, and for squelching sexual freedom.

Although the theories of European authors such as Friedrich Nietzsche and Sigmund Freud undercut the ideal of the rational person celebrated by the early liberals, the publication and dissemination of their works served the liberal argument: Their circulation must be allowed for the sake of human freedom, and because the sexual knowledge they meant to convey addresses the longing for human happiness. Modern authors such as George Bernard Shaw, James Joyce, and D. H. Lawrence produced works that attracted the censors' wrath and the critics' acclaim. At the very moment when self-censorship of the film industry was taking place over liberal protest, federal judges began to free admired literary work from the censors' strictures. The duty of society to prevent harmful speech eventually fell before the liberals' confidence that censorship was generally, maybe always, more harmful than any speech itself could be.

The commonsense observation that the allure of vice is often enhanced by its suppression—and the observed success of literary productions known to have attracted censorial interest, because of that interest—seemed to confirm the liberals' argument in favor of free expression: Even if censorship was not wrong in principle, it was futile in practice, so prudence confirmed what prurience sought, the abandonment of restrictions on what could be read and seen.[19]

---

19 For a typical "Whig" account of the rise of liberal ideas on sexuality and its portrayal, see Hyde, *A History of Pornography*; for a typical account of the rise of liberalism in First Amendment law, see Thomas I. Emerson, *The System of Freedom of Expression* (New York: Vintage Books, 1971). The liberal viewpoint was vindicated in the 1970 report of the President's Commission on Obscenity and Pornography, which didn't find any link between pornography and antisocial behavior. See also Harry M. Clor, *Obscenity and Public Morality: Censorship in a Liberal Society* (Chicago: University of Chicago Press, 1969).

Actually, the case for censorship usually had depended upon assumptions of social inequality, and these played themselves out in America in a curious way. When obscene material was available only to the wealthy or the privileged, it was thought unnecessary to restrain it by law; precisely as technology equalized the access of social classes to obscenity, the call for regulation had been raised.

This is exemplified by the different treatment accorded movies and literature in the 1930s. As mass entertainment, movies were seen as especially dangerous in their potential effects, and so in their potential to corrupt; literature took effort and so could be granted wider liberty, its tendency to corrupt being outweighed by its promise to uplift. But precisely the more sophisticated literary classes were likely to take an interest not only in literature but in constitutional law, and to understand its political potential. First in the doctrine of speech, then in the doctrine of sexual license, dubbed "privacy," courts began to enforce as constitutional commands the liberal ideals of personal freedom. Defended as responses to social evolution, they effectively closed paths of social development: After all, when a policy has been declared unconstitutional, legislative power is constrained and all subsequent political action has to take into its calculations the potential cost of lawsuits and the likelihood of their failure.

Liberalism not only succeeded in winning over the most sophisticated social classes, but it entrenched their authority over what was permissible. Moreover, since liberalism came for similar reasons to dominate the academy and the press, today it takes a bold effort at recovery in academic discourse even to formulate reasons why anyone ever thought otherwise.

As actions follow thoughts, so the case for freedom of thought brought in its train the case for freedom of action. And the dynamic proceeded even as the character of liberalism itself morphed: Freedom of speech, originally celebrated as the avenue to truth, came to be seen as the only plausible position in a climate of pervasive skepticism, while sexual freedom, originally presented as nature's rebellion against the strictures of convention, came to seem all the more cogent as the authority of natural standards was increasingly subjected to doubt.

Neo-Conservatism. As Supreme Court doctrine enforced permissiveness in the 1960s and as liberalism grew increasingly relativistic in character, a secular case for censorship was made by several scholars who are best described as neo-conservatives. They accepted the premises of liberal democracy as the practical basis of what they called the American regime, but they questioned whether the constitutional republic could thrive if the polity showed no concern whatsoever for the character of its citizens. Though students of classical political philosophy, they did not suggest restoring virtue rather than liberty as the end of political life in modern America, but they did argue that a free society depends upon a certain virtue in its citizens and to that extent adopted the language of classical republicanism.

They found the recent involvement of the Supreme Court in enforcing a liberal, or rather libertarian, doctrine of free speech that effectively removed all censorship of obscenity to be doubly problematic in relation to citizen virtue. The Court's decisions permitted material that tended to corrupt those who needed instruction in noble deeds, not base ones, and it took from the people the decision about how to preserve their own liberty and virtue.

The neo-conservative account of obscenity was a sophisticated one: Walter Berns, for example, concludes his essay by explaining the value of the obscene in great art, citing as an example Edmund's "stand up for bastards!" speech in Shakespeare's *King Lear,* showing how artistic use of obscenity serves to ennoble and asserting that art itself thrives in an atmosphere of partial censorship more readily than in a world where everything is permitted and no one publicly cares to distinguish art from trash.[20] Berns is no Comstock who would brag how many trainloads of smut he had captured and destroyed; it is enough for him that it be returned to a place under the counter or behind a screen.

Feminism. The fourth set of ideas about pornography and censorship belongs to modern feminism, which defines pornography as writings or images that depict the sexual subordination of women. Not all scholars who describe themselves as feminists would agree that such pornography ought to be suppressed. Feminist volumes have been produced opposing the movement among some feminists to penalize pornography, and those on both sides of the issue would agree that liberalization of speech about sexuality in the twentieth century was critical to the emergence of the more radical forms of feminism in the latter decades of that century.[21]

Andrea Dworkin and some others drew a distinction between pornography and erotica, rejecting only the former. Catharine MacKinnon drew a parallel between

---

20 Walter Berns, "Beyond the (Garbage) Pale, or Democracy, Censorship, and the Arts," in *Censorship and Freedom of Expression: Essays on Obscenity and Law,* ed. Harry M. Clor (Chicago: Rand McNally, 1971).

21 See Drucilla Cornell, ed., *Feminism and Pornography* (Oxford, U.K.: Oxford University Press, 2000).

feminism and Marxism, with liberalism serving similarly as a stage in development that needed to be put behind.[22] Even among those who favored use of the law to suppress pornography there was little enthusiasm for censorship itself; indeed, to Susan Griffin, the censor is like the pornographer he torments in that the aim of both is the silencing of women.[23]

Nevertheless, drawing on a model of civil rights, anti-pornography feminists believed that law could be used to effect change, restricting liberty of expression in the name of equality of rights. The target was clearly defined as pornography, not obscenity, the depiction of women as sexual objects or sexual slaves, not portrayal of the filthy or the disgusting. The aim was not to restore an old regime that was part and parcel of the problem, but instead to redefine the new.

Now, these four perspectives—Christian moralism, liberalism, neo-conservatism, and feminism—can mix in complex ways. I mentioned that feminism, though critical of liberalism, in fact depended on liberal freedom for its own emergence and growth. Likewise, neo-conservatives, though friendly to censorship of obscenity in the 1970s and the 1980s, developed a wary eye once they found themselves on the receiving end of censoriousness in the age of "political correctness," even if the pressure on speech was largely social, at least outside of academic institutions with their arcane rules.

Moreover, emerging ideas and constituencies endorsing them will influence the debate in ways that are impossible to ignore in any political calculation. Candidates include the Catholic discourse that is developing in response to Pope John Paul II's *Theology of the Body* and notions of gay sexuality that cannot be adequately fit into the category of liberalism, even in its more radically libertarian form.

Still, the four categories of Christian moralism, liberalism, neo-conservatism, and feminism are a useful heuristic. The test is in what they can explain.

Feminist anti-pornography ordinances

In 1983 and 1984, city councils in two Midwestern cities considered and passed a new kind of anti-obscenity ordinance. Based on a theory proposed by feminist

---

22 Catharine MacKinnon, *Feminism Unmodified: Discourses on Life and Law* (Cambridge, Mass.: Harvard University Press, 1987).

23 Susan Griffin, *Pornography and Silence: Culture's Revenge Against Nature* (New York: Harper & Row, 1981).

legal scholar Catharine MacKinnon and involving her in hearings in both instances, the cities sought to redefine pornography as the depiction of sexual violence against women, hence as discrimination, and to penalize it on the model of civil rights legislation. (She had been teaching a course at the University of Minnesota Law School at the time of the first proposed ordinance, and apparently some of the impetus in its favor came from her students.)

The laws would allow citizen complaints and suits directed against those who engage in sexual violence either in making pornography or after watching it, or against those who traffic in pornography and thereby, in the theory of the ordinances, discriminate against women. MacKinnon aimed in her draft legislation to apply to pornography the theory of treating sexual harassment in the workplace as a form of sex discrimination, which was simultaneously working its way through the courts and is now established as law.[24]

In the Minneapolis ordinance, pornography was defined as "the sexually explicit subordination of women, graphically or in words," followed by a list of nine offensive depictions, some explicit in the mode prescribed in *Miller v. California* (e.g., "women are presented as sexual objects who experience sexual pleasure in being raped"), some more general (e.g., "women are presented as sexual objects, things, or commodities" or "women are presented as whores by nature"). The Indianapolis version included only five explicit depictions.

Notably missing from either ordinance was any mention of prurience or immorality, nor was there restriction of the offense to the dominant theme of the work taken as a whole. The Supreme Court's obscenity doctrine, in other words, was replaced by what proponents thought a superior approach.[25]

The politics of the ordinances involved an alliance of feminists and conservatives. In Minneapolis, the key figure was an experienced Republican councilwoman and Reagan supporter who worked closely with MacKinnon and took the lead in seeing the ordinance through the council. In Indianapolis, a town that had long had

---

24 See *Meritor Savings Bank v. Vinson*, 477 U.S. 57 (1986); "Facts About Sexual Harassment," U.S. Equal Employment Opportunity Commission, http://www.eeoc.gov/facts/fs-sex.html (accessed 18 March 2010).

25 See Donald Alexander Downs, *The New Politics of Pornography* (Chicago: University of Chicago Press, 1989). The ordinances are described on pages 44 and 114–15, respectively. My discussion of the Minneapolis and Indianapolis cases draws heavily on Downs's extensive case studies.

active groups favoring the suppression of obscenity, some of whom had grown frustrated by recent Supreme Court jurisprudence, many Republicans supported the ordinance, including the progressive Republican mayor. In both cities, testimony before the council or its committees was dramatic and controversial, with open testimony of sexual abuse that was relatively unprecedented at the time.

In both cities there was both support and opposition for the ordinance among Democrats. Donald Fraser, the Democratic mayor of Minneapolis, vetoed the ordinance, convinced of its unconstitutionality, and later vetoed a revised version that was passed the following spring. In Indianapolis, Mayor William Hudnut signed the act into law, only to find himself named in a lawsuit that led to its being overturned in federal district court, with the Sixth Circuit Court of Appeals affirming the decision to strike the ordinance, in an opinion by Judge Frank Easterbrook, a prominent Reagan appointee. The Supreme Court declined to hear the case.

Easterbrook noted that the ordinance eschewed the Supreme Court's definition of obscenity, which meant that the court had to consider the material in question protected speech. While not denying—indeed, precisely because he admitted—the power of the argument about the meaning of pornography as subordinating women, Easterbrook found the statute to aim at "thought control," adding that neither Homer's *Iliad* nor Joyce's *Ulysses* were outside the terms of the act. He concluded:

> Any rationale we could imagine in support of this ordinance could not be limited to [reducing] sex discrimination. Free speech has been on balance an ally of those seeking change. Governments that want stasis start by restricting speech. Culture is a powerful force of continuity; Indianapolis paints pornography as part of the culture of power. Change in any complex system ultimately depends on the ability of outsiders to challenge accepted views and the reigning institutions. Without a strong guarantee of freedom of speech, there is no effective right to challenge what is.[26]

---

26 *American Booksellers Association v. Hudnut*, 771 F. 2d 323 (1985), at 332.

The feminist theory and ordinance captured national attention, and the testimony of the women, controversial in each city, nevertheless seems to have made a lasting impression on those who heard it. But neither ordinance became law, in both cases because of constitutional concerns anchored in liberal jurisprudence. Both the mayor of Minneapolis and the federal courts found that the punishment of pornography as discrimination ran afoul of First Amendment protection. The court did not deny the fact of harm, but treated concern for free speech as trump.

The passage of the ordinances in the councils and the interest taken in them nationally indicated the possibility of a feminist-conservative coalition on the issue, and in fact in 1986 the federal Meese Commission not only revised the 1970 President's Commission findings on the basis of new social science evidence, but also incorporated the feminist perspective on pornography as discriminatory against women. At the same time, the repudiation of both ordinances on constitutional grounds seems to have caught some conservatives by surprise, indicating, in the opinion of the historian of the controversy cited above, either their naïvety or their desperation in grasping at a radically untested approach in the face of liberal legal entrenchment.

If the feminists pressed for the ordinances only to gain national attention and thereby have some influence on the long-term debate, their strategy was probably successful; if they sought to change the regulation of pornography, they seem to have been naïve about the willingness of the courts to radically shift established (even recently established) doctrine. Their initial success in local government suggests the possibility of anchoring the regulation of pornography in affected communities; after all, *Miller* had seemed to vindicate "community standards," and the zoning cases involving red-light districts suggested the value of local government, too.

But the liberalism now accepted as a national doctrine of constitutional scope undercuts the efforts at the local level to address the moral concerns of actual citizens willing to come forward and admit of having suffered genuine harm. And the entrenchment of that liberalism in constitutional doctrine changes the whole character of the politics, for it raises formidable barriers in front of those on the other side of the issue, who could see all their efforts brought to naught by judicial annulment, and at the very least are faced with enormous legal expense to match the inevitable legal challenge.

Indeed, probably one thought behind the feminist proposal to treat pornography as discrimination was to meet constitutional trump with constitutional trump, since the vindication of civil rights is ordinarily the only goal besides urgent needs for security that can win at law over civil liberties. But this time it didn't.

Conclusion

Much has happened since the 1980s, of course, in terms both of the issues faced and of public opinion. As noted above, the easy availability of pornography on the internet facilitates access and thus increases its use. Moreover, we know even more than before about the harm that pornography does, even if the full extent of that harm is difficult to measure.

At the same time, social attitudes seem to have become more permissive. They have become permissive of the depiction of sex—witness, in Cincinnati, a city declared as recently as 1985 the "Anti-Porn Capital of America," the 1990 jury acquittal of those responsible for an exhibit of the sexually explicit and homoerotic photographs of Robert Mapplethorpe.[27] They certainly have become more permissive of public talk about sex, a fact that was excruciatingly evident in the explicitness of media coverage of the events that led to the impeachment of President Bill Clinton. As in so many other areas of life, we have conducted a vast social experiment, in this case an experiment in a sex-saturated society, and the conditions promoted by that experiment now obstruct any effort to respond to its results.

My first conclusion, then, is a need for caution in any regulatory attempt, lest the effort backfire and make future efforts all the more difficult. The division in ideas and interests suggests that any regulatory effort is going to depend on a coalition whose partners are often at odds, even or especially on related issues such as abortion, gay marriage, or hate speech. It will require negotiation to find common ground. For example, neo-conservatives still feel strongly about the character of the citizenry and the need for fostering sexual self-restraint, but now they also are vigilant against politically motivated suppression of speech, finding themselves already—or imagining themselves potentially—vulnerable to attack by majority opinion. Likewise, Christian moralists and feminists agree on the need to protect women

---

27 The epithet is recorded in Donald Alexander Downs, *The New Politics of Pornography*, 28; on the acquittal, see Isabel Wilkerson, "Cincinnati Jury Acquits Museum in Mapplethorpe Obscenity Case," *New York Times*, 6 October 1990, http://query.nytimes.com/gst/fullpage.html?res=9C0CEFDF113DF935A35753C1A966958260 (accessed 18 March 2010).

from pornographic assault, but they often have fundamentally different expectations of the protectors and the protected.

Conversely, liberalism is unlikely to be defeated if attacked head-on, whether by challenging federal jurisprudence or by ignoring widespread public sentiment in favor of expressive freedom—but it may be open to regulations that address aspects of the problem from an angle liberals might otherwise endorse, focusing, for example, on the regulation of commercial speech.

Partly this caution is a plea to recognize constitutional politics: The costs of taking on the federal courts is very high, and appeals that call for the overturning of established doctrine are not apt to succeed unless well-prepared, for the Supreme Court rarely reverses its decisions outright, but often allows them to be chipped away step by step. Partly it is counsel to remember public opinion, which needs to be well-formed, at both the elite level and at the level of the ordinary citizen.

Second, it is important to be clear about what is really new and what is perennial. The oldest story in pornography and its regulation is, paradoxically, the challenge of new technology. The internet makes access to pornography much easier, but so did mass printing, movies, and videocassettes. Innovative responses might soon enough be antiquated, but sometimes they have success: The move toward zoning had genuine importance in constitutional doctrine and real effect in breaking up porn zones—for example, Times Square in New York—and that suggests to me that creative thinking might have real policy results. Rather than seeking to suppress what the courts are determined to protect, perhaps it is possible legally to reduce or eliminate the profitability of pornography—for example, by adjustments to copyright protection for obscene and maybe even for indecent materials.

Finally, since public opinion is so crucial in all matters of morals—indeed, it is almost all that is at stake, since the complete suppression of vice is impossible—it is critical to consider what can be done, with or without the law, to restore to pornography its bad name. Here I want to suggest the importance of the way we use language and countenance its use, and what I want to recommend is not a return to Comstockian prudery but a deliberate restoration of modesty in talking about sexual things.

This can be done playfully and ironically—a teacher can tell you that you'll get a good laugh if you dance around a sexual reference with a surprising circumlocution before a class of modern students who expect explicitness—and it also can be done seriously, by sacrificing a need to know or say explicit details of sexual scandal for the sake of preserving decorum. A lack of modesty in describing sexual things tends to erase the distinction between human beings and animals, to treat ourselves as only bodies, not persons. By contrast, the antiquated social practice in pre-Oprah America of never publicly discussing sexuality also disregarded the specific character of human beings, for the sexual act is also animalistic if mute in its anticipation and in its aftermath, if its role in a complete human life cannot be explained.

To acknowledge the political difficulty of the situation of those who would protect against pornography is to introduce a certain modesty into the discussion of what ought to be done. But the restoration of modesty, not to say awe, in the face of sexual passion and power would be already a healthy first step.

INDUSTRY SIZE, MEASUREMENT, AND SOCIAL COSTS

K. Doran

In order to estimate the effect of pornography on societal well-being we must study *how* it is distributed and consumed, and the effects on individuals and society of this distribution and consumption. In this paper, I attempt to make an initial contribution to the study of these areas by drawing on many underutilized sources of data regarding a relatively new and significant branch of pornography: internet pornography.

First, I explain the main mechanisms of distributing pornography on the internet. Next, I demonstrate that although the industry's own estimate of $2.5 billion in annual revenue from internet pornography is often considered an exaggeration, it corresponds well with independent data—and in fact significantly underestimates total consumption, because between 80% and 90% of internet pornography consumers seem primarily to consume free internet pornography.

My analysis suggests that there is not yet any convincing *statistical* evidence that the consumption of pornography has either positive or negative effects, but that several promising techniques exist for improving this research. The study concludes by considering the possibility of regulating pornography. The relatively large market for help overcoming pornography addiction strongly suggests that there are large personal costs to pornography consumption, which opens up the possibility of welfare-improving government regulation. Eliminating copyright protections for pornographic materials will only succeed in limiting pornography consumption under certain conditions, but regulation of Internet Service Providers (ISPs) could quickly reduce pornography consumption, especially the vast majority of such consumption that occurs for free.

Distribution and consumption

Internet pornography does not differ substantially from other pornography in the manner of production, but rather in the manner of distribution. Today, with high-speed internet connections quite common across the United States, it consists of (sometimes quite large) digital files containing videos or photographs, distributed to consumers through as many as 40,634 websites around the world.[1] Some videos and photographs are identical to those that can be purchased through pornographic print media or pornographic video vendors, but others are only distributed through the internet.

Pornographic photographs either can be downloaded and stored on the consumer's computer or viewed directly from the website without downloading. Some videos can be downloaded and stored on the consumer's own computer, but others, presented in a "streaming" format, can be viewed but not downloaded. Some streaming videos claim to be live video feeds from a "webcam" that is currently filming pornographic activity.

The websites that distribute this pornography may roughly be divided into three categories: pay sites that allow users to consume pornographic content for a fee, often paid for by credit card; free sites that allow consumers to view either samples or the full photographs and videos without paying; and various versions of YouTube that cater to pornography consumers.

The pay sites usually charge anywhere from $10 to $100 per month for access.[2] Some are connected with massive webs of gateway sites. Users who stumble upon one of these gateway sites will be led by a series of links to the main site, where they will have the opportunity to pay for pornographic content.[3] The sites that give away pornography for free may be for-profit ventures typically supported by advertising or personal homepages that contain (sometimes illegally copied) pornographic content without earning any advertising revenue to pay for their maintenance. The pornographic versions of YouTube are for-profit ventures, and the pornographic content on them is sometimes produced by amateurs.

Thus, there are three revenue models for internet pornography: the end-user model (in which pay sites charge customers for personal access), the advertiser model (in which websites distributing pornography support themselves by selling

---

1 Bill Tancer, *Click: What Millions of People Are Doing Online and Why It Matters* (New York: Hyperion, 2008).

2 Caslon Analytics, "Adult Content Industries," http://www.caslon.com.au/xcontentprofile.htm (accessed February 2008).

3 Ben Edelman, "Domains Reregistered for Distribution of Unrelated Content: A Case Study of 'Tina's Free Live Webcam,'" http://cyber.law.harvard.edu/archived_content/people/edelman/renewals/ (accessed February 2008).

advertising space, sometimes to other pornography sites), and the model of various free pornography sites that may not be profitably supported by either end-user subscriptions or advertising.

Consumption for payment and for free

Before one can analyze the likely effects of pornography on society, it is important to get an estimate of the industry's total revenues to make progress in understanding its effects—without reliable numbers, there is little hope for assessing its impacts. The industry publication *AVN* reports that total internet pornography revenues for 2005 were about $2.5 billion.[4] Although many mainstream news sources take *AVN*'s numbers at face value, some academic sources claim that the pornography industry has enough of an incentive to exaggerate revenues that their numbers simply cannot be trusted.[5] In light of this problem, it is necessary to evaluate the industry's revenue reports using independent data.

First, using information from the US Census Bureau on 2005 e-commerce revenues by industry sector, the reported $2.5 billion amounts to 18% of the total e-commerce revenues earned from publishing, arts, entertainment, and recreation services, 2.5% of the total e-commerce revenues earned from all business-to-consumer "service" industries combined, and 1.3% of the total e-commerce revenues earned from all business-to-consumer industries combined.[6] These percentages do not seem too large.

Furthermore, a simple ratio can determine the reliability of both the *AVN* revenue numbers and the Pew Internet and American Life (PIAL) Project's internet pornography consumption numbers. According to the PIAL 2005 May tracking poll, 66% of Americans age 18 and over used the internet, and 11.25% of those (about 16.7 million) accessed pornography. According to the May 2004 tracking poll data, 20% of internet pornography consumers admit to paying for online content, which, combined with PIAL's finding on consumption, yields about 3.3 million paying internet pornography consumers in 2005.

---

4 David Cay Johnston, "Indications of a Slowdown in Sex Entertainment Trade," *New York Times*, 4 January 2007, final edition.

5 Dan Ackman, "How Big Is Porn?" *Forbes.com*, 25 May 2001, http://www.forbes.com/2001/05/25/0524porn.html (accessed February 2008).

6 US Census Bureau, *2005 E-commerce Multi-Sector Report* (25 May 2007); US Census Bureau, *E-stats* (16 May 2008).

These numbers could be an underestimate, because people may fear revealing themselves as an internet pornography user during a telephone survey.[7] But dividing the revenue estimate by the pornography consumer estimate helps evaluate whether either of them seems to be biased in the directions we fear.

So I divide the $2.5 billion by 3.3 million consumers to get $737 per paying customer per year, or $61 per month. Pay sites charge $10 to $100 per month (in 2007, for example, Vivid.com charged $30 per month), so $61 per month is a fairly reasonable average.[8] Thus, the $2.5 billion in annual internet pornography revenue and the 3.3 million internet pornography paying customers seem reasonable estimates. Since this was calculated using the Pew pornography consumption data, it indirectly suggests that Pew's 11%-to-15% rate of total internet pornography consumption is also not too low.[9]

These numbers reveal a potentially important fact about internet pornography consumption: Most users are using it for free. Of the 14% who admitted to consuming it during the May 2004 Pew survey, only 20% said that they pay for it.[10] In the February 2007 Pew survey, 4.5% of internet users admitted to watching online adult videos, but only 10% of them said that they ever pay to access them.[11]

Finally, "hits" on internet pornography websites are broadly distributed, with "the top five hundred sites account[ing] for only 56% of all visits to the adult category," even though only a few firms bring in most of the revenue.[12] These two facts can be

---

7 Tancer, *Click*.

8 Caslon Analytics, "Adult Content Industries."

9 Some examples might make this logic more clear. Suppose that the industry revenue numbers were correct, but that twice as many consumers actually view pornography as admitted it in the surveys, and rather than 20% of them paying for it, *all* of them paid for it. This would result in each person paying $6.14 per month. This is outside the range of monthly rates reported by Caslon Analytics, although it could be obtained if people use the cheapest sites and only subscribed half their months. But if the revenue numbers were also ten times too large, each person would be paying $0.61 per month. This seems much too small. Thus, the data for both revenue and consumption are probably not both severely biased in the directions sometimes feared in the literature on pornography.

10 See the Pew Research Center Survey Reports at http://people-press.org/.

11 Ibid.

12 Caslon Analytics, "Adult Content Industries."

reconciled if a large number of the hits on pornography sites are users downloading free material. It is also possible to reconcile them by noting that some central sites register innumerable gateway sites that link to the central site.[13]

In short, the evidence suggests that a large number of internet pornography consumers—probably the vast majority—are usually consuming free internet pornography. This free material consists of samples of the pay material, illegally copied versions of the pay material, and amateur material.

Who is consuming internet pornography?

The number of consumers and the total dollars of revenue both can be estimated fairly reliably by combining independent data sources, in spite of the potential for aggregate measurement error. But in order to analyze the demographic characteristics of these consumers, I would have to evaluate whether measurement error is distributed unequally across demographic groupings. For instance, are men more willing to admit the truth about their pornography consumption than are women?

It is impossible to do justice to this question in this paper, but comparing results across independent sources of data can provide an answer. Claims about pornography usage consistently reported within each of these sources over time and across each are less likely to be the results of chance or survey methodology, and are more likely to be accurate. There are three main sources of data: the General Social Survey (GSS), administered since 1972 across the United States; the PIAL Project telephone surveys, which have occurred several times a year since 2001; and data from ISPs, collated by Bill Tancer of the internet tracking firm Hitwise.[14]

Table 1 collects pornography usage data from the May 2004 PIAL survey and the GSS. In both surveys, men more frequently claim to be pornography users than do women, and the young more often than the old, while the married and the widowed are less likely than people of other marital status to claim to use it. Each of these patterns is largely confirmed by data from four other PIAL surveys dating from February 2001 through May 2005. Furthermore, the data from ISPs, which may be less likely to have differential measurement error across demographic groups,

---

13 Edelman, "Domains Reregistered for Distribution of Unrelated Content."

14 Tancer, *Click*.

confirms that men are more likely to use internet pornography than are women.[15] Table 1 shows that admitted pornography consumption varies considerably across religious groups.

All three sources are consistent with a decline over the last several years in the proportion of people consuming pornography. Figure 1a shows a small decrease between 2004 and 2006 in the proportion of respondents who claim to have seen an X-rated movie during the past year. Figure 2 shows a small decrease from May 2004 to May 2005 in the proportion of respondents who report using the internet to visit adult websites. Finally, Figure 3 shows that the pornographic website market share has declined from 17% of all visits to websites in September 2005 to 11% in September 2007.

This decline in market share is consistent with constant consumption of pornography and an increase in the consumption of other services, but it is also consistent with a continued decline in pornography consumption. Nevertheless, as shown in Figure 1a, over the long term, the consumption of pornography has increased since a low point in the late 1970s up until the latest year of 2006. This is even more obvious in Figure 1b, where 54% of men age twenty-nine or under used pornography in 2006 (the most recent pornography usage figure), almost twice the usage during the low point in 1978.

Summary facts

There are at least 40,634 websites that distribute pornographic material on the internet. About 11% of all internet visits are to one of these sites. About 14% of the online population in America (17 million Americans) visits these sites, spending on average 6.5 minutes per visit.[16] About 80% to 90% access only free pornographic material. This free material consists of samples of the pay material, illegally copied versions of the pay material, and amateur material.

The remaining three million Americans who pay for internet pornography pay an average of about $60 per month. This generates $2.5 billion in annual revenues for the internet pornography industry, making its revenues a very small percentage of total e-commerce revenues. While this number is frequently cited as an overestimate,

---

15 Ibid.

16 The minutes-per-visit number is taken from Tancer, *Click*.

it is reasonable when estimated by independent data sources, and in fact severely underestimates the total amount of consumption, because of the prevalence of free material. Most of these revenues are apparently earned by a small number of top firms.[17]

Most of the consumption, on the other hand, is spread widely across a number of websites, with the top 500 of these 40,000 websites earning only 56% of the total traffic. Consumption of pornography is spread unevenly according to gender, age, marital status, and religion, and has no clear relationship with education or income. In spite of a recent decrease in consumption, a considerably higher proportion of the population consumes pornography than it did at the recent low point in the late 1970s, especially among young men.

The effects of consumption

Does consuming pornography affect behavior? There is not yet convincing *statistical* evidence in favor of either a yes or a no answer. In an ideal experiment (ideal for identification, not ethics), people would be randomly exposed to pornography and their sexual and criminal behavior (if any) observed. Without doing this, some random variation in access to, exposure to, or temptation to use pornography must be found—that is, a variation in the "price" of consuming pornography that can be correlated with behavior. This is the most difficult requirement in studying the effects of the consumption of pornography (positive or negative). Two recent papers claim to have found such variation, and with it evidence that pornography does affect behavior, but their evidence is not convincing.

The first, a working paper by Todd Kendall, formerly an assistant professor at Clemson University, uses variation in state internet usage over time to proxy for variation in the "price" of accessing pornography.[18] His first claim is that the difference in the speed of internet adoption between states is largely attributable to reasons unrelated to rape. His second is that this variation led to variation in the rate of rapes across states. His final claim is that internet pornography consumption caused the link between internet usage and rape.

---

17 Caslon Analytics, "Adult Content Industries."

18 Todd Kendall, "Pornography, Rape, and the Internet" (working paper, John E. Walker Department of Economics, Clemson University, 2007).

Each of these claims is difficult to prove empirically, and the fact that Kendall has found some evidence in support of them is impressive. Nevertheless, there remain important concerns about his approach. The first problem is an old one: endogeneity. In Kendall's natural experiment, differing rates of usage of the internet should create differing rates of access to pornography. But changes in internet usage could be caused by changes in other variables related to rape, such as preferences and unobserved demographics. Normally, what a researcher would do in this circumstance is find an "instrument" for internet access: a variable that would lead to random variation in internet usage but that would not directly affect outcome variables such as rape. Kendall could not find such a variable, so he relied on the older technique of simply including controls for whatever potentially related variables he could find. Given the prospect for omitted variable bias here, this is a serious issue.

The second problem is an odd one: Kendall controls simultaneously for changes in the internet and computer usage within states over time. So the results are driven by states in which internet usage has risen by either more or less than their increase in computer usage. Since we do not know why some states experience slower increases in internet usage (relative to their increase in computer usage) than others, we cannot assume that this variation in relative internet usage is unrelated to important variables Kendall did not include.

The second paper, by Winai Wongsurawat, is entitled "Pornography and Social Ills: Evidence from the Early 1990s," and was published in 2006.[19] Wongsurawat uses variation in availability of post office boxes as an instrument for variation in the overall psychological "cost" of subscribing to *Penthouse* magazine. The theory is that, *ceteris paribus*, greater ease of obtaining a private post office box will make other people less likely to notice one's *Penthouse* consumption, thereby lowering the psychological cost of subscribing, and that if pornography affects behavior, then places where post office boxes are more easily acquired will have higher rates of rape. In order for this instrument to reliably reveal something about the effect of pornography, the effect of post office box availability on subscriptions must have a statistically significant effect on *Penthouse* consumption, and not be related through another mechanism to the incidence of rape.

19 Winai Wongsurawat, "Pornography and Social Ills: Evidence from the Early 1990s," *Journal of Applied Economics* 9, no. 1 (May 2006): 185–213.

In the previous paper there wasn't any instrument, but in this paper the instrument is not convincing. Wongsurawat demonstrates that in fact post office box availability does not have a strong effect on *Penthouse* subscriptions, but rather has a borderline-strong effect on subscriptions *and* individual (e.g., newsstand) sales. This implies that availability mainly affects the individual sales, which strongly suggests the existence of an unmeasured third variable affecting *both* post office boxes and individual sales. Furthermore, he admits that the F-statistic on the joint significance of the instruments is not quite at the level sometimes used as a rule of thumb for avoiding the weak instrument problem. Finally, Wongsurawat finds that the availability of post office boxes has a statistically significant and apparently positive effect on *Discover* magazine subscriptions, and thus has no way of ruling out the possibility that subscriptions to *Discover* magazine rather than *Penthouse* connects availability to rape.

While both papers point out inadequacies in much of the statistical evidence that consumption of pornography does not affect behavior, their own evidence that it does is not convincing. In both cases, their results are driven strongly by their techniques for obtaining variation in the "price" of pornography consumption, and in both cases this variation is unlikely to be exogenous. Therefore, their results are not a substantial improvement on the older literature that showed positive effects of pornography consumption on rape.

Nevertheless, more can be done to use statistical evidence to measure the effect of pornography consumption. The first step would be to find a useful instrument for pornography availability or consumption: one that has a strong and measurable effect on pornography usage, and is also unlikely to have an independent effect on the behavior being measured. One example of this would be variation in broadband internet availability that comes from a known source. Another example would be using the similarity in take-up rates of technology over time.[20] In fact, this approach is being used in ongoing work.[21]

---

20 Betsey Stevenson, "The Internet and Job Search," in *Studies of Labor Market Intermediation*, ed. David H. Autor (Chicago: University of Chicago Press, 2007), 67–86.

21 K. Doran and Joseph Price, "The Effect of Internet Pornography on Marital Intimacy," in progress.

Consumption theory and consumption effects

Samuel Cameron asks, "Why . . . should we be spending time trying to define porn in the first place? If individuals are rational utility maximizers, then why do they need to be barred from pornography?"[22] The answer, as Cameron himself later admits, is that pornography may be addictive, and thus it may be optimal for the state to attempt to reduce consumption. "We're seeing it [addiction] with epidemic proportions now, particularly with regards to cybersex," says Mark Schwartz, psychologist and former director of the Masters and Johnson Institute in St. Louis, Missouri.[23]

Consumption theory typically assumes that anything a person chooses to consume will be the precise choice (subject to the relevant scarcity constraints) that makes that person best off. This assumption implies that those who choose to consume pornography are improving their own well-being by doing so. Thus, adding an additional constraint to their decision-making (such as raising the price of pornography or making consumption a punishable offense) would necessarily reduce their well-being by decreasing the frequency of their choosing pornography.

In fact, there is a lot of money being made helping people overcome their "sex-addiction," a condition that increasingly refers to the use and abuse of internet pornography.[24] There are numerous self-help books on breaking pornography addiction, in addition to numerous internet filters designed to prevent temptation. People feel the costs of their addiction are so high that they pay for services such as X3 Pure's $165 counseling sessions for married men, or Covenant Eyes®' $55 per year accountability software. There isn't any money being made helping people with tooth-brushing addiction, or kite-flying addiction. All of this evidence should be sufficient to convince us that using pornography can result in great costs for the person consuming; costs not incurred by truly innocuous activities such as brushing one's teeth.

---

22 Samuel Cameron, "The Economics of Pornography," in *Economics Uncut: A Complete Guide to Life, Death, and Misadventure*, ed. Simon W. Bowmaker (Cheltenham, U.K.: Edward Elgar Publishing Limited, 2006), 171–92.

23 Elizabeth Landau, "When Sex Becomes an Addiction," *CNN.com*, 5 September 2008, http://www.cnn.com/2008/HEALTH/09/05/sex.addiction/index.html (accessed September 2008).

24 Ibid.

But we are left with a contradiction. It appears that the same person is willing to spend a positive amount of money to consume pornography, and a positive amount of money to be prevented from consuming pornography. The first expense would imply that a constraint to prevent him from consuming pornography would have negative value to him, but the second expense implies that such a constraint would have positive value. Clearly, researchers need to make use of various models of addiction to properly understand the effects of pornography consumption, and we can assume that the most relevant theoretical research on pornography will make use of addiction theories in the future.

Summary facts on the effects of pornography usage

There isn't any convincing *statistical* evidence that consumption of pornography does or does not affect behavior. However, some people do appear to have a strong incentive to prevent themselves from consuming pornography, and to pay more for this prevention than for the pornography itself. This suggests that there may be large personal costs of consumption associated with pornography, and opens up the possibility that it may be optimal for the state to use regulation to limit the distribution and consumption of pornography.

The regulation of pornography

Between 80% and 90% of the people who consume internet pornography generally consume free content. Thus, if we want to know the effects on consumption of eliminating copyright protections, the most important question is: Will the large number of consumers currently accessing free content still be able to do so after elimination of copyright?

This free content is a combination of legally posted content supported by advertising, legally posted content serving as an advertisement (e.g., samples), illegally posted pay content, and amateur content. Only the first two categories possibly could be negatively affected by elimination of copyright: Illegally posted material will be instantly turned into legally posted material, and amateur material will be posted for the same reasons it already has been. I have not found what portion of free pornography consumption comes from these two sources, but whatever level it is at will be a lower bound for the amount of free pornography consumption that can persist after elimination of copyright.

The revenues for the first two categories primarily will come from end-users, since much of the advertising on pornography sites is from other pornography sites.[25] So it remains to find out whether the end-user revenue model can persist after elimination of copyright, whether some other source of revenue can be found, or whether these first two categories of free content will disappear entirely.

A useful way of answering this question is to ask whether there already exists an industry that distributes public domain works and supports itself through its own revenues. The answer is yes. There is money to be made from reworking public domain books and selling them, often over the internet.[26] Many major publishers sell large numbers. They are not printing and distributing these works out of charity—the revenues must be greater than the costs. Jane Austen's *Pride and Prejudice* long has been in the public domain. At least fifteen editions are currently available as new purchases, including several by major publishing houses, even though the complete text is available for free online. The bestselling Dover thrift edition of three Austen works packaged together has a sales rank of 2,140, and this implies yearly sales of about 3,300 copies.[27] It is therefore clear that the fact that *Pride and Prejudice* is in the public domain has not reduced its availability for consumption whatsoever. In fact, it is currently quite cheap to consume *Pride and Prejudice*, and it would be much more expensive if it was still under copyright.

How can this be? The answer is that publishing houses can make money on public domain works by distinguishing their product from the other versions currently available. Many editions of *Pride and Prejudice* contain special annotations and essays to make the text more readable and interesting. Some contain illustrations, or are printed or digitally stored in an especially attractive format. This is likely to be what would happen to the internet pornography industry were copyright to be revoked. Some websites would package and organize the pornographic material in

---

25 Caslon Analytics, "Adult Content Industries."

26 Lisa Beers, "Making Easy Profit with Public Domain," *ArticleAlley.com*, 18 June 2006, http://www.articlealley.com/article_64452_81.html (accessed February 2008); Paul Sloan, "Free and Easy. How Material in the Public Domain Can Be Turned into Your Own Private Revenue Stream," *CNNMoney.com*, 15 March 2007, http://money.cnn.com/magazines/business2/business2_archive/2006/12/01/83949 75/index.htm (accessed February 2008).

27 See "Amazon Sales Ranks for Books," http://www.fonerbooks.com/surfing.htm (accessed February 2008).

a better way than others. They would make an extra effort to ensure that the digital videos and photographs on their site were free of computer viruses. They would develop interfaces that were easier and more pleasant to use. It is likely that their profits would go down. But there still would be profits to be made from high-quality distribution. The price would likely decline, and the consumption of pornography would either remain constant or increase.

The same cannot be said for production. In the absence of copyright protection, the service that is being profitably sold is efficient distribution, not quality production, since any well-produced product can be taken and distributed by anyone. Thus, there would be little incentive to continue to produce works for profit. If the moral costs of producing pornography are high, then eliminating copyright will reduce the social costs of pornography. However, elimination of copyright will, in the short term at least, either leave constant, or increase, consumption, as the price of consumption decreases.

The one possibly good effect of copyright elimination will be that, as decades pass, the lack of new production will make the available material seem dated. Few people now consume the pornographic postcards of the late nineteenth century. Thus, after the changes in tastes that occur over generations, it is possible that elimination of copyright will succeed in reducing consumption of pornography.

An easier way to reduce consumption

If eliminating copyright protection will not reduce the consumption of pornography, is there another legal change that might do so? It is possible that regulating what information could be transferred by ISPs would be an effective way to reduce internet pornography. At least 80% of internet users nationwide make use of the top twenty-five ISPs,[28] and it thus would be relatively simple to prevent large numbers of consumers from accessing internet pornography by regulating the degree to which internet lines can be used to transmit obscene material, and heavily enforcing this regulation for the top one hundred ISPs around the country.

---

28 Alex Goldman, "Top 23 U.S. ISPs by Subscriber: Q3 2008," 2 December 2008, http://www.isp-planet.com/research/rankings/usa.html. This is an underestimate of the market share of top ISPs because it was not possible to obtain data for several key players.

It is unlikely that the vast majority of internet pornography consumers (especially those who only consume free internet pornography) would be willing to risk using a black market ISP just to access pornography. We already know the 80% to 90% of internet pornography consumers who consume free pornography are unwilling to pay rates as low as $10 or $30 per month in order to obtain higher-quality pornography from subscription sites. This suggests that they also would be unwilling to pay for a black market ISP just to consume pornography.

THE MORAL BASES FOR LEGAL REGULATION OF PORNOGRAPHY

Gerard V. Bradley

Although we are accustomed to think that pornography is completely "free" and unregulated, it is regulated quite intensively—but many regulations have nothing to do with the lurid nature of the material. It is regulated, under various non-moral descriptions and for diverse, non-moral reasons. A pornographic book is subject to copyright and commercial laws. A pornographic movie theater must conform to fire safety and construction codes. A pornographic stage show must meet legal standards for employment. In some places bordellos are regulated for sanitary and commercial purposes.

I put these sorts of regulations aside. Here I am interested in the legal regulation of pornography as a special sort of printed or visual material that seeks to sexually stimulate the viewer.

Pornography as such is an elusive legal concept. Supreme Court Justice Potter Stewart famously confessed in a 1964 concurrence that he could not define "pornography," not even the "hard-core" kind. He insisted nonetheless that he "knew it when he saw it."[1] Call this the conceptual vagueness of pornography. But vagueness is not a problem so long as precision is neither needed nor demanded. And for a very long time American law did not demand it. Our laws up to the 1960s typically banned "filthy," "lewd," "indecent," and "immoral" material, and provided no further definition of these terms.[2]

There was, it is true, more consensus about moral norms in those days than there is now. But there was disagreement then, too. There always has been lively disagreement about how far legal restrictions of sexually explicit material should go, lest mature but nonetheless valuable books, magazines, and movies be censored.

The difference between today and back in the day lies as much in the law as it does in the culture. The difference-that-law-has-made arises from an important value

1 *Jacobellis v. Ohio*, 378 U.S. 184, 197 (1964).

2 *Roth v. United States*, 354 U.S. 476 (1957).

choice made by our legal elites, particularly judges and professors, starting about fifty years ago. Before then, the law's overriding commitment was to protecting the moral character of the weaker among us, including but not limited to minors, against corruption.[3] With that end in view, our law in effect warned any writer or performer who ventured near the casually drawn forbidden zone—demarcated as "filthy" or "lascivious"—that he took his chances.

The thought was this: Someone who flitted so near the flame of lust was probably not doing anyone any genuine good, and he was tempting many people by exposing them to materials they were too morally weak to resist. In the law's eyes, this writer or performer was not a misunderstood *artiste*, or a member of an oppressed moral minority. He was a misguided adventurer, even an immoral tempter. He was, from the moral point of view, a misanthrope. Scaring him off the margins of decency in order to help the morally weak, even if doing so meant using "vague" legal terms, served the common good.

Our law started to make a Copernican revolution in 1957, in the leading case of *Roth v. United States*. It was the first time the Supreme Court sought to provide a concrete definition of obscenity. The Court rejected the common law test for obscenity, derived from the English case *Regina v. Hicklin* in 1868 that "allowed material to be judged merely by the effect of an isolated excerpt upon particularly susceptible persons."[4] In its place, the Court applied a community standards test: "whether to the average person, applying contemporary community standards, the dominant theme of the material taken as a whole appeals to prurient interest."[5]

The law's overriding concern then began to be, and since has surely become, the writer's or performer's putative rights and not the consumer's moral well-being. *Roth* inverted the law's traditional moral preference for protecting the character of the easily tempted, even at the expense of censoring material with some genuine literary or social value. It established that "[a]ll ideas having even the slightest redeeming social importance" were fully protected by the First Amendment.[6] So long as salacious material was surrounded by some sort of intellectual content it enjoyed constitutional protection. Before long *Roth's* thin tether to "social" values

---

3 Ibid., 488, 489.
4 Ibid., 489.
5 Ibid., 484.
6 Ibid.

gave way to the prevailing emphasis upon the writer's or performer's "freedom of expression."

The countervailing public interest is almost always called "public morality." The legal regulation of pornography today takes place at the intersection of something called *public morality* and the emergent colossus *freedom of expression*. The "freedom of opinion and expression" affirmed in the Universal Declaration of Human Rights is limited in its "exercise" by the "just requirements of morality, public order, and the general welfare."[7] The European Convention for the Protection of Human Rights and Fundamental Freedoms says that "[e]veryone has the right to freedom of expression," but that this right may be subject to limits derived from "the prevention of disorder or crime" and "the protection of health or morals," among other reasons.[8] The universal right to *religious* liberty—or "religious expression" if you prefer—affirmed by Vatican II in *Dignitatis Humanae*, its Declaration on Religious Freedom, is limited by the responsibility of civil authority for the "proper guardianship of public morality."[9] Our Supreme Court has affirmed that freedom of expression is limited by "the right of the Nation and the States to maintain a decent society."[10]

But what is this public morality? Its stable definition has been a challenge to our law, but not because it is inherently vague, as is the case with pornography. It instead has been regularly confused with other bases for the legal regulation of pornography, and in particular with arguments from public decency, consent, the combating of injustices, the combating of the particular injustice to children of child pornography, and judicial adherence to rules already laid down.

These bases can be combined into a productive working alliance with public morality, all the better together to serve the common good. At root, though, they are unrelated to public morality, and they cannot do the job that needs to be done all by themselves. Yet they ever threaten totally to eclipse the concept of public morality.

---

7 Universal Declaration of Human Rights, Articles 19 and 29, adopted by the United Nations General Assembly on 10 December 1948, www.un.org/en/documents/udhr (accessed 17 February 2010).

8 Counsel of Europe, *European Convention for the Protection of Human Rights and Fundamental Freedoms* (Strasbourg: 1998), 10.

9 *Dignitatis Humanae*, 7 December 1965, section 7, http://www.vatican.va/archive/hist_councils/ii_vatican_council/documents/vat-ii_decl_19651207_dignitatis-humanae_en.html (accessed 17 February 2010).

10 *Jacobellis v. Ohio*, 378 U.S. 184, 199 (1964).

In Part I of this essay I describe these surrogates for public morality as moral bases for regulating pornography. In Part II I take up another basis, not quite moral but not altogether amoral: inherited constitutional doctrine. These two parts reveal this unfortunate fact: American constitutional law does not possess any concept or definition of what's *harmful* about pornography—even about the hard-core pornography or "obscenity," which still enjoys *no* First Amendment protection. Part III considers more specifically the concept of "public morality," and argues that it includes what is more commonly called "culture," the broader patterns of belief and action that constitute our social world. The law has an important but usually secondary role in making this culture a morally healthy influence upon our lives. Part IV is more prescriptive than all of the preceding parts. It contains a legal strategy for morally stigmatizing the transmission and consumption of obscene materials.

I. Surrogates for public morality

The first entangling alliance of public morality is with *public decency*. Public decency laws protect the sensibilities of persons who are involuntarily exposed to acts that should be performed in private. Restricted "indecent" acts include urinating in public, excessive public displays of affection (even by married couples), nude sunbathing, and loud parties. None of these acts is in itself immoral. Some are positively good. None is pornographic in any familiar sense of that term.

Now, it is true that *feelings* help to clarify what both public decency laws and public morality laws are for. But they are different feelings. Indecency tends to induce revulsion or disgust. Pornography is defined by its tendency to excite *lust*—sexual arousal apart from any genuine interpersonal act of a sexual kind. Because "indecent" acts performed in private cannot give offense, they should not be regulated to promote public decency. Pornography is a different matter.

The second entangling alliance is with *consent*. Consent laws protect everyone's choices and tastes as they bear upon erotic materials. In canonical form, this basis of regulation could be stated as: "The state has constitutional power to protect unwilling adults from being exposed to pornography." Or, as a reworking of the first entangling alliance: "People should be protected—within limits—against the *uninvited* intrusion (and consequent disgust) of erotic imagery."

Thus an "adult emporium" may not be closed by the police as a menace to morals. But the police may and should see to it that the emporium's pleasures are limited to those, and only to those, adults who really go for that sort of thing. The law may and should require that advertising be discrete, that signage be bland, and that entrances be clearly marked, so that anyone who enters knows what to expect. None of these regulations need presuppose that the act or material at issue is genuinely immoral, or that the experience willing customers seek is harmful to them.

The question about this regulatory authority is not its legitimacy, for every member of the Supreme Court and virtually all of the commentators affirm it. The question is whether it marks the outer limit of state authority to limit pornography. Is the state's interest in regulating pornography *exhausted* once it is ascertained that those indulging are, indeed, consenting adults? The Supreme Court seemed to adopt this idea in *Stanley v. Georgia,* a 1969 case that immunized possession of "obscene" materials *in the home,* even though "obscene" materials always had been deemed to be altogether outside the First Amendment's protections.[11] *Stanley* still stands as a valid precedent, and I shall have more to say about it in due course. But its inchoate proposal to make consent the limiting principle of state regulation was soon rejected by a Court populated with the nominees of Richard Nixon.[12] I say more about that rejection in Part III.

The third entangling alliance with public morality is the everyday warrant that our public authorities possess to combat injustices. Though I think that it is dogmatic to hold *ex ante* that pornography is, at worst, a "victimless" immorality, it is nonetheless the fashion to treat it just that way. So, when jurists and commentators refer to "injustices" and "pornography" in the same sentence, they mean something other than the injustice of manipulating other people's passions and corrupting their character for financial gain or to satisfy one's own passion for exhibitionism.

What today's legal thinkers mean is illustrated by Justice David Souter's concurring opinion in *Barnes v. Glen Theatre* (1991).[13] That decision upheld an Indiana law that banned nude bar-room dancing (in the event, in South Bend's Kitty Kat Lounge). The complaining dancers said that their "erotic message" was stifled by G-strings and pasties; the Court decided that they would have to send their message with some "opaque" covering.

---

11 *Stanley v. Georgia,* 394 U.S. 557, 568 (1969).

12 *Paris Adult Theatre I v. Slaton,* 413 U.S. 49, 66 (1973); *Miller v. California,* 413 U.S. 15, 24 (1973).

13 *Barnes v. Glen Theatre, Inc.,* 501 U.S. 560 (1991).

Justice Souter supplied the necessary fifth vote. The decision rested, he said, "not on the possible sufficiency of society's moral views to justify the limitations at issue, but on the State's substantial interest in combating the secondary effects of adult entertainment establishments." These statistically predictable "secondary effects" included "prostitution, sexual assault, and other criminal activity," all of which the state rightly sought to suppress.[14] Though these "secondary" acts are all (more or less) obviously immoral, and though they are all (by some metric) correlated with nude dancing, *nothing* in Justice Souter's position implies or entails that nude dancing is itself morally dubious. Indeed, he makes explicit that he does *not* adopt any such premise.

The content and interlocking character of the three lines of regulatory authority is reflected in Justice Antonin Scalia's cogent argument in favor of the law. While the dissent "confidently asserts . . . that the purpose of restricting nudity in public places in general is to protect non-consenting parties from offense," he notes that,

> there is no basis for thinking that our society has ever shared that Thoreauvian "you may do what you like so long as it does not injure someone else" beau ideal—much less for thinking that it was written into the Constitution. The purpose of Indiana's nudity law would be violated, I think, if 60,000 fully consenting adults crowded into the Hoosier Dome to display their genitals to one another, even if there were not an offended innocent in the crowd. . . . In American society, such prohibitions have included, for example, sadomasochism, cock-fighting, bestiality, suicide, drug use, prostitution, and sodomy. . . . [T]here is no doubt that, absent specific constitutional protection for the conduct involved, the Constitution does not prohibit them simply because they regulate "morality."[15]

The fourth entangling alliance is a variant of the third, covering the very particular injustice of child pornography. The law's treatment of kiddie porn is quite different from its handling of the adult variety, in two ways. First, the Supreme Court in *Osborne v. Ohio* (1990) held that neither the First Amendment nor any

14 Ibid., 582.
15 Ibid., 574, 575.

other constitutional provision precluded criminalizing the possession of "child pornography" anywhere.[16] So, the *Stanley* case still protects someone's possession of adult-themed obscenity at home, but our laws about child pornography extend all the way to possession in one's abode, even to the hard drive of one's personal computer.

Second, child pornography need not be "obscene" according to the prevailing grown-ups' test; it is illegal even if it only includes images of children that, were they portrayals of adults, would be protected by the First Amendment.

The Court's stated reason for this large authority to combat child pornography has nothing to do with public morality, even though there is a strong social consensus that child pornography is morally degenerate and should be banned for that reason alone.[17] The reason proffered by the *Osborne* Court was to protect the "victims of child pornography." These "victims" were not children in general, whom, one could reasonably argue, were put at greater risk of being viewed as objects of sexual desire and satisfaction. Nor were they the sometimes hapless and invariably diminished consumers (usually adults) of child pornography. The Court's "victims" were exclusively the children depicted in the materials. The stated reason for the sweeping *Osborne* authority was the "hope to destroy a market for the exploitative use of children" in *making* kiddie porn.[18]

This rationale was recently confirmed by seven members of the Court. In *U.S. v. Williams*, decided in June 2008, they wrote that "[c]hild pornography harms and debases the most defenseless of our citizens."[19] That case made explicit a certain implication of *Osborne*: *only* material "depicting *actual* children engaged in sexually explicit conduct" counts as "child pornography." *Only* that material—and not sexually explicit material with adult actors who look like children or life-like "virtual" children—involves the exploitation of society's "defenseless." The state's authority to combat "child pornography" has nothing to do with sexual perversion or lust or age-inappropriate attractions, or even the possible stimulation of sexual predators to act. The rationale would apply equally to a total ban on possession of

16 *Osborne v. Ohio*, 495 U.S. 103 (1990).

17 Oliver Lewis, "Fear of Online Crime," Pew Internet news release, 2 April 2001. http://www.pewinternet.org/Press-Releases/2001/Fear-of-Online-Crime-aspx (accessed 17 February 2010).

18 *Osborne v. Ohio*, 495 U.S. 103, 109 (1990).

19 *United States. v. Williams*, 553 U.S. 285 (2008), 128 S.Ct. 1830, 1846 (2008).

snuff movies, which have nothing to do with sexual immorality. *Osborne* is about child labor practices.

II. Inherited constitutional doctrine

There is a fifth line of authority for the legal regulation of pornography entangled with public morality. This one has moral underpinnings, but is not itself a principle of political morality, public policy, or even an aspect of the common good. It is a matter of following *authority,* of judicial adherence to the rules laid down.

In 1957 the Supreme Court, in the case of *Roth v. United States,* looked back at the constitutional tradition. The Court observed that there are "certain well-defined and narrowly limited classes of speech, the prevention and punishment of which have never been thought to raise any constitutional problem."[20] "Obscenity" was one such category: "Implicit in the history of the First Amendment is the rejection of obscenity as utterly without redeeming social importance."[21] The Court then articulated a test for what counts as obscenity. That test persists, in slightly modified form, to this day.

Roth and *Butler v. Michigan,* both decided on the same day, departed from the ancient doctrine laid down in 1868 by the King's Bench in *Regina v. Hicklin.* In that famous English decision, Lord Chief Justice Cockburn defined the test of "obscenity" as "whether the tendency of the matter charged as obscenity is to deprave and corrupt those whose minds are open to such immoral influences, and into whose hands a publication of this sort may fall."[22] As the Supreme Court phrased it in the *Roth* case, *Hicklin* "allowed material to be judged by the effect of an isolated excerpt upon particularly susceptible persons."[23]

This standard was judged in *Roth* to be "unconstitutionally restrictive of the freedoms of speech and press" because it "might well encompass material legitimately treating with sex."[24] In *Butler,* Justice Felix Frankfurter, writing for the Court, described the state's use of *Hicklin* as "quarantining the general reading public against books not too rugged for grown men and women."[25] The challenged law,

---

20 *Roth v. United States,* 354 U.S. 476, 485 (1957).

21 Ibid., 484.

22 *Butler v. Michigan,* 352 U.S. 380, 381 (1957).

23 *Roth v. United States,* 354 U.S. 488, 489 (1957).

24 Ibid.

25 *Butler v. Michigan,* 352 U.S. 380, 383 (1957).

Frankfurter said, reduces "the adult population of Michigan to reading only what is fit for children. . . . Surely this is to burn the house to roast the pig."[26]

Fair enough. It appears (to me, at least) that the Court in 1957 was guided, not by any desire to free up smut peddlers, but to save passably good literature from the heavy hand of blue-nosed censors. Through the mid-1960s, the justices were animated by that intention, supplemented by the conscious desire to protect materials that dealt, even in a frank and visually explicit but non-pornographic way, with sex. Then, in 1966, in *Memoirs v. Massachusetts,* the Court made what *Roth* declared to be a *reason* obscenity lacked constitutional protection—it was "utterly without redeeming social value"[27]—part of the *test* for obscenity. The case, which concerned the eighteenth-century novel *Fanny Hill,* thus burdened public authorities with proving an almost impossible negative.

Now, here is the regnant "test" for obscenity as it was articulated in the 1973 decision *Miller v. California:* only those works are obscene, "which, taken as a whole, appeal to the prurient interest in sex, which portray sexual conduct in a patently offensive way and which, taken as a whole, do not have serious literary, artistic, political, or scientific value."[28] *Miller* expressly limited the "obscenity" to "works which depict or describe *sexual* conduct" (emphasis added). It also revised the third part of the *Roth* test, as *it* had been modified in the *Memoirs* case.

Roth, Miller, and their progeny set a boundary between "free expression" and prohibitable "obscenity." Beyond that boundary, no public official may go.[29] Within the universe populated by works that satisfy the *Miller* test, public officials *may* regulate. And since 1957 the Supreme Court has consistently, though with the notable exception of *Stanley v. Georgia,* stood by this boundary line.

It is important to note that the *Miller* standard by itself does not call for, much less ensure, that any "obscene" act or work will be prosecuted or legally hampered in any other way. Not any lawmaker or executive official—federal, state, or local—is *required* by *Roth, Miller,* or any other case or constitutional provision to clamp down on even the grossest immorality. One might say that persons and the people have a natural, moral right to live in a decent society. But that right is not constitutionally

---

26 Ibid.

27 *A Book Named "John Cleland's Memoirs of a Woman of Pleasure" et al. v. Attorney General of Massachusetts,* 383 U.S. 413, 419 (1966).

28 *Miller v. California,* 413 U.S. 15, 24 (1973).

29 For the sake of public morality, that is. As we saw in the opening paragraph, all sorts of pornographic conduct and works are regulated for non-moral reasons.

enforceable. In other words, the constitutional standard I have described here distinguishes material which public officials *may*, but do not have to, prohibit.

My judgment is that, if the legacy of our constitutional tradition was not that obscenity lacked First Amendment protection, it is doubtful that the Court at any time since 1957 would have minted such a doctrine. I say so largely because the Court in fifty years since has not produced a cogent moral justification for it; that is, the Court has *not* articulated, much less defended, any claim about what is wrong with obscenity.

The Burger Court in 1973 took a strong stand, to be sure, *against* reducing public morality to the four entangling strands described in Part I of this essay. The 1973 cases express well *what* public morality really is. In them the Court no doubt meant to permit communities (towns, cities, and states) that wanted to rid themselves of obscenity to do so. The Court rulings since 1957 are nonetheless suffused with high hosannas to the inestimable role that "freedom of expression" plays in the good life of man and in a democracy. There isn't any corresponding testimony to the moral harm that obscenity visits upon its consumers, harm that does not discriminate between willing and unwilling users. There isn't any parallel witness to the inestimable role that a decent regard for public morality plays in the good life of the human person, and of that person's democracy.

III. Public morality and culture

The four lines of lawmaking authority described in Part I are all sound, valid, and true. All have an important role to play in regulating pornography. But *public morality* is more than the sum of these four parts. And without any concept of what is wrong with obscene material, this important authority is severely hampered. This whole complex of ideas is missing a central element: a sound concept of "public morality."

Public morality is an overarching collective or common good, maintainable by public authority. It is a centripetal force that depends for its meaning and justification upon no one's unwilling participation or upon anyone's insulted sensibilities. Everyone may justly be made to conform to its legally stipulated requirements; no one may rightly claim to not owe any obligation to society's shared moral ecology.

As Alexander Bickel, one of America's greatest constitutional scholars, wrote, in words adopted by the Supreme Court in 1973: "Even supposing that each of us can, if he wishes, effectively avert the eye and stop the ear (which in truth, we cannot), what is commonly heard and done intrudes upon us all, want it or not."[30] Or as Justice Scalia wrote in the 1991 Kitty Kat Lounge case: "[O]ur society prohibits, and all human societies have prohibited, certain activities, not because they harm others but because they are considered, in the traditional phrase, '*contra bonos mores*,' i.e., immoral."

Neither Bickel nor the Burger Court justices who relied upon him, nor Justice Scalia used the word *culture*. But that is exactly what they were all talking about. *Culture* is a human production. It consists of what people do and say, congealed over time into a stable set of social practices. Culture is the collective and settled projection of meaning, including what it means to be a decent human being, and how a decent human being conducts himself or herself, sexually speaking. Culture nonetheless confronts each one of us as a massive objective reality, a formative influence we cannot escape, and that we cannot call into being according to our lights.

We possess, as it were, a common life that contributes in ways known and yet to be understood to my identity and to yours. Our personalities and our characters are not reducible to those features or traits that we acquire in voluntary transactions. We are not the authors of *all* that we think and believe. "To each his own thing" is an intrinsically naïve and empirically unavailable proposal by which to settle the meaning and scope of public morality. We are all, to some significant extent, the products of our culture.

The civil law plays an important, but secondary, role in making this inescapably common force a wholesome one.[31] A sound understanding of public morality does not involve straightforward moral paternalism, even where restrictive laws are enforced against persons who dissent from the law's moral judgments. Paternalism is coercion of an individual for the sake of that individual's moral improvement. Public morality involves the maintenance of a morally wholesome public realm. Just as in order to stabilize prices, Congress forbids farmers to grow certain crops even for home consumption, so too might the law prohibit private possession of all pornographic material to suppress that market. That may have the effect, by helping

---

30 Alexander Bickel, "Dissenting and Concurring Opinions: I," *Public Interest* 22 (Winter 1971): 25–26; see *Paris Adult Theatre I v. Slaton*, 413 U.S. 49 (1973).

31 Robert P. George, *Making Men Moral: Civil Liberties and Public Morality* (Oxford, U.K.: Clarendon Press, 1993).

to break someone's habitual use of it, but that benefit is, or at least it should be, a welcome side effect of laws justified on other grounds.

Public morality presupposes that the state is competent to make sound moral judgments about sexual conduct, and to act on the basis of those judgments. The relevant moral judgment is that pornography morally harms the people who consume it because (a further moral judgment) lustful feelings that are unconnected to any morally upright relationship are subversive of good character. These judgments could of course be mistaken. But they do not depend for their validity upon any consumer's agreement with it, at least no more than do the validity of the state's judgments that prostitution and drug use are wrong and for that reason made crimes, regardless of consumer preferences.

But this public morality is fragile. It depends upon there being an objective right and wrong, which judgment would have to be nested within a larger web of moral judgments. The problem is that our constitutional law is now tilted toward a minority-veto: If material has *any* serious value to anyone it is immune to legal regulation. One standing threat to any adequate state power to protect public morality is therefore the unavailability of such objective moral judgments. The threat is real. Our constitutional law has flirted with a perilous moral subjectivism for several decades; indeed, *Stanley* nearly consummated the affair.

Let me start with an avant-garde expression of this acidic agent. It is an excerpt from Justice Douglas' dissenting opinion in the *Ginzburg* case (1966), in which the Supreme Court affirmed the conviction of a New York publisher for "pandering" *Eros* magazine.[32] The important point of law established there is that, in the case of a publication hovering on the border of obscenity, the fact that it was marketed as sure to titillate ("pandered"), could tip the scales of judgment against it.

In *Ginzburg*, Douglas took an extreme view of what democracy entails and advocated what sociologists call a "bottom up" theory of obscenity; in short, he was an egalitarian on steroids. But reader be warned: Do not scoff or giggle and be done with it. For Douglas' oration is *not* a period piece. It is not a daguerreotype of the Age of Aquarius. It is not the curious product of Justice Douglas' (admittedly) fertile imagination. (He famously loved the ladies.) It is instead a colorful anticipation of what has become a constitutional principle. He began by noting that "Some of the tracts for which these publishers go to prison concern normal sex, some homosexuality,

---

32 *Ginzburg v. United States*, 383 U.S. 463 (1966).

some the masochistic yearning that is probably present in everyone and dominant in some." Masochism, he continued,

> is a desire to be punished or subdued. In the broad frame of reference, the desire may be expressed in the longing to be whipped and lashed, bound and gagged, and cruelly treated. Why is it unlawful to cater to the needs of this group? They are, to be sure, somewhat off-beat, nonconformist, and odd. But we are not in the realm of criminal conduct, only ideas and tastes. Some like Chopin, others like "rock and roll." Some are "normal," some are masochistic, some deviant in other respects, such as the homosexual.

Why, Douglas asked, are these groups to be denied the freedom of the press and expression everyone else enjoys and denied the freedom to communicate in symbolisms important to them?

> When the Court today speaks of "social value," does it mean a "value" to the majority? Why is not a minority "value" cognizable? The masochistic group is one; the deviant group is another. Is it not important that members of those groups communicate with each other? Why is communication by the "written word" forbidden? If we were wise enough, we might know that communication may have greater therapeutical value than any sermon that those of the "normal" community can ever offer. But if the communication is of value to the masochistic community or to others of the deviant community, how can it be said to be "utterly without redeeming social importance"? "Redeeming" to whom? "Importance" to whom?[33]

Douglas gave voice to a profound moral subjectivism: At least when it comes to sexual satisfaction, whatever works for the individual is *perforce* morally acceptable for that individual. There is neither "right" nor "wrong" beyond individual preference, at least so long as one does not conscript an unwilling other into one's sexual fantasy. From the viewpoint of public authority, there isn't any practical difference between

---

33 Ibid., 489, 490.

holding that morality is individuated and saying that (unless a non-consenting party enters the picture) there isn't any morality at all. This nihilism is a standing mortal threat to legal regulation of pornography for the sake of public morality.

How so?

Moral subjectivism is a mortal threat because it grossly inflates the scope and presumptive legitimacy of "expression." As Douglas suggests, "freedom of expression" extends effortlessly to whatever individuals and non-government groups *want* to say or otherwise "express" through spoken or written word, by other communicative conduct, and by symbolic representations (art). Thus a gyrating pole dancer who aims to excite customers enough to part with their money is an "artist."

This sort of subjectivism is a mortal threat also because it explodes the concept of public morality. Where there isn't any negative, objective moral judgment that a sexual act (sadomasochism, for example) is wrong, an aspiring legal regulator could not judge any work genuinely harmful. Without such judgments, a proposed morals law is nothing more than the imposition of a majority's preferences upon an unfairly maligned minority, which simply prefers different but equally valid things. Because an objective moral judgment isn't possible, there isn't any possibility of a genuine *common good* to which all members of society could, in justice, be made to contribute. There can only be—as Douglas suggests—aggregations (larger and smaller) of individuals who happen to share the same interest or taste, some for marriage, and some for bondage.

I counseled against scoffing at Douglas' essay. The reason is that events made him a prophet. I am not here referring to the bacchanal turn of our culture since 1966, which he may have anticipated and which he surely welcomed. I refer to our constitutional law, where an acidic nihilism has come (probably to Douglas' surprise, if there are indeed surprises in the hereafter) to define "freedom of expression." This development was succinctly captured in the June 2008 child pornography case, *U.S. v. Williams*, by dissenting Justices Souter and Ginsburg: "True, what will be lost is short on merit, but intrinsic value is not the reason for protecting unpopular expression."[34] The judgment that some "expression" qualifies for constitutional protection does *not* include a moral evaluative criterion of any kind.

---

34 *United States v. Williams*, 553 U.S. 285 (2008), 128 S.Ct. 1830, 1854 (2008).

IV. A LEGAL STRATEGY FOR REGULATING PORNOGRAPHY

> It is not for this Court thus to limit the State in resorting to various weapons in the armory of the law. Whether proscribed conduct is to be visited by a criminal prosecution or by a *qui tam* action, or by an injunction, or by some or all of these remedies in combination, is a matter within the legislature's range of choice. If New York chooses to subject persons who disseminate obscene "literature" to criminal prosecution and also to deal with such books as deodands of old, or both, with due regard, of course, to appropriate opportunities for the trial of the underlying issue, it is not for us to gainsay its selection of remedies.[35]
>
> — *Kingsley Books, Inc., v. Brown*

Kingsley Books, decided the same day as *Roth,* is still good law: Legal regulation of pornography is *not* limited to what can be accomplished by and through criminal prosecution. This is good news, because one can now expect scant return on criminal prosecutions. The reasons they are nearly obsolete have little to do with the legal changes we've examined and almost everything to do with technological and cultural developments over the last decade, especially the internet. Legal regulation of pornography today must chart a distinctive course. In brief conclusion, I shall describe the legal situation today, and then suggest three steps to develop more creative and effective civil policies to regulate pornography.

The legal rules governing prosecutions have undergone little relevant change since 1957. Police officers' access to evidence (such as porn DVDs and the like) is limited, as it always has been, by restrictive rules governing search and seizure; for example, by the Fourth Amendment's requirement of judicial approval of warrants based upon probable cause, which often required judges to view a purloined copy of the suspect film or book before signing the warrant. Convictions have always depended upon the unanimous verdict of twelve jurors on evidence beyond a reasonable doubt. The constitutional doctrines of vagueness (rooted in Due Process) and overbreadth (a First Amendment test) have long placed the burden of clearly distinguishing obscenity from mere pornography on the State, not on the defendant.

---

35 *Kingsley Books, Inc., v. Brown,* 354 U.S. 436, 441 (1957).

There are and always have been a very limited number of public prosecutors. They long have had a monopoly on initiating criminal cases, and many other pressing demands upon their attention. Never did they mount a numerically impressive number of criminal cases against pornographers.

One possible change that has only made such prosecutions even more difficult is that, given the widespread and largely shameless use of pornography today, jurors may hesitate now as they never did before to return guilty verdicts against even those who sell obscene materials, so long as the material was traded between consenting adult users. (Child pornography cases are another matter.) But this is simply to say that *cultural* changes can affect jurors' decisions. Jury nullification would be further encouraged by the use of enforcement techniques that intruded upon the home, or that interfered with the lawful use of the internet. But this is simply to say that evolving notions of privacy and technological change can affect criminal trials.

On the demand side, it has been the case for forty years that at-home consumers of material that meets the *Miller* test for "obscenity" cannot be prosecuted. That is the legacy of the *Stanley* case (1969). This odd decision did not, however, extinguish "demand-side" prosecutions altogether. In 1969, pornography consumers could not be couch potatoes. They had to go to a disreputable theater or, at least, to a stag party to see a porn-film. They had to find a seedy bookstore in Times Square to acquire the latest skin magazine. Even where there weren't any police lurking, exposure and shame were constant menaces. (Recall the scene in Woody Allen's *Bananas,* where an embarrassed Fielding Melish used *Time* and *Newsweek* to conceal his copy of *Orgasm* from the other customers.) Now would-be consumers can find everything they want at home, on the internet or even Facebook. *Stanley* is thus a real roadblock to demand-side prosecutions: One's home may now be one's porn-castle.

On the supply side, police authorities (including postal inspectors and customs officials) could until relatively recently target certain specific areas and persons for supply-side prosecution, and have an appreciable impact upon supply if they succeeded. (Indeed, to an extent few yet appreciate, this country's porn industry was, until the 1980s, very much controlled by organized crime families.) Bookstores, movie theaters, and warehouses could all be closed down; materials from overseas distributors could be stopped at customs. Now it is all quite different. There aren't any choke points of entry to be watched, consortiums of powerful producers or distributors to break up, few places of public amusement to padlock. Instead, entry costs for production are minimal—anyone can post an obscene video on a website. Overseas distributors of internet porn are beyond the reach of our law.

The takeaway from all these considerations is this: Public authority is not any time soon going to attempt to prosecute more than a tiny fraction of the vast universe of obscenity cases, not nearly enough for the occasional conviction to deter other users.

But these limitations on potential criminal law enforcement are not the death knell for the possibility of reducing pornography through the criminal law. Any conduct defined as a crime is usually thereby morally stigmatized, and—even if the cases are rarely prosecuted—that stigmatization sometimes stimulates social and cultural disapproval. During the last generation the criminal law's crackdown on drunk driving has, in my judgment, instigated and not just reflected the cultural marginalization of a practice that was not long ago winked at. Viewed as a percentage of real-world occurrences, prosecutions for recreational drug consumption are rare. But the presence of the pertinent criminal laws on the books nonetheless reinforces the social message that doing drugs is bad for you. And these criminal laws make possible the many collateral legal and social sanctions for drug use, such as questions about it on government job applications and the "zero-tolerance" policies of schools.

The law's contribution to public morality has nonetheless always been secondary to that of cultural authorities and popular mores. The law has an important but subsidiary role in culturally marginalizing pornography. It is time for more creative civil—that is, non-criminal—legal policies designed to do just that.

This new strategy would rely upon a proliferation of non-governmental *initiators* and *initiatives* to combat pornography by morally stigmatizing it. These proposed legal tools would not traffic in the strict standards of proof in criminal proceedings, nor would they depend upon police methods of obtaining evidence. They would shift the burden of vagueness—the gray area of uncertain definition at the border of soft- and hard-core pornography—to enforcement targets and away from those seeking to protect public morality. One might compare this allocation of the risk of uncertain application of law to that encountered in cases of alleged sexual harassment. To be sure that they do not incur the costs of a successful action for harassment, many institutions in our society impose a "risk management" perimeter around possibly suspect conduct. Thus the birth of house rules against coarse or suggestive language, and unwanted gestures and the like. Finally, this new strategy does not depend for its success upon any change in the present First Amendment landscape, including the unfortunate and anomalous *Stanley* holding.

Here are three proposals, broadly described.

First, call upon legislatures to create a new private (civil, not criminal) right of action, called the "negligent exposure of a minor or an unwilling adult to obscene materials." This civil action would expand and toughen the reach of existing criminal laws against endangering the moral welfare of minors, and perhaps of civil suits to recover for emotional offense to adults. The proposed cause of action would be provable by a preponderance of the evidence and would—because of the inherent difficulty of calculating a money award adequate to making a plaintiff "whole"—have to carry stipulated damages—*at least* a five-figure award—sufficient to deter such misconduct.

This new legal provision could stipulate further that a "pattern" of such negligence consisting of two or more specific acts or omissions which meet the definition of the civil wrong would result in the kind of catastrophic damages presently recoverable under RICO (Racketeer Influenced and Corrupt Organizations Act). The effect of this new law could be expanded by adapting the British definition of obscenity to serve as a pleading and proof requirement: any material that appeals predominantly to the prurient interest and is patently offensive. That this provisionally obscene matter possessed serious value would be provable by the accused as an affirmative defense. Because we would not be dealing here with a criminal offense, it might be possible to adopt this approach without having to persuade the Supreme Court to change the meaning of *Miller.*

Second, as an exercise of its spending power, Congress, or a particular state, could make a condition of *any* money grant that the grantees enact, publish, and enforce policies governing the use of any computers under the recipient's control, which policies effectively eliminate the use of grantee's facilities to visit obscene websites, to receive obscene messages and images, and to prevent their use in any other way to connect to obscenity. The recipients would have to impose effective penalties for any violation of these policies. They would be further advised that their workplace is subject to unannounced inspections, and that their policies and procedures will be regularly audited. The penalty for institutional failure to comply would be the revocation of the grant.

Third, individuals who seek government employment for which moral character is especially relevant—say, as a federal prosecutor or a public school teacher—could be required to pledge that they will not knowingly visit an obscene website or download obscene materials during the time they are employed in the character-sensitive job. The long-standing legal definition of obscenity that has never been accorded First Amendment protection could be included within the job description as constituting the forbidden, or no-fly zones. After a while, the requirement could be expanded to include additional positions and an affirmation that one has not visited such a site in, say, the preceding year.

CONTRIBUTORS

Hadley Arkes is the Edward Ney Professor of American Institutions at Amherst College, where he has been on the faculty since 1966. He has published five books with the Princeton University Press—*Bureaucracy, the Marshall Plan, and the National Interest* (1972), *The Philosopher in the City* (1981), *First Things* (1986), *Beyond the Constitution* (1990), and *The Return of George Sutherland* (1994)—and he now has published two books with Cambridge—*Natural Rights and the Right to Choose* (2002) and *Constitutional Illusions and Anchoring Truths: The Touchstone of Natural Law* (2010). Professor Arkes has become known to a wider audience through his writings in the *Wall Street Journal*, the *Washington Post*, the *Weekly Standard*, *National Review*, *Crisis*, and *First Things*. Active in the pro-life cause, he was the main advocate, and architect, of the bill that became known as the Born-Alive Infants Protection Act of 2002. Professor Arkes is the founder of the Committee for the American Founding at Amherst, and he served, in 2002–2003, as Visiting Professor of Public and International Affairs in the Woodrow Wilson School of Public and International Affairs, and as Vaughan Fellow in the James Madison Program in American Ideals and Institutions, both at Princeton University.

Gerard V. Bradley has been Professor of Law at the University of Notre Dame since 1992. He began teaching law in 1983 at the University of Illinois. Prior to that, Professor Bradley was a trial lawyer in the Manhattan District Attorney's Office. He graduated summa cum laude from Cornell Law School in 1980. At Notre Dame, Professor Bradley is co-director of the Natural Law Institute, and is editor-in-chief (with John Finnis) of *The American Journal of Jurisprudence*. He is Chair of the Academic Committee of the William E. and Carol G. Simon Center on Religion and the Constitution at the Witherspoon Institute (in Princeton, New Jersey), and is a visiting fellow at the Hoover Institution of Stanford University. Professor Bradley served for many years as President of the Fellowship of Catholic Scholars.

Ana J. Bridges is an Assistant Professor of Clinical Psychology at the University of Arkansas. She received her BS from the University of Illinois at Urbana-Champaign, her MS from Illinois State University, and her PhD from the University of Rhode Island. Dr. Bridges also completed her predoctoral training in clinical psychology at the Medical University of South Carolina. She has authored or co-authored more than forty articles, book chapters, and conference presentations in the areas of sexuality, ethnic diversity, and assessment. Dr. Bridges' research has been funded by agencies such as the Society for the Scientific Study of Sexuality. Recognized for her contributions to the field of sexuality, Dr. Bridges' research has been featured in publications such as *Psychology Today, Guardian UK, Glamour* magazine, and *The Price of Pleasure*, an educational documentary film about the pornography industry.

Norman Doidge is a psychiatrist, psychoanalyst, researcher, and essayist, and serves on the Research Faculty at the Columbia University Center for Psychoanalytic Training and Research, in New York, and in the University of Toronto's Department of Psychiatry. His book, *The Brain That Changes Itself: Stories of Personal Triumph from the Frontiers of Brain Science* (New York: Viking Penguin, 2007), has been a #1 best seller in Canada and Australia, and is a *New York Times* best seller, on the extended list for eleven months. The book is available in over seventy countries, and it is also a documentary film. It was chosen as one of the top science books of 2007 by amazon.com.

K. Doran is a graduate of Harvard and Princeton and is a 2009–2010 Bradley Visiting Fellow at the Witherspoon Institute.

Donna M. Hughes is a professor and holds the Eleanor M. and Oscar M. Carlson Endowed Chair in Women's Studies at the University of Rhode Island. She is an internationally leading researcher on sex trafficking. Professor Hughes has completed research on the trafficking of women and girls for sexual exploitation in the United States, Russia, the Ukraine, and Korea. She is frequently consulted by governments and nongovernmental organizations on policies related to the trafficking of women and girls for sexual exploitation. Professor Hughes researched and wrote two reports for the Council of Europe on the use of new information technologies for the trafficking of women and girls. She is currently researching sex trafficking in the production of pornography. Professor Hughes has testified before the United States House International Relations Committee, the Senate Foreign Relations

Committee, the Moscow Duma, and the Czech Parliament. She is a co-founder of Citizens Against Trafficking. Professor Hughes teaches undergraduate and graduate courses on human trafficking and sexual violence.

Mary Anne Layden is a psychotherapist, Director of Education, and Director of the Sexual Trauma and Psychopathology Program at the Center for Cognitive Therapy in the Department of Psychiatry at the University of Pennsylvania. Dr. Layden specializes in the treatment of victims and perpetrators of sexual violence, sexual addicts, and sex industry members. She has co-authored with Linnea Smith a chapter titled "Adult Survivors of the Child Sexual Exploitation Industry" in *Medical, Legal, and Social Science Aspects of Child Sexual Exploitation: A Comprehensive Review of Pornography, Prostitution, and Internet Crimes*. Dr. Layden has testified before the United States Congress on five occasions, focused on issues of sexual violence, the sexual exploitation industry, and the media. She has lectured extensively both in the United States and abroad on cognitive therapy, childhood sexual trauma, sexual addiction, the sexual exploitation industry, and imagery techniques.

Jill C. Manning is a Licensed Marriage and Family Therapist who specializes in clinical work related to pornography and problematic sexual behavior. She has been featured in television programs and documentaries, and on radio talk shows. Dr. Manning has authored numerous book chapters and academic journal articles on the subject of pornography. In 2005, she was selected to be a visiting Social Science Fellow at the Heritage Foundation in Washington, DC, and as a result of her research there, Dr. Manning testified before a Senate Subcommittee on the Harms of Pornography. A native of Calgary, Alberta, Canada, she currently resides in Denver, Colorado, with her husband and daughter.

Pamela Paul is an author and journalist who writes about social and cultural issues, demographic trends, consumer culture, psychology and health, and family. Her first book, *The Starter Marriage and the Future of Matrimony*, was named one of the best books of 2002 by the *Washington Post*; her second book, *Pornified*, was named one of the best books of 2005 by the *San Francisco Chronicle*. Ms. Paul's latest book, *Parenting, Inc.*, an investigation of the "parenting" business, was published in April 2008 by Times Books. Her work has appeared in the *Economist*, the *New York Times*, *Time* magazine, the *New York Times Book Review*, the *Washington Post*, the *National Post*, *Psychology Today*, and other national and international publications.

Roger Scruton is a writer, philosopher, and public commentator. In July 2009 he became an Adjunct Scholar of the American Enterprise Institute in Washington, DC. Prior to that, Professor Scruton was Research Professor for the Institute for the Psychological Sciences. He is also a Fellow of Blackfriars Hall in Oxford. Professor Scruton has specialized in aesthetics, with particular attention to music and architecture. He engages in contemporary political and cultural debates from the standpoint of a conservative thinker. Professor Scruton's two new books published in 2009 are *Beauty* (Oxford University Press) and *Understanding Music* (Continuum International).

James R. Stoner, Jr., is Professor of Political Science at Louisiana State University, where he has taught since 1988; he chairs the Department of Political Science, and is serving as Acting Dean in the Honors College, where he is also the 2010 Sternberg Professor. He is the author of *Common Law and Liberal Theory: Coke, Hobbes, and the Origins of American Constitutionalism* (University Press of Kansas, 1992) and *Common-Law Liberty: Rethinking American Constitutionalism* (University Press of Kansas, 2003), as well as a number of articles and essays. With Samuel Gregg, Professor Stoner co-edited *Rethinking Business Management: Examining the Foundations of Business Education* (The Witherspoon Institute, 2008). He received his AB from Middlebury College in Vermont, and his MA and PhD degrees from Harvard. In academic year 2002–2003, Professor Stoner was a Visiting Fellow in the James Madison Program in American Ideals and Institutions at Princeton University. He served from 2002 to 2006 on the National Council on the Humanities. Professor Stoner is a senior fellow at the Witherspoon Institute.

Hamza Yusuf is the co-founder of Zaytuna College, in Berkeley, California. He has been studying and teaching classical Islamic disciplines for over thirty years and is recognized as a leading proponent of interreligious tolerance and respect. Mr. Yusuf is a co-president of Religions for Peace. He was also a special adviser to the United Nations Alliance of Civilizations, and one of the original thirty-eight scholars who sent an *Open Letter to His Holiness, Pope Bernedict XVI.* Mr. Yusuf is licensed to teach in several subjects in the classical Islamic curriculum and has been a student of Shaykh Abdallah bin Bayyah, who is one of the greatest living authorities in both Islamic jurisprudence and legal theory as well as the Arabic language. He serves as an adviser in Stanford University's Program in

Islamic Studies as well as Berkeley's Graduate Theological Union Islamic Studies Program. Mr. Yusuf's books include *Purification of the Heart, The Content of Character, The Creed of Imam al-Tahawi,* and *Agenda to Change Our Condition.* He resides in the Greater Bay Area of California with his wife and five children.

APPENDIX:
SELECTED RESEARCH FINDINGS

Compiled by Mary Anne Layden

The Butner Study Redux: A report of the incidence of hands-on child victimization by child pornography offenders

Subjects were 155 imprisoned child pornography offenders. Information known at the time of sentencing was compared with information known at the end of their treatment program in prison. At the time of sentencing, 115 (74%) subjects didn't have any documented hands-on victims. The number of victims known at the time of sentencing was 75, or an average of 1.88 (SD=1.88) victims per offender. By the end of treatment, 24 (15%) subjects denied they had committed hands-on sexual abuse, and 131 subjects (85%) admitted they had at least one hands-on sexual offense, a 59% increase in the number of subjects with known hands-on offenses. The number of reported victims known at the end of treatment, among all offenders, was 1,777, an average of 13.56 (SD=30.11) victims per offender. When analyzed separately, we found that the 40 subjects who had known histories of hands-on sexual offending at the time of sentencing disclosed an average of 19.4 victims during their treatment period. In comparison, the 115 subjects with no known histories of these crimes ultimately disclosed an average of 8.7 victims.

In fact, of the 24 subjects in our sample who denied they had committed a hands-on offense at the end of treatment, nine were polygraphed, and only two "passed." In other words, less than 2% of subjects who entered treatment without known hands-on offenses were verified to be "just pictures" cases. It is noteworthy that both of these offenders remarked that while they had not molested a child prior to their arrest for the instant offense, with access and opportunity they would have been at risk for engaging in hands-on molestation. This calls into question whether it is pragmatically, not to mention theoretically, useful to discriminate between "child pornographers" and "child abusers" or even "pedophiles."

Bourke, Michael, and Andres Hernandez. "The Butner Study Redux: A Report of the Incidence of Hands-On Child Victimization by Child Pornography Offenders." *Journal of Family Violence* 24 (2009): 183–191.

Exposure to sexually explicit websites (SEWs) and adolescent sexual attitudes and behaviors

Adolescents exposed to sexually explicit websites (SEWs) were more likely to have multiple lifetime sexual partners, to have had more than one sexual partner in the last three months, to have used alcohol or other substances at last sexual encounter, and to have engaged in anal sex. Adolescents who visit SEWs display higher sexual permissiveness scores compared with those who never have been exposed, indicating a more permissive attitude.

Braun-Courville, Debra, and Mary Rojas. "Exposure to Sexually Explicit Web Sites and Adolescent Sexual Attitudes and Behaviors." *Journal of Adolescent Health* 45 (2009): 156–162.

X-rated sexual attitudes and behaviors associated with US early adolescents' exposure to sexually explicit media

Correlates of use and subsequent sexual attitudes and behaviors predicted by exposure to sexually explicit content (i.e., pornography and erotica) in adult magazines, X-rated movies, and the internet were examined in a prospective survey of a diverse sample of early adolescents (average age at baseline = 13.6 years; N = 967). Longitudinal analyses showed that early exposure for males predicted less progressive gender role attitudes, more permissive sexual norms, more sexual harassment perpetration, and having oral sex and sexual intercourse two years later. Early exposure for females predicted subsequently less progressive gender role attitudes, and having oral sex and sexual intercourse.

Brown, Jane, and Kelly L'Engle. "X-Rated: Sexual Attitudes and Behaviors Associated with U.S. Early Adolescents' Exposure to Sexually Explicit Media." *Communication Research* 36 (2009): 129–151.

Sexualized innocence: Effects of magazine ads portraying adult women as sexy little girls

Subjects were shown magazine ads that contained images of nature or adult sexy women or adult sexy women portrayed as little girls. They were then given the Child Sexual Abuse Myth Scale. There was more acceptance of child sexual abuse myths for those who saw the sexy women portrayed as little girls and for those who saw the sexy adult women when compared with those who saw nature images. In addition, the greater the acceptance of child sexual abuse myths, the more normal the subject thought it was to be attracted to young girls and the less concerned the subject was about women posed as young girls in various media.

Machia, Marty, and Sharon Lamb. "Sexualized Innocence: Effects of Magazine Ads Portraying Adult Women as Sexy Little Girls." *Journal of Media Psychology* 21, no.1 (2009): 15–24.

"Boys will be boys" and other gendered accounts: An exploration of victims' excuses and justifications for unwanted sexual contact and coercion

One in five women who reveal an incident of sexual victimization excuse or justify their situation by suggesting that male sexual aggression is natural, normal within dating relationships, didn't hurt anyone, is caused by outside factors such as alcohol, isn't really rape unless there were physical injuries, or was the victim's fault. In addition, only 19% of victims reported the incident to the police.

Weiss, Karen. "'Boys Will Be Boys' and Other Gendered Accounts: An Exploration of Victims' Excuses and Justifications for Unwanted Sexual Contact and Coercion." *Violence Against Women* 15 (2009): 810–834.

Generation XXX: Pornography acceptance and use among emerging adults

Almost two-thirds (67%) of young adult males find pornography use acceptable, while 49% of young adult females find it acceptable. More young adult males use pornography (87%) than do young adult females (31%). While 31% of males use pornography never or less than once a month, about 5% of males use pornography daily or almost daily. Young adult females use pornography infrequently; 69% never use it, 21% use it less than once a month, and only .2% use it daily or almost every day. For males, more pornography use is correlated with more sex partners, more alcohol use, more binge-drinking, greater acceptance of sex outside of marriage for married individuals, greater acceptance of sex before marriage, and less child-centeredness during marriage.

Carroll, Jason, Laura Padilla-Walker, Larry Nelson, Chad Olson, Carolyn McNamara Barry, and Stephanie Madsen. "Generation XXX: Pornography Acceptance and Use Among Emerging Adults." *Journal of Adolescent Research* 23, no.1 (2008): 6–30.

Does watching sex on television predict teen pregnancy? Findings from a national longitudinal survey of youth

Teens who were exposed to high levels of television sexual content (90th percentile) were twice as likely to experience pregnancy in the subsequent three years, compared with those with lower levels of exposure (10th percentile). Teens' base rate of media consumption was measured when they were 12–17 years old, and the outcome measures were taken when they were 15–20 years old.

Chandra, Anita, Steven Martino, Rebecca Collins, Marc Elliott, Sandra Berry, David Kanouse, and Angela Miu. "Does Watching Sex on Television Predict Teen Pregnancy? Findings from a National Longitudinal Survey of Youth." *Pediatrics* 122 (2008): 1047–1054.

Pornography use and sexual aggression: The impact of frequency and type of pornography use on recidivism among sexual offenders

In this study, we examined the unique contribution of pornography consumption to the longitudinal prediction of criminal recidivism in a sample of 341 child molesters. After controlling for general and specific risk factors for sexual aggression, pornography added significantly to the prediction of recidivism. Statistical interactions indicated that frequency of pornography use was primarily a risk factor for higher-risk offenders, when compared with lower-risk offenders, and that content of pornography (i.e., pornography containing deviant content) was a risk factor for all groups. For those who viewed deviant pornography, the predicted odds for criminal recidivism increased by 177%, the predicted odds for violent (including sexual) recidivism increased by 185%, and the predicted odds for sexual recidivism was 233%.

Kingston, Drew, Paul Fedoroff, Philip Firestone, Susan Curry, and John Bradford. "Pornography Use and Sexual Aggression: The Impact of Frequency and Type of Pornography Use on Recidivism Among Sexual Offenders." *Aggressive Behavior* 34, no. 4 (2008): 341–351.

Linking male use of the sex industry to controlling behaviors in violent relationships

Male domestic violence offenders who utilize the sex industry (pornography and strip clubs) use more controlling behaviors, and engage in more sexual abuse, stalking, and marital rape against their partners then do males who do not use the sex industry.

Simmons, Catherine, Peter Lehmann, and Shannon Collier-Tenison. "Linking Male Use of the Sex Industry to Controlling Behaviors in Violent Relationships." *Violence Against Women* 14 (2008): 406–417.

The role of cognitive distortions in pedophilic offending: Internet and contact offenders compared

Contrary to the expectation that contact offenders would have more cognitive distortions, it was found that internet offenders had more cognitive distortions that children are sexual beings.

Howitt, Dennis, and Kerry Sheldon. "The Role of Cognitive Distortions in Paedophilic Offending: Internet and Contact Offenders Compared." *Psychology, Crime and Law* 13, no. 5 (2007): 469–486.

Adolescents' exposure to a sexualized media environment and their notions of women as sex objects

Exposure to sexually explicit online movies was significantly related to beliefs about women as sex objects for both male and female 13–18-year-old Dutch adolescents.

Peter, Jochen, and Patti M. Valkenburg. "Adolescents' Exposure to a Sexualized Media Environment and Their Notions of Women as Sex Objects." *Sex Roles* 56 (2007): 381–395.

Cross-sectional predictors of sexual assault perpetration in a community sample of single African American and Caucasian men

Almost a quarter (24.5%) of men acknowledged committing an act since the age of 14 who met standard legal definitions of attempted or completed rape; an additional 39% had committed another type of sexual assault involving forced sexual contact or verbal coercion. The number of sexual assaults perpetrated by participants was associated with the effects of childhood sexual abuse, adolescent delinquency, alcohol problems, sexual dominance, positive attitudes about casual sexual relationships, and pressure from peers to engage in sexual relationships. Additionally, empathy buffered the relationship between sexual dominance and perpetration so that the greater the empathy the males showed the less likely they were to engage in perpetration at each level of sexual dominance. Of the 40 subjects whose behavior met the legal definition of rape or attempted rape, only 5 called it rape.

Abbey, Antonia, Michele Parkhill, Renee BeShears, A. Monique Clinton-Sherrod, and Tina Zawacki. "Cross-Sectional Predictors of Sexual Assault Perpetration in a Community Sample of Single African American and Caucasian Men." *Aggressive Behavior* 32 (2005): 54–67.

Use of pornography and self-reported engagement in sexual violence among adolescents

Reading and viewing pornographic material (magazines, comics, films, and videos) was linked to perpetrating sexual violence (both sexual harassment and forced sex) for both male and female adolescents. Reading and viewing pornographic material was linked to being a victim of sexual violence (both sexual harassment and forced sex) for female adolescents. Reading and viewing pornographic material was linked to being the victim of forced sex for male adolescents.

Bonino, Silvia, Silvia Ciairano, Emanuela Rabaglietti, and Elena Cattelino. "Use of Pornography and Self-Reported Engagement in Sexual Violence Among Adolescents." *European Journal of Developmental Psychology* 3, no. 3 (2006): 265–288.

Exhibitionistic and voyeuristic behavior in a Swedish national population survey

In a Swedish survey of 2,450 randomly selected 18–60-year-olds, 3% reported at least one incident of exhibitionistic behavior; 8% reported at least one incident of voyeuristic behavior. Both exhibitionism and voyeurism were correlated to increased pornography use. Both exhibitionists and voyeurs had an increased likelihood of engaging in other atypical sexual behaviors such as sadomasochism or cross-dressing. Exhibitionists and voyeurs showed increased sexual fantasies that mirrored their behavior, but they also showed an increase in sexual fantasies in other atypical sexual behaviors as well. While exhibitionists had more exhibitionistic sexual fantasies than did voyeurs or normals, they also had more voyeuristic sexual fantasies than did normals. Voyeurs had more voyeuristic sexual fantasies than exhibitionists or normals, but they also had more exhibitionist sexual fantasies than did normals.

Långström, Niklas, and Michael C. Seto. "Exhibitionistic and Voyeuristic Behavior in a Swedish National Population Survey." *Archives of Sexual Behavior* 35 (2006): 427–435.

The mass media are an important context for adolescents' sexual behavior

The media that teenagers watch has a high level of sexual content. The majority of sexual content in the media depicts risk-free, recreational sexual behavior between non-married people. Adolescents who are exposed to more sexual content in the media, and who perceive greater support from the media for teen sexual behavior, report greater intentions to engage in sexual intercourse and more sexual activity.

L'Engle, Kelly Ladin, Jane Brown, and Kristin Kenneavy. "The Mass Media Are an Important Context for Adolescents' Sexual Behavior." *Journal of Adolescent Health* 38, no. 4 (2006): 186–192.

Child pornography offenses are a valid diagnostic indicator of pedophilia

Individuals who have been charged with a child pornography offense and have offended against children and individuals who have been charged with a child pornography offense and have not offended against children are more likely to be pedophiles than individuals who have offended against adults or individuals who have offended against children but who do not use child pornography. Therefore, being charged with a child pornography offense is a better indicator of who might get the diagnosis of pedophilia than having sexually molested a child.

Seto, Michael C., James Cantor, and Ray Blanchard. "Child Pornography Offenses Are a Valid Diagnostic Indicator of Pedophilia." *Journal of Abnormal Psychology* 115, no. 3 (2006): 610–615.

Transvestic fetishism in the general population: Prevalence and correlates

In a Swedish survey of 2,450 randomly selected 18–60-year-olds, 3% reported having at least one incident of transvestic fetishism. Transvestic fetishism was found to correlate with increased pornography use. Transvestic fetishism was strongly related to experiences of sexual arousal from using pain, spying on others having sex, and exposing one's genitals to a stranger.

Långström, Nicklas, and Kenneth Zucker. "Transvestic Fetishism in the General Population: Prevalence and Correlates." *Journal of Sex and Marital Therapy* 31 (2005): 87–95.

Pornified

At the 2003 meeting of the American Academy of Matrimonial Lawyers, a gathering of the nation's divorce lawyers, attendees documented a startling trend. Nearly two-thirds of the attorneys present had witnessed a sudden rise in divorces related to the internet; 58% of those were the result of a spouse looking at excessive amounts of pornography online.

Paul, Pamela. *Pornified: How Pornography Is Damaging Our Lives, Our Relationships, and Our Families*. New York: Henry Holt and Co., 2005.

The criminal histories and later offending of child pornography offenders

Two hundred and one adult male child pornography offenders were examined for re-offending. Child pornography offenders with prior criminal records were significantly more likely to offend again in any way during the follow-up period. Child pornography offenders who had committed a prior or concurrent contact sexual offense were the most likely to offend again, either generally or sexually.

Seto, Michael C., and Angela Eke. "The Criminal Histories and Later Offending of Child Pornography Offenders." *Sexual Abuse: Journal of Research and Treatment* 17, no. 2 (2005): 201–210.

Watching sex on television predicts adolescent initiation of sexual behavior

Youth ages 12–17 in the 90th percentile of TV sex viewing had a predicted probability of intercourse initiation that was approximately double that of youth in the 10th percentile.

Collins, Rebecca, Marc Elliott, Sandra Berry, David Kanouse, Dale Kunkel, Sarah Hunter, and Angela Miu. "Watching Sex on Television Predicts Adolescent Initiation of Sexual Behavior." *Pediatrics* 114, no. 3 (2004): e280–e289.

Older adolescents' positive attitudes toward younger adolescents as sexual partners

Subjects were 710 Norwegian 18–19-year-olds attending non-vocational high schools. Some likelihood of having sex with preadolescents (less than 12 years old) was reported by 5.9% of the males; 19.1% of the males indicated some likelihood of having sex with a 13–14-year-old.

The 19.1% who were willing to have sex with a 13–14-year-old reported:

- More high-frequency drinking
- More alcohol-related problems
- Earlier sexual initiation
- More conduct problems
- Poorer psychosocial adjustment
- More high-frequency pornography use
- Having more friends who are interested in child pornography and violent pornography
- Greater use of coercion to obtain sexual favors
- More buying and selling of sex

Hegna, Kristinn, Svein Mossige, and Lars Wichstrom. "Older Adolescents' Positive Attitudes Toward Younger Adolescents as Sexual Partners." *Adolescence* 39, no. 156 (2004): 627–651.

When words are not enough: The search for the effect of pornography on abused women

The use of pornography (by the batterer) significantly increases a battered woman's odds of being sexually abused. Use of pornography and alcohol increases the odds of sexual abuse. Pornography alone increases the odds of sexual abuse by a factor of almost 2, and the combination of pornography and alcohol increases the odds of sexual abuse by a factor of 3.

Shope, Janet Hinson. "When Words Are Not Enough: The Search for the Effect of Pornography on Abused Women." *Violence Against Women* 10, no. 1 (2004): 56–72.

Adult social bonds and use of internet pornography

Persons ever having an extramarital affair were 3.18 times more apt to have used cyberporn than ones who had not had affairs. Further, those ever having engaged in paid sex were 3.7 times more apt than those who had not to be using cyberporn.

Stack, Steven, Ira Wasserman, and Roger Kern. "Adult Social Bonds and Use of Internet Pornography." *Social Science Quarterly* 85 (2004): 75–88.

Child pornography and the internet: Perpetuating a cycle of abuse

Interviews were conducted with 13 men who were convicted of downloading child pornography with a view to understanding how they talked about the photographs and the function such talk played in their accounts. Quotations are used from the interviews to illustrate the analysis.

Their selection of images for sexual purposes was influenced by superficial cues, which allowed the viewer to believe that the children in the pictures were consenting and enjoyed being photographed: "no kids being hurt," "and they had to look happy. I mean, I wasn't looking for rape or anything."

Accessing the images appeared to reinforce existing fantasies, and was used to give permission to act on them: "It made me want to do the things I wanted to do. It gave me more courage to do them . . . knowing that I've seen it there . . . they were doing it . . . I can do it."

Teaching skills: "I copied what I'd seen on the computer."

Tolerance: "It seemed to be getting younger and younger . . . as the more I got into the sites and the more I diversified the more you could . . . you know . . . the harder the pornography got . . . seemed to be getting harder and harder."

Internet effect: "The children side of it came into being when I discovered this stuff on the internet." "So I then got into this kind of regime of finding hard-core porn . . . the sort that if I had . . . the nerve I would have bought a magazine that showed this kind of material in a shop but then there'd be a problem of sneaking the magazine back into the house and then accessing that material privately."

Quayle, Ethel, and Max Taylor. "Child Pornography and the Internet: Perpetuating a Cycle of Abuse." *Deviant Behavior* 23, no. 4 (2002): 331–361.

Exposure to X-rated movies and adolescents' sexual and contraceptive-related attitudes and behaviors

Black females ages 14–18 were questioned about their exposure to X-rated movies. Exposure to X-rated movies was associated with being more likely to have negative attitudes toward using condoms, to have multiple sex partners, to have sex more frequently, to not have used contraception during the last intercourse, to not have used contraception in the past six months, to have a strong desire to conceive, and to test positive for chlamydia.

Wingood, Gina, Ralph DiClemente, Kathy Harrington, Suzy Davies, Edward Hook III, and M. Kim Oh. "Exposure to X-Rated Movies and Adolescents' Sexual and Contraceptive-Related Attitudes and Behaviors." *Pediatrics* 107, no. 5 (2001): 1116–1119.

Exploring the connection between pornography and sexual violence

Subjects were 100 women who presented to a rape crisis center. Twenty-eight percent said that their abuser used pornography; 58% did not know if he used pornography or not. Of those whose abuser used pornography, 40% said the pornography was part of the abuse incident being used either during the abuse or just prior to it, and 43% said that it affected the nature of the abuse. None of the women thought that it decreased the frequency of the abuse, 21% thought that it increased the frequency of the abuse, and 14% believed that it increased the level of violence. In fact, 18% thought that their abuser became more sadistic with the use of pornography.

Of the total sample, 12% said the abuser imitated the pornography, and 14% said someone had tried to force them to do something they had seen in pornography.

Bergen, Raquel, and Kathleen Bogle. "Exploring the Connection Between Pornography and Sexual Violence." *Violence and Victims* 15, no. 3 (2000): 227–234.

Pornography and sexual aggression: Are there reliable effects, and can we understand them?

Males who were high in hostile masculinity and sexual promiscuity, and who used pornography frequently were significantly more likely to have physically and sexually aggressed (7.78) than did males who were low in these factors (.4).

Malamuth, Neil M., Tamara Addison, and Mary Koss. "Pornography and Sexual Aggression: Are There Reliable Effects and Can We Understand Them?" *Annual Review of Sex Research* 11 (2000): 26–68.

Child pornography and the internet

Almost one-third of subjects thought that downloading child pornography from a newsgroup was legal, although it is illegal.

McCabe, Kimberly. "Child Pornography and the Internet." *Social Science Computer Review* 18 (2000): 73–76.

Effects of internet pornography and individual differences on men's attitudes toward women

The likelihood of sexually harassing another is significantly correlated with volume of past exposure to sexually explicit materials.

Barak, Azy, William Fisher, Sandra Belfry, and Darryl Lashambe. "Sex, Guys, and Cyberspace: Effects of Internet Pornography and Individual Differences on Men's Attitudes Toward Women." *Journal of Psychological and Human Sexuality* 11 (1999): 63–92.

Focusing on the clients of street prostitutes: A creative approach to reducing violence against women

Men who go to prostitutes are much more likely to have watched a pornographic movie over the last year (66%) than a national sample (33%). Men who go to prostitutes frequently are even more likely to have seen a pornographic movie (74%) than those who have gone to a prostitute only once (53%). The same pattern is seen with the use of pornographic magazines; men who go to prostitutes frequently are more likely to have seen a pornographic magazine in the last year (75%) than men who have gone to a prostitute only once (56%).

Monto, Martin. "Focusing on the Clients of Street Prostitutes: A Creative Approach to Reducing Violence Against Women," final report for the National Institute of Justice, Grant #97-IJ-CX-0033, June 2000.

Pathways in the offending process of extrafamilial sexual child molesters

Two pathways to offending were identified: the non-coercive pathway and the coercive pathway. Subjects using the non-coercive pathway generally had used pornography (50%), had deviant sexual fantasies before their offenses (71%), and had cognitive distortions (64%).

Proulx, Jean, Christine Perreault, and Marc Ouimet. "Pathways in the Offending Process of Extrafamilial Sexual Child Molesters." *Sexual Abuse: A Journal of Research and Treatment* 11, no. 2 (1999): 117–129.

Deviant sexual behavior in children and young adolescents

In a sample of 30 juveniles who had committed sex offenses, exposure to pornographic material at a young age was common. The researchers reported that 29 of the 30 juveniles had been exposed to X-rated magazines or videos; the average age at exposure was about 7.5 years.

Wieckowski, Edward, Peggy Hartsoe, Arthur Mayer, and Joianne Shortz. "Deviant Sexual Behavior in Children and Young Adolescents: Frequency and Patterns." *Sexual Abuse: A Journal of Research and Treatment* 10, no. 4 (1998): 293–304.

Women in strip clubs speak out

Abuse by customers

91%	Verbally abused
52%	Called cunt
61%	Called whore
85%	Called bitch
88%	Arm grabbed
73%	Breast grabbed
91%	Buttocks grabbed
27%	Hair pulled
58%	Pinched
24%	Slapped
36%	Bitten
76%	Customers flicked cigarettes, ice, coins
70%	Customers followed them home
42%	Customers stalked them

Abuse by managers or male staff

85%	Verbally or physically abused
21%	Called cunt
18%	Called slut
33%	Called bitch
12%	Pinched
12%	Slapped

Women who work in strip clubs are abused by both customers and management.

Holsopple, Kelly. "From the Dressing Room: Women in Strip Clubs Speak Out." *Whisper* 9 (1995): 9.

The relationship between pornography usage and child molesting

Approximately 93% of child molesters reported having some fantasies about committing sexual offenses against children. The child molesters were far more likely to have used more pornography in adulthood, and the most common type of materials were "soft-core" materials, which involved nudity or consenting sexual activities between adults. Some child molesters reported a cathartic effect from viewing pornography, but this perception was not supported by other results of this study, in that over one-third of the child molesters reported using pornographic materials shortly before committing a sexual offense.

Wheeler, David L. "The Relationship Between Pornography Usage and Child Molesting." *Dissertation Abstracts International Section A: Humanities and Social Sciences* 57, no. 8-A (1996): 3691.

The ages of fathers in California adolescent births, 1993

School-age mothers have partners who are older. Men who have finished their schooling father two-thirds of the infants born to school-age mothers. These men are on average 4.2 years older than senior-high mothers, and 6.8 years older than junior-high mothers.

Males, Mike, and Kenneth Chew. "The Ages of Fathers in California Adolescent Births, 1993." *American Journal of Public Health* 86 (1996): 565–568.

Self-reported sexual interest in children: Sex differences and psychosocial correlates in a university sample

A sample of 180 female and 99 male university students were surveyed regarding their sexual interest in children. Males reported sexual attraction to at least one child more often than did females. Both males and females reported very low rates of sexual fantasies about children, masturbation to such fantasies, or potential likelihood of sexual contact with a child. Males' sexual attraction to children was associated with:

- Lower self-esteem
- Greater sexual conflicts
- More sexual impulsivity
- Lower scores on the Socialization Scale of the California Psychological Inventory
- Greater use of pornography depicting consenting adult sex
- More self-reported difficulty attracting age-appropriate sexual partners

Smiljanich, Kathy, and John Briere. "Self-Reported Sexual Interest in Children: Sex Differences and Psychosocial Correlates in a University Sample." *Violence and Victims* 11, no. 1 (1996): 39–50.

A meta-analysis summarizing the effects of pornography II: Aggression after exposure

A meta-analysis of 33 studies revealed that exposure to either violent or non-violent pornography increased behavioral aggression.

Allen, Mike, Dave D'Allessio, and Keri Brezgel. "A Meta-Analysis Summarizing the Effects of Pornography II: Aggression After Exposure." *Human Communication Research* 22 (1995): 258–283.

Pornography and rape myth acceptance

There was an increase in attitudes supporting sexual violence following pornography exposure. Violent pornography increased these attitudes even more than did non-violent pornography.

Allen, Mike, Tara Emmers, Lisa Gebhardt, and Mary Giery. "Pornography and Rape Myth Acceptance." *Journal of Communication* 45 (1995): 5–26.

Comparative analysis of juvenile sexual offenders, violent nonsexual offenders, and status offenders

Juvenile sexual offenders (juvenile rapists and juvenile child molesters) were more likely to have been exposed to pornography (42%) than were juvenile nonsexual offenders (29%). Juvenile sexual offenders also were exposed at an early age (5–8 years old). Juvenile child molesters had been more frequently exposed to pornography.

Ford, Michelle, and Jean Ann Linney. "Comparative Analysis of Juvenile Sexual Offenders, Violent Nonsexual Offenders, and Status Offenders." *Journal of Interpersonal Violence* 10, no. 1 (1995): 56–70.

The effects of exposure to filmed sexual violence on attitudes toward rape

Males who viewed sexual violence obtained higher scores on scales measuring acceptance of interpersonal violence and rape myth acceptance when compared with males who viewed either a physically violent film or a neutral film.

Weisz, Monica, and Christopher Earls. "The Effects of Exposure to Filmed Sexual Violence on Attitudes Toward Rape." *Journal of Interpersonal Violence* 10 (1995): 71–84.

Pornography and sexual aggression: Associations of violent and non-violent depictions with rape and rape proclivity

All types of pornography (soft-core, hard-core, violent, and rape) were correlated with using verbal coercion, drugs, and alcohol to sexually coerce women.

All types of pornography other than soft-core were correlated with rape. Those reporting higher exposure to violent pornography use were six times more likely to report having raped than those in the low-exposure group.

Likelihood of forcing a woman sexually was correlated with hard-core, violent, and rape pornography use but not with soft-core pornography use. Likelihood of rape was correlated with all types of pornography use.

Boeringer, Scot. "Pornography and Sexual Aggression: Associations of Violent and Nonviolent Depictions With Rape and Rape Proclivity." *Deviant Behavior* 15 (1994): 289–304.

Pornography and abuse of women

Forty percent of abused women indicated that their partner used violent pornography. Of those whose partners used pornography, 53% indicated that they had been asked or forced to enact scenes they had been shown. Forty percent had been raped, and of these, 73% stated that their partners had used pornography. Twenty-six percent of the women had been reminded of pornography during the abuse.

Cramer, Elizabeth, and Judith McFarlane. "Pornography and Abuse of Women." *Public Health Nursing* 11, no. 4 (1994): 268–272.

Effects of violent pornography upon viewer's rape myth beliefs: A study of Japanese males

Japanese males who were exposed to a rape depiction in which the woman appeared to have enjoyed the rape were more likely to believe that women in general enjoy rape and to make false accusations of rape when compared with males who were exposed to a rape depiction in which the women displayed pain.

Ohbuchi, Ken-Ichi, Tatsuhiko Ikeda, and Goya Takeuchi. "Effects of Violent Pornography Upon Viewer's Rape Myth Beliefs: A Study of Japanese Males." *Psychology, Crime, and Law* 1 (1994): 71–81.

Correlates of attitudes toward sexual harassment among early adolescents

Early adolescent males who viewed mostly R- and X- (NC-17) rated films had a more accepting attitude toward sexual harassment than did males who viewed mostly G, PG, and PG-13 films. Early adolescent females who listened to more pop music were more accepting of sexual harassment than were females who listened to little pop music.

Strouse, Jeremiah, Megan Goodwin, and Bruce Roscoe. "Correlates of Attitudes Toward Sexual Harassment Among Early Adolescents." *Sex Roles* 31 (1994): 559–577.

The research on women and pornography: The many faces of harm

Twenty-four percent of women surveyed indicated that they were upset by someone trying to get them to do something that they had seen in pornography. Those women who answered "yes" were more likely to have been victims of threatened or actual sexual assault.

Senn, Charlene. "The Research on Women and Pornography: The Many Faces of Harm." In *Making Violence Sexy*, ed. Diana E. H. Russell. New York: Teachers College Press, 1993.

Women's attitudes and fantasies about rape as a function of early exposure to pornography

Women who were exposed to pornography as children were more likely to accept the rape myth and to have sexual fantasies that involved rape.

Corne, Shawn, John Briere, and Lillian Esses. "Women's Attitudes and Fantasies About Rape as a Function of Early Exposure to Pornography." *Journal of Interpersonal Violence* 7, no. 4 (1992): 454–461.

Is sexual erotica associated with sexual deviance in adolescent males?

Juvenile sexual offenders were questioned about their use of sexually explicit material. Only 11% said that they did not use sexually explicit material. Of those who used it, 74% said that it increased their sexual arousal.

Becker, Judith, and Robert Stein. "Is Sexual Erotica Associated With Sexual Deviance in Adolescent Males?" *International Journal of Law and Psychiatry* 14 (1991): 85–95.

Pornography as a source of sex information

Men rated seven sources of sex information. The highest sources of sex information for males were (1) friends, (2) media, (3) books, and (4) pornography. The lowest sources of sex information for males were (5) school, (6) parents, and (7) church. Females rated the same seven sources of sex information. For females, the highest sources of sex information were (1) friends, (2) books, (3) parents, and (4) school. For females, the lowest sources of sex information were (5) media, (6) pornography, and (7) church.

Duncan, David, and J. William Donnelly. "Pornography as a Source of Sex Information for Students at a Private Northeastern University." *Psychological Reports* 68 (1991): 782.

Dissociation and abuse among multiple-personality patients, prostitutes, and exotic dancers

	Strippers	Prostitutes
Sexual abuse	65%	55%
Multiple-personality disorder	35%	5%
Borderline-personality disorder	55%	11%
Depression	60%	60%
Substance abuse	40%	80%

Strippers and prostitutes suffer from a number of psychiatric disorders. Childhood abuse often precedes their entry into the sexual exploitation industry.

Ross, Colin, Geri Anderson, Sharon Heber, and Ron Norton. "Dissociation and Abuse Among Multiple-Personality Patients, Prostitutes, and Exotic Dancers." *Hospital and Community Psychiatry* 41, no. 3 (1990): 328–330.

University males' sexual interest in children: Predicting potential indices of "pedophilia" in a nonforensic sample

A survey was administered to 193 male undergraduate students regarding their sexual interest in children, as well as their responses to a number of questions theoretically relevant to pedophilia. In total, 21% of subjects reported sexual attraction to some small children, 9% described sexual fantasies involving children, 5% admitted to having masturbated to such fantasies, and 7% indicated some likelihood of having sex with a child if they could avoid detection and punishment. These sexual interests were associated with negative early sexual experiences, masturbation to pornography, self-reported likelihood of raping a woman, frequent sex partners, sexual conflicts, and attitudes supportive of sexual dominance over women. The data did not, however, support clinical theories regarding sexual repression or impulse-control problems among potential pedophiles.

Note: Sexual interest in children did not correlate with use of pornography but did correlate with masturbation to pornography.

Briere, John, and Marsha Runtz. "University Males' Sexual Interest in Children: Predicting Potential Indices of 'Pedophilia' in a Nonforensic Sample." *Child Abuse and Neglect* 13 (1989): 65–75.

The effects of repeated exposure to sexually violent pornography, non-violent dehumanizing pornography, and erotica

High pornography users were higher than low pornography users on scales measuring rape myth acceptance, acceptance of violence against women, adversarial sex beliefs, reported likelihood of committing rape and forced sex acts, and sex callousness.

High pornography users who were shown non-violent, dehumanizing pornography showed higher scores in reported likelihood of committing rape, sex callousness, and sexually aggressive behaviors than did high pornography users who weren't shown pornography.

Check, James V. P., and Ted Guloien. "The Effects of Repeated Exposure to Sexually Violent Pornography; Nonviolent, Dehumanizing Pornography; and Erotica." In *Pornography: Recent Research, Interpretations, and Policy Considerations*, eds. Dolf Zillmann and Jennings Bryant. Hillsdale, N.J.: Lawrence Erlbaum Associates, 1989.

The use of sexually explicit stimuli by rapists, child molesters, and non-offenders

Sex offenders show a high rate of use of hard-core pornography: child molesters (67%), incest offenders (53%), and rapists (83%), compared with non-offenders (29%). Child molesters (37%) and rapists (35%) were more likely to use pornography as an instigator to offending than were incest offenders (13%). The material used to instigate offending was often adult and consensual pornography.

Marshall, William. "The Use of Sexually Explicit Stimuli by Rapists, Child Molesters, and Non-Offenders." *Journal of Sex Research* 25, no. 2 (1988): 267–288.

I never called it rape

Men who engaged in date rape rated as "very frequently" how often they read *Playboy, Penthouse, Chic, Club, Forum, Gallery, Genesis, Oui,* or *Hustler.*

Warshaw, Robin. *I Never Called It Rape*. New York: HarperCollins, 1988.

Use of pornography in the criminal and developmental histories of sex offenders

Child molesters when compared with rapists indicated:

- More exposure to pornography as an adult
- More use of pornography prior to criminal offenses
- More use of pornography during criminal offenses

- More use of pornography to relieve the impulse to commit an offense
- More overall influence of pornography on life

Carter, Daniel Lee, Robert Alan Prentky, Raymond Knight, Penny Vanderveer, and Richard Boucher. "Use of Pornography in the Criminal and Developmental Histories of Sex Offenders." *Journal of Interpersonal Violence* 2, no. 2 (1987): 196–211.

An empirical investigation of the role of pornography in the verbal and physical abuse of women

Battered women experienced significantly more sexual violence than did non-battered controls. In addition, 39% of the battered women indicated that their partners had tried to get them to act out pornographic scenes they had been shown as compared with 3% of the controls.

Sommers, Evelyn, and James V. P. Check. "An Empirical Investigation of the Role of Pornography in the Verbal and Physical Abuse of Women." *Violence and Victims* 2, no.1 (1987): 189–209.

Shifting preferences in pornography consumption

Male and female students and non-students were shown videos for one hour each week for six weeks. Half of these subjects were shown pornography that was non-violent and included common sexual practices. Half were shown videos that didn't have any pornography or violence and were innocuous. Two weeks after they stopped, all of the subjects were given an opportunity to watch videos in private. Those who saw the pornography were significantly more likely to pick harder-core pornography, which included sex with animals and sex that included violence. Those who had seen the innocuous videos were unlikely to pick the pornographic videos to watch. They were especially unlikely to pick the hard-core pornographic ones.

Watching pornographic videos increases the interest in watching pornographic videos that are more hard-core and contain unusual and/or pathological sexual behaviors.

Zillmann, Dolf, and Jennings Bryant. "Shifting Preferences in Pornography Consumption." *Communication Research* 13, no. 4 (1986): 560–578.

An empirical assessment of some feminist hypotheses about rape

One group of males saw a portrayal of a woman who was aroused by sexual violence. A second group saw control materials. Both groups then were exposed to pornography that involved rape. The first group who had seen a woman aroused by sexual violence was more likely than the second group who did not see those images to say that the woman in the rape pornography suffered less and enjoyed it, and that women in general enjoy rape.

Check, James, and Neil M. Malamuth. "An Empirical Assessment of Some Feminist Hypotheses About Rape." *International Journal of Women's Studies* 8 (1985): 414–423.

Sexual stratification, pornography, and rape in the United States

The correlation between rape rates and circulation rates for eight pornographic magazines (*Playboy, Hustler, Oui, Chic, Club, Forum, Gallery,* and *Genesis*) in 50 states was +.64. States with higher circulation rates had higher rape rates.

Baron, Larry, and Murray Straus. "Sexual Stratification, Pornography, and Rape in the United States." In *Pornography and Sexual Aggression*, eds. Neil M. Malamuth and Edward Donnerstein. New York: Academic Press, 1984.

Sex and violence: A ripple effect

In South Australia the pornography laws were liberalized, which saw a 284% increase in rape. During the same time period in Queensland, Australia, there were in place conservative pornography laws, and they experienced only a 23% increase in rape.

In Hawaii, pornography laws were liberalized and then became more restrictive, and then they were liberalized again. The rape curve followed the same pattern of increasing, then decreasing, when the restriction on pornography occurred, and then increasing again when the restrictions were lifted.

Court, John. "Sex and Violence: A Ripple Effect." In *Pornography and Sexual Aggression*, eds. Neil M. Malamuth and Edward Donnerstein. New York: Academic Press, 1984.

Pornography: Its effects on violence against women

Males were either angered or not, and then either they were shown a pornographic movie in which a female was distressed throughout a sexual assault or they were not shown a movie. The males who were angered and saw the movie gave more electric shocks to a female than did the males who were not angered and didn't see the movie.

Males were either angered or not, and then either they were shown a pornographic movie in which a female was portrayed as becoming sexually aroused at the end of the movie or not shown a movie. The males who saw the movie gave more electric shocks to a female whether they had been angered or not.

Donnerstein, Edward. "Pornography: Its Effects on Violence Against Women." In *Pornography and Sexual Aggression*, eds. Neil M. Malamuth and Edward Donnerstein. New York: Academic Press, 1984.

Effects of massive exposure to pornography

Exposure to "massive pornography" (4 hours and 48 minute) leads to changes in beliefs and attitudes; for example, reduced support for the women's liberation movement, reduced belief that pornography needs to be restricted for minors, reduced recommended jail sentences for rapists, increased callousness toward woman, and beliefs of increased frequency of pathological sex (such as sex with animals and sex with violence).

Zillmann, Dolf, and Jennings Bryant. "Effects of Massive Exposure to Pornography." In *Pornography and Sexual Aggression*, eds. Neil M. Malamuth and Edward Donnerstein. New York: Academic Press, 1984.

Self-reported likelihood of sexually aggressive behavior: Attitudinal versus sexual explanations

Sixty percent of males said that there was some likelihood that if they thought they wouldn't get caught, then they would be willing to force a women to do something she really didn't want to do and/or rape her.

Briere, John, and Neil M. Malamuth. "Self-Reported Likelihood of Sexually Aggressive Behavior: Attitudinal Versus Sexual Explanations." *Journal of Research in Personality* 17 (1983): 315–323.

Sexual experiences survey: A research instrument investigating sexual aggression and victimization

The more frequently men used pornography, and the more violent the pornography they used, the more likely they were to be involved in various types of coercive sex, including physical coercion.

Koss, Mary, and Cheryl Oros. "Sexual Experiences Survey: A Research Instrument Investigating Sexual Aggression and Victimization." *Journal of Consulting and Clinical Psychology* 50 (1982): 455–457.

Rape fantasies as a function of exposure to violent sexual stimuli

Males were exposed to either an arousing rape slide-audio presentation, or an arousing non-rape slide-audio presentation. Later they were asked to try to describe fantasies they would use to try to reach as high a level of sexual arousal as they could without providing any direct stimulation to the penis. Those who had been exposed to the rape presentation created more sexually violent fantasies than did those exposed to the non-rape presentation.

Malamuth, Neil M. "Rape Fantasies as a Function of Exposure to Violent Sexual Stimuli." *Archives of Sexual Behavior* 10 (1981): 33–47.

Experimentally induced "sexual fetishism": Replication and development

Males can learn to get sexually aroused to the image of a woman's boot by seeing images of nude women associated with a boot.

Rachman, Stanley, and R. J. Hodgson. "Experimentally Induced 'Sexual Fetishism': Replication and Development." *Psychological Record* 18 (1968): 25–27.

INDEX

A NOTE ON THE WITHERSPOON INSTITUTE

The majority of the papers in this volume were presented to an audience of scholars, professionals, journalists, and non-profit leaders at a consultation of the Witherspoon Institute, held in Princeton, New Jersey, in December 2008.

The Witherspoon Institute works to enhance public understanding of the political, moral, and philosophical principles of free and democratic societies. It promotes the application of these principles to contemporary problems.

The Institute is named for John Witherspoon (1723–1794), a leading member of the Continental Congress, a signer of the Declaration of Independence, the sixth president of Princeton University, and a mentor to James Madison. As important as these and his other notable accomplishments are, however, it is Witherspoon's commitment to liberal education and his recognition of the dignity of human freedom, whether it be personal, political, or religious, that inspire the Institute's name.

In furtherance of its educational mission, the Witherspoon Institute supports a variety of scholarly activities. It sponsors the research and teaching of its fellows; organizes consultations, lectures, and colloquia on contemporary issues and problems; and encourages and assists scholarly collaboration among individuals sharing the Institute's interest in the foundations of a free society. The Witherspoon Institute also serves as a resource for the media and other organizations seeking comment on matters of concern to the Institute and its associated scholars.

For more information about the work of the Witherspoon Institute, please visit www.winst.org.

A NOTE ON THE SOCIAL TRENDS INSTITUTE

The Social Trends Institute is a non-profit research center that offers institutional and financial support to academics of all fields who seek to make sense of emerging social trends and their effects on human communities.

STI focuses its research on four subject areas: Family, Bioethics, Culture and Lifestyles, and Corporate Governance. Primarily it organizes Experts Meetings, which bring together various scholars to present and discuss each others' original research in an academic forum. These meetings are intended to foster open intellectual dialogue between scholars from all over the world, of various academic backgrounds, disciplines, and beliefs. At times, STI helps to publish a collection of the meeting papers in a single volume, revised and reviewed in light of the discussion.

STI hopes to promote research and scholarship of the highest academic standards. In so doing, it aims to make a scholarly contribution toward understanding the varying and complex social trends that are intertwined with the modern world. STI is committed, then, to that which makes such scholarship possible: intellectual freedom, openness to a diversity of viewpoints, and a shared commitment to serve the common good.

Founded in New York City, STI also has a delegation in Barcelona, Spain. For more information about the Social Trends Institute, please visit www.socialtrendsinstitute.org.

A NOTE ON THE INSTITUTE FOR THE PSYCHOLOGICAL SCIENCES

The Institute for the Psychological Sciences is an institution of higher education offering master's and doctoral degrees in clinical psychology.

The Institute seeks to provide an effective academic and educational environment that incorporates the integral understanding of the person with the psychological sciences. IPS trains students intellectually and professionally through teaching the knowledge and clinical skills necessary to prepare them to respond to their calling as mental health professionals.

As part of its mission, IPS organizes colloquia, conferences, special seminars, and various scholarly activities to enrich the academic life of the students. The eighth John Henry Cardinal Newman Lecture Series along with the Monograph Series published by the IPS Press exemplify the Institute's commitment to interdisciplinary dialogue engaging the culture at large.

For more information about the Institute for the Psychological Sciences, please visit www.ipsciences.edu.